T0339416

Entrepreneurship and the Creation of Organization

When re-imagining, re-thinking, and re-writing entrepreneurship in this book, the authors have come to the conclusion that the concept that describes it most precisely is one that signifies a process that includes imagining, seductively describing, playfully organizing, political agility in navigating common sense, and business sensibility before possible commerce.

This book develops a process theory of entrepreneurship by exploring how key concepts in such a theory – affect, desire, assemblage – allow us to think about entrepreneurship differently. This makes a significant contribution to bridging the fields of entrepreneurship and organization studies. Using literature and literary characters and their stories as main sources, entrepreneurship research is here revitalized, and the result provides students of entrepreneurship processes with new conceptual opportunities. The book is also a contribution to a multi-disciplinary research tradition in social sciences more broadly, where humanities is a key "conversation partner."

Undergraduates in entrepreneurship PhD students, and entrepreneurship and organization scholars will find this to be a refreshing renewal of research into entrepreneurship and the creation of organization.

Daniel Hjorth is a Professor at the Department of Management, Politics and Philosophy, Copenhagen Business School, Denmark, and Professor of Entrepreneurship, Innovation Management, and Organization Theory at Nottingham Business School, UK.

Robin Holt is a Professor of Entrepreneurship and Organisation at the Department of Management, Politics and Philosophy, Copenhagen Business School, Denmark.

Routledge Studies in Entrepreneurship

This series extends the meaning and scope of entrepreneurship by capturing new research and enquiry on economic, social, cultural and personal value creation. Entrepreneurship as value creation represents the endeavours of innovative people and organisations in creative environments that open up opportunities for developing new products, new services, new firms and new forms of policy making in different environments seeking sustainable economic growth and social development. In setting this objective the series includes books which cover a diverse range of conceptual, empirical and scholarly topics that both inform the field and push the boundaries of entrepreneurship.

Women and Global Entrepreneurship
Contextualising Everyday Experiences
Edited by Maura McAdam and James A. Cunningham

Digital Entrepreneurship and the Sharing Economy
Edited by Evgueni Vinogradov, Birgit Leick and Djamchid Assadi

Entrepreneurship in India
Alexander Newman, Andrea North-Samardzic, Madhura Bedarkar and Yogesh Brahmankar

Entrepreneurship in Indonesia
From Artisan and Tourism to Technology-based Business Growth
Edited by Vanessa Ratten

Driving Entrepreneurship in Southeast Asia
Edited by Vanessa Ratten

Entrepreneurship and the Creation of Organization
Daniel Hjorth and Robin Holt

For more information about this series please visit: www.routledge.com/ Routledge-Studies-in-Entrepreneurship/book-series/RSE

Entrepreneurship and the Creation of Organization

Daniel Hjorth and Robin Holt

Routledge
Taylor & Francis Group

NEW YORK AND LONDON

First published 2022
by Routledge
605 Third Avenue, New York, NY 10158

and by Routledge
4 Park Square, Milton Park, Abingdon, Oxon, OX14 4RN

Routledge is an imprint of the Taylor & Francis Group, an informa business

© 2022 Taylor & Francis

Library of Congress Cataloging-in-Publication Data
A catalog record for this title has been requested

ISBN: 978-1-138-88697-1 (hbk)
ISBN: 978-1-03-224737-3 (pbk)
ISBN: 978-1-315-71445-5 (ebk)

DOI: 10.4324/9781315714455

Typeset in Sabon
by Newgen Publishing UK

For Gustaf, my son, who is on his way to find out what to explore in the world

- Daniel

For Iris and Peter

- Robin

Contents

Acknowledgements

Many people have, in one way or another, helped this book towards its finalization. Colleagues involved in organizing the Organization Studies Summer Workshops and Process Symposia have been important in providing multiple opportunities to meet, discuss, and present. Colleagues at the Department of Management, Politics and Philosophy, Copenhagen Business School, colleagues at Nottingham Business School, Nottingham Trent University, and colleagues at the Graduate School of Management, Kyoto University, have all contributed to the creation of a valuable intellectual space where fragments of this book could be presented and discussed. Eva Pallesen has generously shared feedback from reading chapters, and the people at Routledge have shown great patience. Thank you all for making the creation of books like this a joyful process.

Introduction

Much in the way of entrepreneurship inquiry has become stuck in a to and fro discussion of whether to ground explanation and understanding in the entrepreneur or the wider economic conditions. Do we go big or small, macro or micro, prioritize economic-structural, personal-psychological, or micro-sociological processes in our analyses? There are those that, in Brian Massumi's words, "conjure away society with the fiction of an atomistic flock of individuals who forge a relation with one another on the basis of a normative recognition of shared needs and common goals."[1] And there are others that more or less invert this individual-foundationalist approach by finding in structures and institutional forces the conditions by which the individual entrepreneur is an already determined being.

The question of whether to go for the macro or the micro that continues to engross many entrepreneurial theorists feels very similar in nature to the internecine controversy Jonathan Swift's Gulliver found raging in Lilliput between those who favoured opening their boiled eggs from the big end, and those preferring the little.[2] In Swift's satirical take on warring religious sects, The Big Endians (Catholics) had enjoyed historical ascendency, but in recent times, the emperor's son having hurt himself wrestling with an especially large egg, the Little Endians (Protestants) became dominant, eventually forcing the Big Endians into exile on the nearby island of Blefuscu from where they continued to agitate for their "macro approach."[3]

The Big Endians in the entrepreneurial inquiry have been the economists committed to the macro analysis of structural conditions such as established and emerging markets, capital flows, and regulatory environments. Here, if entrepreneurial agents appear at all, they do so fleetingly, as secondary effects instituted by primary forces of which they have no direct control or even awareness. In contrast the Little Endians, such as behavioural theorists, look for patterns of human activity and thought distinguishing entrepreneurial agency. Here structural conditions (the restless shifts in technology, e.g., or the availability of investment capital) are acknowledged as the collective residue of agent-based reasoning.

DOI: 10.4324/9781315714455-1

Entrepreneurship is either a macro condition of structural order or micro condition of individual decision-making.

As in Swift's story, the tangles arising from these differing commitments are rife. How, for example, do those committed to examining the cognitive patterns associated with individual decision-making explain characteristics that emerge from, and seem inherent to, a collective order? The sheer preponderance of entrepreneurial firms clustering in certain geographic regions, for example, gives rise to a collective form of disciplinary identity based on forces of trust or reputation that cannot possibly be reduced to an amalgam of individual abilities and decisions. The trust and regulation are unplanned and often unarticulated and yet can govern the strategic direction of the business venture in fundamental ways. The entrepreneurs find themselves thrown into something larger, a system of economic exchange that is itself ungraspable and which itself is stitched into other systems: cultural traditions, weather patterns, architectural and legal structures, tax regimes, streams of available investor capital, or prevailing demographic trends. In combination these systems create an atmospheric pressure that colour how the entrepreneur thinks, feels, and acts. Silicon Valley, the population is male dominated, the investment capital is as endless as the sunny days are long, the technological development as rapid as the fast food, the dress code is as lax as the regulatory environment, the infrastructure is tight-packed, and the rents as high as the ambition writ into the blue sky. In such a space a human history emerges: there are characters, events, and rules of thumb, but no central narrator, and the stories circulate as a form of collective memory in which the locals become inured (as of their cognition is embodied, and spatially distributed), it becomes their place, and they are both its guardians and prisoners. The limits defining the edge of this density of connexion and memory is impossible to define, but its lingering disciplinary force is unmistakable and as real as the bright, leasehold cars that ply the ever-full highways, moving from innovation to innovation, deal to deal, without end.

Whilst it might confound a Little-Endian analysis with its emphasis on solitary agents, lingering with such the atmospheric condition of a place like Silicon Valley does not endear itself to a Big-Endian study either. The community or collective forces are not at all totalizing, or even obviously determining. The clustering of regional forces cannot structure entirely what is permissible by way of accepted behaviour, no matter how much the structural offices, routines, and ritual processes take precedence over specific performances; the atmosphere is not that of a casino where probability reigns. Moreover, the discipline is as much one of encouraging an intensity of individual autonomy as it is collective propriety: the entrepreneur is a willing supplicant to their own self-willed subjection.

At its most predictable the order emerges through stochastic feedback, whether that of positive intensification (e.g., repeated hires of typified employees accentuates demographic skews, which in turn warrants further typified hires) or negative correction (technological failure yields diminished income). Yet these feedback loops are more arcs of influence than they are consistent patterns, and disturbance is ever-present. Entrepreneurial ventures can leave to set up outside the region, or agitate for change from within, with the entrepreneurs themselves ever conscious of, but not necessarily in control of, the effect of such on their ability to say and do things. Indeed, it would seem to be in the very nature of "being entrepreneurial" that this should be a possibility.

The atmosphere is always absorbing its being a contingent order whose systemic parts are extrinsically rather than intrinsically dependent on its form. Humans, climates, symbols, regulatory structures, all of which/ whom, as systems, occupy a vast ecology of enriching and denuding, opening and constraining, typified and unusual relations. The character of each system is contingent on its continuous interactions with other systems, yet entirely dependent on it because there is always something (potentially) beyond and hence autonomous (but never unrelated) from the interactions that can be pulled in: traces of becomings, memories, strange attractors.

"If there are relations of power in every social field," Michel Foucault pointed out, "this is because there is freedom everywhere."[4] Freedom means potential movement and it is in enquiry into the nature of this movement that entrepreneurship studies can, we argue, dissolve the big end/little end controversies. It is a movement that we understand as desire, the desire that is bound to will, to imagination, to acting in ways that actualize what is of value to others, and which is achieved by creating organization – a process we and others call entrepreneuring, the result of which is entrepreneurship.

To inquire into the creation of new organizational forms, then, whilst it makes full use of concepts, models, and theoretical ideas, is to do so with a nod to the priority of passage over position. It is to do so not simply out of ontological curiosity for a world of forces, affect, and fluxing motion, but equally from abeyance to a phenomenon that is in nature inherently restless. With any entrepreneurial venture the empirical things in play (the workspace, the roles adopted, investments secured, business plans drafted, and technologies subjected to) are very obviously always being shadowed by the virtuality (multiple differential relations of potentialities) out of which any new organization might become "this" or "that." What *did* become actual, what *was* actualized, is just one of the multiple differential potentials that could have been so. The actualization process means selections and incisions being made, resulting in a form that only retrospectively can be described as the one that was possible; it only comes into view historically, so to speak. It is the dynamic movement from # that makes § emerge into crystalized, concrete form, and landing at § reveals * underneath. In historical light this can be told as an A–B–C move, where the names (A, B, and C) seem logically related as belonging to one system (such as the alphabet). And what is virtual is not simply the new form being categorized, but the multiple ways in which this could have come about: the different individuals touched, the different stories that might be told of its growing pains, the differing visions, the open and uncontrollable effects of trying to persuade others of its viability, the playful moves into spaces not yet occupied, the bumping into established, institutionalized common sense, all of which in some un-orchestrated coming-together results in commerce.[5]

In our emphasis on process – the coming to be of the virtual in the midst of already actualized actualities – we assume that everything that has been actualized and has concrete form and bothers us, that occupies us in everyday practices, and that has taken form and shares the world with us, always has a shadow, a doubling of multiple differential relations, a swarm of virtualities that could have been actualized or individuated instead. Actualization in entrepreneurship happens on the plane of intensity/individuation where an organizational creation, via difference and selection, emerges as it enters into relationships, becomes established, and takes its part as a form of organization amongst already organized forms. This actual world, visible and present to us, is better understood, whereas the world of intensities, the world of the virtual, of potentialities is less so. Yet, it is alongside this sensed potential that entrepreneurial forms appear to thrive, the entrepreneurial, as distinct from the managerial or institutional, is a place of opportunities in which the virtual becomes vivid. It is a place modified by small movements, a chance (yet still structured) meeting of people, for example, through which, for a moment, everything changes, if only slightly, when an idea emerges in conversation – and it might amount to something. The entrepreneurial here is a condition of receptivity and spontaneity, of being receptive to and moved by the potential of momentary changes, and allowing these to affect others such that their desire to move with you is mobilized. These conditions are not fully graspable through inquiry and reasoned argument. They cannot be planned for or hunted down. They dawn as conditions of affect and atmospheres, they are felt (by bodies with power to be affected) in their incipiency and when being an affirmation of chance they carry with them an almost playful quality.[6] Play affirms, and affirmation is to become active, to participate in the incarnation of virtualities in their concrete forms: e.g. new ventures.

It is in this, in the passage from the virtual to the actual, that we intend to frame the entrepreneurial condition: the creation of proto-organizational forms – assemblages – that can, might, and sometimes do become new organizations; proto-organizational forms realized through intensities and affect, and held together by desire. In committing to this framing we do not leave the field of entrepreneurship studies but intensify our study thereof. Indeed, we take seriously the established concern of the field of entrepreneurship studies with understanding both the individual entrepreneur and the structural forces of which they are a part. Working processually, however, we find nothing oppositional in the distinction: individuality is a conditional, socially and politically structured achievement, and structural forces constrain individuality insofar as they are embodied in particular, ordinary, individual actions. Some in the field of entrepreneurship research, such as Helene Ahl, Saras Sarasvathy, Sarah Jack, Sarah Drakopoulo Dodd, Alistair Anderson, Denise Fletcher, Susan Marlow, Chris Steyaert, Pascal Dey, Stratos Ramaglou, and Dimo Dimov, also sense the coming together of subjective desire and structural pressure, finding in entrepreneurship a phenomenon that in wilfully and actively naming a nexus of power, knowledge, and norms brings it into questionability. Entrepreneurship materializes in the realization that reality cannot be reduced to what is materialized.[7] This is active self-understanding and the desirous and sometimes provocative summoning of what is beyond habit. Human bodies are individuated as entrepreneurs socially, and that sociality is composed by an affective engagement that draws assemblages together.[8]

To give event to this intimacy of subject and subjection, and to better apprehend its implications for entrepreneurship studies, we begin by taking a sustained foray into Romanticism. Romanticism provides one of the most thoroughgoing excursions into the nature of human individuality, affect and desire, and the creative refusals of habit and necessity it entails. We show how, from within its circuitous patterns, self-expression becomes an imaginative, fragmentary experience of desiring to be elsewhere, one which involves, and relies upon, the mobilization of others. Though we limit our reading to its European forms,[9] Romanticism is, we argue, a genre of thinking about oneself that feels very pertinent to an understanding of entrepreneurship wherever it might occur. Framed through Romanticism, entrepreneurs carry distinction only insofar as they are uncomfortable with certainties and so curious about what lies beyond the established ways of doing things. They (often this is a group of people) are figures who have what Foucault called a "limit attitude" as they, first, make visible the habituated routines by which subjects are organized, and second, in making the limits visible, they bring their constraining force into a state of questionability from which transgression and hence new organizational form can emerge. This emergence is far from heroic, and it need not be hugely impactful. The myth of world gyrating genius finds little truck amongst Romantic writers, though some have been accused of being self-obsessed, like some entrepreneurs, and with both there is substance to the critique. Typically, though, the Romantic is too alive to the fragility, contingency, and dependency of their creation to believe themselves in any way superior to the condition in which they find themselves. Indeed they reserve their spleen for those who attempt to goad others with visions and organizational structures so glassily transparent and properly judged that disturbance and experiment are little more than sources of shame. To write and believe in the myth of self-sufficient prowess or organizational perfection is to shrink and enclose the world in an image, it is to be convinced that the world is as it is because of you and your ilk, and it is, in our reading, as far from the entrepreneurial spirit as you can be. So in its intense interest with individuality, Romanticism is alive to its corruptions, as too should entrepreneurship be. It is the kind of corruption that has entrepreneurs on the cover of ghost-written books, each a story of overtaking and triumph, each an exercise in sophistry, each a well-packaged assembly line of exaggeration and hyperbole.

Entrepreneurs, we argue, like Romantic writers, are tacticians, and as such have to travel lightly, aware of depending on fellow travellers, never capitalize on what they won (in order to stay light and fast), and be constantly on the move. They do not operate on the strategic model of occupying a place atop a mound of possessions. Such a position is far too settled and content to allow for the receptivity and spontaneity of desire by which the creation process is being moved along, this way then that: it may be slowly or with haste, meandering or direct, but it is always with a sense of the place being a space with a prospect whose limits are in kept view.

Having acquainted ourselves with Romanticism (Chapters 1 and 2), letting the Romantic writers help us grasp individuality, we move on to Chapter 3, where the two grounding theoretical concepts (or constructs) emerge and are developed for the purpose of our inquiry (to review the study of entrepreneurship by developing a process theory of entrepreneuring as organization-creation): desire and assemblage. With these as a ground, Chapter 4 uses these concepts to develop a process theory of entrepreneurship, i.e. of entrepreneuring, as organization-creation. We do this using process thinking as a philosophically natural way of thinking about the becoming of ventures (venturing) or firms (firming) as an organization-creation process. Chapter 4 culminates in a model of the entrepreneurial process. The model is composed of the four related atmospheric-affective aspects that, we argue, best evoke the organization-creation process: *Seduction – Play – Common sense – Commerce*.

Given we argue, in Chapters 1 and 2, that to understand entrepreneurship as the creation of a new organizational form is nearly always, empirically, an exercise in the retrospective study, we have turned to literature. Though fictional, the literary has the advantage of sustaining speculative inquiry into the nature of human experience with a density and precision that explicitly (because they are narrated) reveals the limit conditions of human practice. The texts describe affect, desire, force, relation, potentiality, and creation in ways that, conceptually speaking, crystallize, or distil as fragments what otherwise dissipate into generalities.

Our choice of literature as empirical material for this book's study and theorization of entrepreneurship requires some contextualization too. The best way to describe our reasoning here is to refer to our model of the entrepreneurship process (see Chapter 4) and to say that we try to be performative in our writing, i.e. to apply the model in our own process of making this book. Thus, we use Romanticism to open up to what we find is central for the emergence of the character of the entrepreneur, the subjectivity or subject-position of the entrepreneur in everyday language and in academic discourses. The modern idea of individuality emerges into ripeness through Romanticism, at least the version of it that complicates the stable, inner subjective entity and its rational mind envisaged in social contract theories. This is where the possibilities and challenges associated with the "free individual" are taken on as the Romantics imagine what it will be to be elsewhere, to be both dependent on and yet beyond the present, to throw themselves into what we describe as becoming-other. However, having made that opening for us, historically, and for this book's purpose of developing a new conceptualization and model of the entrepreneurship process, we turn to a more selective material to analyse and to use in order to substantiate our conceptual development. Thus, we have rather aimed for precision and resonance when selecting literature. Precision in the sense that we find it hard to imagine our key concepts without the story/character that brings it alive in literature. Resonance follows from discovering the potential precision with which literary sources of concepts we find indispensable for renewing our thinking of and understanding of entrepreneurship affects us as interpreters. The discovery is one accompanied by wonder, a glimpse of the actual that the potential provides. Our method draws upon Foucault's interpretive analytics, this combination of genealogy and archaeology that gives priority to the cultural-historical when using concepts to understand what discursive practices mean and do. This is present in Geertz' interpretive analytics, analysed by Greenblatt, and picked up by Agamben as he develops[10] the concept of dispositif from Foucault: "... a set of strategies of the relations of force supporting, and supported by, certain types of knowledge."[11] We might also say, using Agamben's more general term for describing his method, that we have traced the signature[12] of key concepts for understanding the entrepreneurship process in the literary as a way to place greater emphasis on a cultural (genealogical) understanding of this that we believe has been overlooked in entrepreneurship research.[13]

This initial "encounter," and the wonder that is how it is affectively sensed in us as readers, sets off a process of discovery that gradually builds resonance. Just as wonder is one (or indeed the) start of philosophy,[14] the start of entrepreneurship processes is often the wonder that follows from desire bringing you to the brim of what is actualized (Chapters 3 and 4) and the urge to know how moving beyond is made possible. "... [T]he experience of wonder continually reminds us that our grasp of the world is incomplete."[15] To entrepreneurship, that's an opportunity.

Granted, that's mainly the wonder part. What follows from wonder – resonance – is more the result of actualizing, showing how this object of wonder, this piece of literature, holds great power when it comes to helping us think entrepreneurship anew. Greenblatt again:

> By resonance I mean the power of the object [literary text] displayed
> [read] to reach out beyond its formal boundaries to a larger world,
> to evoke in the viewer [reader] the complex, dynamic cultural forces
> from which it has emerged and for which as metaphor or more simply
> as metonymy it may be taken by a viewer to stand.[16]

Resonance is thus the result of a kind of ethnographic thickness brought
in by the interpreter and analyst (us in this case), and for which imagination is part of establishing the resonance as much as framing.

We thus study Seduction (Chapter 5) via Kierkegaard's writing on
Don Juan, as he finds it in Mozart's Don Giovanni, and in Shakespeare's
Othello and its central character, Iago. Both Don Giovanni and Iago
are beautifully poised, compressed descriptions of seduction. Play
(Chapter 6) brings us to the worlds of Virginia Woolf's Mrs Dalloway
and Astrid Lindgren's Pippi Longstocking. Those, in different and com-
plementary ways, show how life's potentiality, what could become,
and what one's power to be affected can bring to life that is not yet,
but could become. This makes it necessary to understand the impact of
common sense (Chapter 7), which is where the seductive and playful
entrepreneuring process is put to the test: can the force of actualizing the
new find its ways between the routines, habits, customs, practices, and
institutions? Can it mobilize support, convince, negotiate, and bring life
beyond the limit of the present? This is what entrepreneurship does – rigs
life in (possibly) joyful speculative anticipation of what could be reached
beyond the boundary of the actual. This is where the multiple differential relationships, the virtualities that shadow the actual, need action to
pave the way for the difference. Who would be better teachers in this art
of finding ways through and around than Elisabeth Bennett from Jane
Austen's *Pride and Prejudice* (the expert of common sense, custom, tradition, practice), or Chichikov from Gogol's *Dead Souls*? The reward, for
the entrepreneuring process, is commerce (Chapter 8) and Stendhal's
character Julien Sorel (from the novel *The Red and the Black*) knows
all about how to fixate on it, whereas Patricia Highsmith's *Talented Mr
Ripley* knows how to explore commerce as approach, philosophy, attitude, and method.

Again, the choice of these texts, and the decision to concentrate on
characters, are made on the basis of wonder and resonance. They are
selected due to the precision with which they show how seduction,
play, common sense, and commerce are – to us – inevitable parts of the
organization-creation process that is entrepreneurship. However, some,
and especially Don Giovanni, Iago, Chichikov, Sorel, and Mr Ripley are
in their different ways, also quite dubious characters. Don Juan seduces
as a pathological practice in his life (according to the ancient Spanish
myth), and Mozart's Don Giovanni takes advantage of vulnerability and
seems to do so for a short-term "win." Iago is driven and consumed by
revenge as he leaves a trail – as Shakespeare was inclined to do in his

tragedies – of bodies that, albeit acting on their own, were misconceived into thinking they had to. Chichikov is, in comparison, a less dramatic exploiter of circumstances. He makes use of the bureaucracy and invents an in-between category that makes him the owner of capital that is not there (dead serfs that can be used as collateral when getting a loan to buy land). With Mr Ripley the stakes are considerably higher again, as we witness a pathological mythomaniac skilled in the art of self-deception hard at work. Whether Ripley always knows who he is and which one of his characters does what is sometimes deliberately vague, such that the only real certainty is when his amorality strikes through the text like a bright, dark light through the pinhole of a small statement.

These are extreme examples, and their thoughts and actions are often ethically indefensible. The question is: Can we still learn from them, and do they show us (perhaps even with great precision) what seduction, common sense, and commerce are? Rhetorically stating the questions, we are sure they do teach us. They are exceptionally precise in showing us lived versions of these key concepts in our model of entrepreneurship. This is where we take advantage of literature for it brings us life in a condensed form that metaphorically or metonymically has resonance with our lived lives. Indeed, by stepping over lines they reveal the mundane but vitally important skill of knowing where lines are being drawn in everyday life, and why. There is no doubt that entrepreneurship is also, in the ethical sense (apart from social, cultural, and psychological) a liminal practice, and that this is a difficulty in researching it.[17] We have also seen that concepts like "acting-as-if" and "organization-creation" (that we work with here) are concepts that seek to capture the transgressing of existing orders for the benefit of opening up new possibilities. Though framed by tragedy, irony, or comedy, the actions of Iago, Ripley, Don Giovanni, Sorel, or Chichicov remain delinquent in ways that draw critique. But as "cases" to learn from, and as characters that work in liminal space, we find them provoking both wonder and resonance.

On the basis of this, Chapter 9 will conclude on these studies (Chapters 5–8) and return to the opening part of the book and substantiate our theorization of entrepreneuring and our model of the entrepreneuring process. This is where we affirm and make use of our analyses of the condensed lives brought to us in a vivid form in the literature studied, and develop the learnings for those that, like us, are interested in a renewed, processual theory of the entrepreneuring process, the process of organization-creation, the result of which we call entrepreneurship but the process for which we hitherto have had few concepts to use in our ambition to understand and describe.

Notes

1 Massumi, B. (2002) *Parables for the Virtual – Movement, Affect, Sensation*, Durham and London: Duke University Press, p. 68.

2 Swift, J. (2002) *Gulliver's Travels*, New York: Norton, p. 41.

3 For a detailed foray into the symbolism in Swift's metaphorical satire and his association of big and little Endians with the Protestant and Catholic causes, see Real, H.J. (2010) *Ab Ovo*: Swift's Small-Endians and Big-Endians and Transubstantiation. In Burton, J., Marx, W., & O'Mara, V. (Eds.), *Leeds Studies in English*, New Series XLI. Essays in Honour of Oliver Pickering, pp. 200–213.

4 Foucault, M. (1997) *Michel Foucault – Ethics; Subjectivity and Truth*, Rabinow, P. (Ed.), *Essential works of Foucault 1954–1984, vol. 1*. New York: The New Press, p. 292.

5 Serres, M. (1982) *The Parasite*, Transl. L.R. Schehr, Baltimore: John Hopkins University Press, pp. 224–234; Latour, B. (1993) *We Have Never Been Modern*, Transl. C. Porter, Cambridge: Harvard University Press, pp. 50–55. Seres talks of a ball that "… catalyzes the play as a whole but is not itself a whole. It attracts and arrays the players, defining their effective role in the game and defining the overall state of the game, at any given moment, by the potential movement of the players with respect to it. The ball moves the players. *The player is the object of the ball*."

6 Deleuze, G. *Nietzsche & Philosophy*, Transl. H. Tomlinson, New York: Columbia University Press.

7 See Ramoglou, S. and Tsang, E. (2017) "In Defense of Common Sense in Entrepreneurship Theory: Beyond Philosophical Extremities and Linguistic Abuses," *Academy of Management Review*, 42(4): 736–744.

8 Hjorth, D. (2013) "Public Entrepreneurship – Desiring Social Change, Creating Sociality," *Entrepreneurship and Regional Development*, 25(1–2): 34–51.

9 Enlightenment-Romanticism was itself set in motion by the encounter with other cultures, India, China, Japan, and the South Pacific in particular, and thus too a result of a "dialogue"; e.g. Franklin, M.J. (2006) *Romantic Representations of British India*, London and New York: Routledge.

10 Agamben, G. (2009) *What Is an Apparatus? And Other Essays*, Stanford: Stanford University Press.

11 Foucault, M. (1980) *Power/Knowledge: Selected Interviews and Other Writings, 1972–1977*, C. Gordon (Ed.), New York: Pantheon Books, p. 196.

12 There are two levels of signature in our study: we trace the signature of entrepreneurship to the concepts of seduction, play, common sense, and commerce. And, we trace the signature of those concepts in literature, where we find, beyond the semiological and the hermeneutic, what is more the conditions for the discursive functions that these concepts have in the entrepreneurship process. See Agamben, G. (2009b) *The Signature of All Things – On Method*, New York: Zone Books; Dean, M. (2013) *The Signature of Power – Sovereignty, Governmentality and Biopolitics*, London: SAGE.

13 And here we would say that we find there is an internal regime of power that directs the way in which our concepts for the entrepreneurship process govern one another to constitute, form, and work in practice as an ensemble (cf. Agamben, 2009a; 2009b).

14 Hadot, P. (2002) *What Is Ancient Philosophy?* Transl. M. Chase, Cambridge and London: The Belknap Press of Harvard University Press.

15 Greenblatt, S. (1991) *Marvelous Possessions: The Wonder of the New World*, Oxford: Clarendon Press.

16 Greenblatt, S. (1992) *Learning to Curse: Essays in Modern Culture,* London: Routledge. Additions made by us.

17 Garcia-Lorenzo, L., Donnelly, P., Sell-Trujillo, L., Imas, J.M. (2018) "Liminal Entrepreneuring: The Creative Practices of Nascent Necessity Entrepreneurs," *Organization Studies,* 39(2–3): 373–395. See also Hannafey, F.T. (2003) "Entrepreneurship and Ethics: A Literature Review," *Journal of Business Ethics,* 46: 99–110.

Part 1

1 Romanticism and wonder

Spinoza and "the self"

For Baruch Spinoza human beings are distinct from all other sentient beings in one basic way: they feel the urge to be elsewhere. Humans are defined, he suggested, by the passion to become rather than be; as partial modifications of a whole they strive to reach towards what is beyond and possibly more than them. Henri Bergson and Gilles Deleuze would later emphasize that this urge is the result of imaginative capacity – "else-where" is imagined in an intense, attractive way, thus the urge to move, and in this move to then sense the self.[1] Self-awareness, Spinoza stresses, is woven from attempts at self-creation, the mind and body entwined in the mobile and active enquiry into possibility driven by what he calls *conatus*: a striving to do and become more and to overcome.[2]

As if to empirically embody this essential restlessness Spinoza was himself always on the move, not just physically – and he certainly got about – but also intellectually. Born in Amsterdam into a family of Spanish-Jewish traders who had found themselves in the commercially primed, repub-lican city they had escaped what they felt as the religious intolerance of their native Portugal. Reared in the exposed enclosure of Jewish tradition, but exposed to a vibrant array of religious dissenters and freethinkers, Spinoza flirted with, and then committed, to a brand of rational thinking whose questioning nature found him cursed and excommunicated from his tightly knit community; it was an exodus from religious belief into open enquiry. As rational beings he believed humans needed to commune with their environment continually, learn from it through exposure, trans-parently and without fear, and always with a collective sense of its being an unending experience of continual modification.

His radicalism, which was embodied in the plain sight of enquiry, attracted the attention of Europe's intellects and intelligentsia, but he refused the offer of endowments from patrons who kept coming his way: to work for someone was to limit the range of intellectual reach. Instead of patronage he ground out a living making optical lenses, the glassy equipment polished with rough sand through which emerged dim passageways into a wider world, whether out into the heavens or inward

DOI: 10.4324/9781315714455-3

into myriad tiny detail. To expound his project he conceived a book on everything: *The Ethics*. It would address both the realm of God and nature, and ultimately it argued these were indistinguishable, a unity held fast by the transforming momentum of endless modification. *The Ethics* aimed to make humans more fully human (always perfecting, but never perfect) by having them realize the profoundly non-anthropological conditions that went by the names God and nature – forget God's representation in human form, forget the idea of a vengeful or loving spirit, forget chains of being and prelapsarian, or uniquely blessed landscapes. Nature (and god) were nothing more than pure structure – the "there-being" that was the world and so everything, the empirically "there" world of things and the spiritually "there" world of feelings were woven into one and the same fabric – and it was with and within this fabric that humans found ourselves folded and from which they might be re-folded anew. Such a being-in-the-world always meant an involved becoming, related to others, and shaped by a mood or affect. Spinoza's was an entire world away from the enjoined, ordained, and familial commitments of a biblical metaphysics that had the world once an Eden and thence Fallen. It was also an entire world away from an utterly determined, mute world of particles moving in hit and miss patterns. Rather, the entirety of the world was to be found within the universal reason found in each human being and which, were it thought about passionately and clearly, is part of a self-explanatory natural order immanent in all things. Being fallible our comprehension of such an order is always partial, but we might remain nevertheless, with disciplined thought, become aware of its being there in its potentiality, not least because it is the only way of freeing life from the arbitrariness of accident and determinism.

The experience of throwing oneself into the world and striving to know what cannot be fully known is, suggested Spinoza, a grounding paradox of human enquiry that should be relished. It was a paradox that Spinoza felt was especially apparent when humans tried to understand themselves. We humans might, for example, believe ourselves essentially free beings because we make conscious choices, and from this think ourselves into a world whose apparently mute and mutable state renders it subservient, a world *for* us. Yet close, reflexive rational enquiry yields the precarious nature of such self-assurance. Each of us is affecting and affected by others, and as each of us is placed *with* the other we find we are bound collectively somehow: we are in communities, cultures and species, groups who abide amid a wider nature that we often experience not as being there for us, but a bundle of forces to which we invariably buckle.

Gilles Deleuze, in his discussion of Spinoza, uses this language of rhythm and force as he describes the mapping of a body (a body can be a human body, an animal body, a body of sounds such as created by bird-song, a mind, an idea) as constitutive of nature:

We call longitude of a body the set of relations of speed and slowness, of motion and rest, between particles that compose it from this point of view, that is, between unformed elements. We call latitude the set of affects that occupy a body at each moment, that is, the intensive states of an *anonymous force* (force of existing, capacity for being affected). In this way we construct a map of a body. The longitudes and latitudes together constitute Nature [...], which is always variable and is constantly being altered, composed and recomposed, by individuals and collectivities.[3]

Examined from the outside, as it were, Spinoza found we are all of us humans constituted and guided by rhythms, movements, and rests, not our own and by which we are influenced, and rather than resent these affects, or try and compensate for them, we ought to relish their disturbing constraint. Why? Well: it is because nature/God are so different from us, and so indifferent, and yet so compelling in being the only place we have in which to live, that our unfinished nature (our felt urge to be elsewhere, *our conatus*, which empirically, if we are honest, we all feel) becomes our own; it is immanent to us, as all things in nature are immanent, an ordering in which each is to find its space and to expand or diminish this space by acting and thinking in ways that always resolve to look beyond the place of present settlement. In our "with-ness," in being always already related to others, we are moved/affected and move/affect through habit, and these habits of socially sanctioned and relationally instituted activity and thought are for many enough of a comfort not to look any further. Their *conatus* is concealed by an orthodox pursuit of possessions, status, and temporary sensual pleasure. If all we do is comply with tradition and expectation (fix ourselves habitually to the actual) we never expand to reveal the edges of our condition to ourselves, and so become incapable of seeing ourselves anew. *The Ethics* was a book to teach us otherwise, to bring us elsewhere.

In the book, Spinoza was careful not to associate such an expansion with a kind of "colonial" spread of one's own inner world. To touch the edges meant keeping them in place. The ethical condition arose when we were thrown into the order of things without the comforts of habit and possession. Instead we were to rely on a more universal passion for encountering and absorbing differences (or otherness) in ways that fused mind, body, and nature into an immanent unity of similarity and difference. An expansion of awareness is created when we learn to treat immediate and everyday passions and experiences as the source of ideas about how to live. In thinking imaginatively the everyday becomes a scene of possible transformation as we look beyond what we are.[4] And through this capacity to create experiences of the unusual by imaginatively looking beyond comforts and norms we begin to build from the restlessness that most closely embodies the distinctiveness of human beings. *Conatus* is thus also about one's capacity to be affected and to affect, which also means one's capacity to joyfully speculate, to assemble, to put together, and to move beyond.[5] There is a striving to increase one's power to act, to do things beyond (what Joseph Schumpeter called) the "pale of routine." Spinoza's thinking, so we suggest, is thus bringing us into an intimate relationship with things entrepreneurial.

Spinoza's thinking was a lure, it shone and twisted in a glassy and opaque world, like his lenses, it opened up new views, new worlds to imagine, pulling the reader on, but to where? For the German Romantics of the late eighteenth century, who were madly filtering his thinking through experiment in literary form, the answer was "nowhere" and this was the point. The writer Novalis was especially enthusiastic. In taking up Spinoza's refrain of committing oneself to an expansive life of continual modification, he found himself most at home when experiencing unhomeliness, and many of his settings and characters attest to a charged upswell of personal disorientation that emerged from sustained enquiry into one's own condition. To feel unhomely was a condition of self-awareness grounded in strangely unsettling mirror play: we are closest to understanding what we are when we struggle imaginatively to distance ourselves from what we are. We are both removed from ourselves and, yet, exercising faculties that remain integral to us. In spectating on ourselves we are remaining ourselves, yet are still unable to understand the totality of who we are because we cannot get out of the sphere that is "us" to then spectate fully on our spectating self.

Novalis – whose real name was Georg Philipp Friedrich Freiherr von Hardenberg, having adopted his *nom de plume* from his ancestors who had called themselves *de Novali*, meaning "clearers of new land" – revelled in such paradoxical curlicues. For here, in this irresolvable clearing between our inexhaustible will to know and our limited knowledge, lay a form of romantic possibility. We cannot know who we are with any certainty because we can only account for the feeling of being alive from the distance of imaginative contemplation and this distance does not get us closer to our essence, but closer to the limits, to the other. So, in striving to know who we are we constitute ourselves in a condition of unhomeliness in which we struggle to represent what resists representation, and it is the struggle itself that best defines us and by which we realize a touching unity with nature: us in the world and the world in us.[6]

With Spinoza the human becomes a figure partaking of the rich multiplicity of the world, encountering the potential of an inseparable body and mind as it wends and wrestles a way through life, without end, and Novalis distils this morphing sensibility by attempting to show how such a protean figure, fully thrown into the world, also puts the world entirely in itself. The sense of "self" emerges both inwardly and outwardly; in encountering something else it encounters also itself, and is affected in one way or the other. If we look for this in ourselves, as Novalis did continually, we sense that we are not wholly what we once were, and we endure a tension between what we were before this spectating experience and what we are now, between what we could only then imagine to what we can now signify.[7] We are drawn in, affected this way or that, and this tension itself becomes a subject of interest. This restlessness of the unknowable consciousness is what marks us: it is our distinction to be searching and striving; we will never be complete, and are always moving in relation to what is not us, including ourselves. Becoming is how we "are" in the world, the only being is the being of becoming.[8]

Spinoza's questioning brought the virtual to the fore, and in doing so the distinctions made in the actual world between part and whole, or self and the world, were obliterated in a convergence of self, nature, and God. For Novalis this questioning was embodied in the passionate figure of the poet and philosopher. Through thinking, writing, and imagery this figure becomes aware of its limits, yet strives regardless to realize a ground or "home" or, as is crucial to Spinoza, strives to assemble forces to act beyond the necessities she experiences. This is done without resentment, indeed the poet and philosopher delights in and is curious about the inherent sense of lack that pervades all attempts to know life as such: "All that is visible clings to the invisible. That which can be heard to that which cannot, that which can be felt to that which cannot. Perhaps the thinkable to the unthinkable."[9] It is on the liminal and limitless edge where representations stop, but action and feeling continue, that the self discovers itself, but only ever as an enigma, not a unit.[10] Again, it is here, beyond the Schumpeterian "pale of routine," that entrepreneurial imagination has such strong appeal on the body (mind, of thought, physical) that it is lured into acting such that the virtual is given a way into the actual. Life is extended by creating the organizational "handles" that incipient newness uses to move beyond the limits of the present.

Fictions, fragments

Where Spinoza dealt in concepts and philosophical, political, and legal enquiry, Novalis also dealt in fiction. Whilst fiction need not refer to a person or events in the actual world – the author and words intrude – it does refer to the general sense being made of the world, it shares the same descriptive and propositional forms, and commonly creates eidetic similarities – a person taking similar form to the narrator's own and experiencing similar events. These characters and events bear the structure of truthfulness – in Emily Brontë's *Wuthering Heights*, for example, the wind howls, and the moor over which Cathy walks is bleak, and the nest of lapwings can go unattended by the parent bird for fear of its being trapped. But there is no empirical need of a woman called Cathy recalling a nest full of little lapwing skeletons to make an excerpt from Brontë's novel work as a means of revealing patterns and values in the nature of things.[11] The world is not simply, nor even fully, revealed on the basis of actual events: full disclosure embraces the fictional, and its very real affective force can touch on the readers' and writer's capacity to imagine themselves into scenes that resonate with life. Imagination is a carrier of experience that is made sense of, and which can be shared without diminishment or repetition. For example, in the case of Cathy recalling how Heathcliff set a trap for lapwings, the image of the ravaged nest reveals the collateral damage to human relationships that can be wrought by the consuming singularity of a love and passion that must speak its name.[12] The real is always the actual plus the virtual; the experienced and the imagined; the physical-material and the affective. What we call fiction helps disclose the real. It is not limited to what can be represented in a measure of statistical certainty. This would only provide us with a retrospective account of the actual. In the realm of business such information is mainly catering to the needs of management, seeking ways to reduce uncertainty in the name of increased predictability, control, and efficiency. The world of entrepreneurship is the actual plus the virtual, and requires knowledge of the ways of imagination.

Romanticism takes the intimacies between reality and fiction and twists them irrevocably into one another, squeezing out the apparent distinctions to the point where adherents are not at all limited by the discussion of whether and how much the fictional and the real match up.[13] Romanticism is an acceptance that there are no boundaries to discover except those that are being made, and in the making something about the human self is revealed. In fictionalized language the experienced reality of social and historical lives and the intelligibility of these lives connects and stays connected. As Jacques Rancière argues, this is not to claim with the Romantic that everything is fiction or a narrative (whether major or minor), rather:

> By declaring that the principle of poetry is not to be found in fiction but in a certain arrangement of the signs of language, the Romantic Age blurred the dividing line that isolated art from the jurisdiction of statements or images, as well as the dividing line that separated the logic of facts from the logic of stories.[14]

The aesthetic age – Romanticism – emerges in gloriously vociferous expressions from writers who got stuck into the historical, symbolic, and material reality of things and signs. Everyone irrespective of their station in life is implicated in making life; all things, even mute things, have a voice, and meaning is a multiplicity in which stable classifications are little more than platforms for a grammatical "breather." It is a realization that "[P]olitics and art, like forms of knowledge, construct 'fictions,' that is to say *material* rearrangements of signs and images, relationships between what is seen and what is said, between what is done and what can be done."[15]

The anthropologist and ethnographer Clifford Geertz reflects on this in his celebrated *The Interpretation of Cultures* from 1973, arguing that "what we call our data are really our own constructions of other people's constructions of what they and their compatriots are up to."[16] Getting to the truth of what people are up to in any culture, the literary theorist Stephen Greenblatt comments, as he reads and quotes Geertz, is a question of acquainting oneself "with the imaginative universe within which their acts are signs."[17] Greenblatt's point is that the literary and the non-literary are each other's thick descriptions: "that both the literary work and the anthropological (or historical) anecdote are texts, that both are fictions in the sense of things made, that both are shaped by the imagination and by the available resources of imagination ..." This is a central principle adhered to in this book's approach to understanding entrepreneurship – that the imaginative universe is key to understand what you study, and that the literary and the non-literary are each other's thick descriptions.

This line of reasoning is also consistent with Paul Ricoeur's development of the role of imagination in interpretation – to say something in terms of another; to understand something through metaphorical description; to make sense of something through semantic innovation.[18] Understanding hermeneutics as "the art of deciphering indirect meanings," Kearney continues, "acknowledges the symbolizing power of imagination."[19] Imagination is important, indeed critical, as agitating for and permitting forms of understanding which, as Ricoeur notes[20] "comes into play in that moment when new meaning emerges from out of the ruins of the literal interpretation." As in Romantic literature, hermeneutic interpretation responds to emerging realities' demand for achieving being by being said, described, expressed in new ways. This is very much the entrepreneurial agenda where organization-creation assembles people, things, and resources in new ways in order for the virtually new to become actualized. Seeing what it could be like, what it could be described as, what images or metaphors that would aid people's grasping of what emerges is greatly helped by imaginative description (as narrative approaches in entrepreneurship studies have shown).

Ricoeur also stresses that it is in the context of work that fiction – such as a strategy, a plan or, in our case, the entrepreneurial story of what could become actual – becomes productive of a world. In this he relates to Kant's analysis of imagination (which we will discuss later, see Chapter 9). He continues: "... to form an image is not to have an image, in the sense of having a mental representation; instead, it is to read, through the icon of a relation, the relation itself."[21] This expresses a process philosophical attention to the being of the middle, the autonomy of the relation, very close to Bergson's and Deleuze's thinking. In his further analysis of fiction, Ricoeur stresses that "When the image is made, it is also able to re-make a world,"[22] which to us suggests that an enquiry into how entrepreneurship shapes the world benefits from analysis of fiction as world-making.

These material re-arrangements, fictions, or things made are never total or complete. Rather they are fragments. With the written fragment of the Romantics we have what Maurice Blanchot called "a new form of completion that mobilizes – renders mobile – the whole through its interruption and through interruption's various modes."[23] These modes – the poems, plays, or prose – are necessarily fragmentary for they all mark and embody (like colour swatches they both indicate the thing and are the thing) continually roaming encounters between the images and idealizations of desire made possible in language and the realism of events. For Novalis fragments are total in the way a seed has complete form and which gives forth beyond itself once in the company of other things: climate, weather, and soil. The seed then produces, it is the source of all life. It is neither a part of anything – it is self-contained – nor is it a whole, for it is only a seed insofar as it becomes other than what it is, it transcends and transforms itself. What marks the novel out as a fragment made up of fragments is the fact of its self-reliance (fiction) being the overture to an entire world that is freed, essentially, from the weight of established truth, that gives the actual over to the virtual. The discontinuous form of the fragment establishes a collective coming and going of one response upon another, serious on playful, languid on vigorous, expansive upon narrow, all of which circulation dissolves the conceits of known facts. Greenblatt sees a similar literary skill and "technique" in Geertz's ability to select, out of the continuous flow of social existence, a fragment of social action and keep it in the "high-resolution area of perception." Only then, and because it is small enough to be held within the narrow boundaries of full analytical attention (as Greenblatt puts it), can it be widened out such that it describes something that is telling, something that is indicative and resonant with and reveals something new about the larger world of the reader.[24]

In calling Novalis' writing fragmentary, Blanchot is making us aware of the strangely potent ontology of the fictional written form, how in describing events, words, and ideas become subsumed by the world to which they refer, whilst at the same time creating this world. There is no possibility of settlement, whether that of positive (real) identification with material things or negative (imagined) idealization of absolute truths, there is only the braided disturbance of image and thought whose imaginary force both creates a world (entirely in language) and remains alive to what appears (is produced) but which is yet to be received by such a self-forming world. What is doing the signifying and what is being signified are folded upon one another, uneasily, and it is in revealing, and revelling in such unease that the Romantic writer excels.[25] The author's intensity of awareness brings forth a fervent sense of involvement with lived life, whilst it's being imaginatively felt negates the reality of such immediate or direct sensation and, instead, appears to conscript meaning to the unreality of a personally configured ideal. The author's imagination brings into being ideas that images cannot fully contain or express, and they spin-off, but if not in the compass of the author – who becomes enticed by and in thrall to, their own imaginary production – then where? To be creating here, in this space of the imaginary, is to be in the company of vision that is both too close and too far to be an object of perception; the vision is, as Maclachlan says, "not something which I *can* see, but something which I cannot *not* see."[26] The visionary escapes the author and yet remains in perpetual encounter with this authoring self, like an impersonal shadow, giving the whole production – the written form – a fleeting and flickering reality whose force is both derivative and generative. Derivative in that it cannot leave the world, generative in its being the creative production of an author whose synthesizing power receives and produces at the same time. Foveation (keep what you study in the high-resolution area of perception) is thus the analyst's work and requires from the analyst-as-author to make this intelligible to the reader.

The human response to this endless mirror-play between the particular feeling of being an "I," the signified declaration of an "I," and the signifying "I," is to imaginatively locate (thrown and throwing) oneself within the endless diversions and divisions of such a condition. Here the ordinary appears extraordinary and what was thought fixed can open up. The more we stay with the experience of being thrown, the more our descriptions of this as floating, as process, hits the mark as realistic, as true to the event of experience. To be aware of oneself is to register first the pull and conformity of habits, and then, following this, the slight absurdity of this "hold," which can then open up space to a possible transformation. To stay with experience is to expose one's apparent limits to how things can become strange, frightening, elusive, and beguiling, if the poetic perceptibility or attentiveness allows them to become so.

Friedrich Schlegel's *Dialogue on Poetry* imagines a conversation amongst a group of Romantics (including a character based on Novalis) that exemplifies such poetic attentiveness. The dialogue is a continual opening up, one that is exemplified in metaphor and allegory in which what is said is meant first one way, then another, then both at the same time, and many others, in endless play, one speech tumbling into others, joining, but as in allegory, never seamlessly or even easily. The imagined conversation plays with language as *Spiel*, the playful speech by which closeness becomes distance, and where sympathy yields difference, and in these paradoxical plays we get a fictional demonstration of that attentiveness which is itself beguiling.

The praise of sensitivity, openness, and attentiveness that characterize the Romantics is a good illustration of how this helps us remain in the flow of becoming, or what an ethnographer like Geertz might describe as staying with and in the flowing river of the empirical. In addition, to us, "It is precisely this aesthetic sensitivity that underpins the unfolding of the entrepreneurial imagination."[27] It takes the study closer to experience. But it also indicates that it is hard work, that it is easier to invent a figure of thought that can control all this flow, and be the stop and start of it – such as the sense of self that emerges from the experiencing, Cartesian subject that is placed outside of events, as an invariant, mental observer of all that is going on "out there." The Romantics eschew the use of such a comforting device, they prefer a messy idea of the subject that belongs to the world. The mind is the site where the connection of experiences takes place, and amongst those connections we find also the idea that there is a subject that makes these connections when, for empiricism of the process-thinking kind, the subject is an effect of such connections; the idea of a subject is an effect of experiences: "[P]ut more concretely, we cannot use the subject and his ideas to *explain* the world of experience; we have to account for how the subject is formed *from experience*."[28]

In his *Dialogue* Schlegel can only show, not tell, and even in showing what he shows he, as an author, does nothing more than the characters who take part in or do his showing, one poetic expression yields another, without end. He is riven with the irony of it all: how in writing there is, in whatever is written, an implied exhortation to disbelief and to breaking free from the text and from the role of author with all its illusions of performativity (technically called *parabis*, as when an author declares herself in the text, or an actor breaks the role of character to speak to the audience). But break free to where? Into nature, which is inherently unknowable save from the particularity of a perspective that hints at infinite, mysterious, and enchanted nature, but which accepts in its reasoned reflection that what is natural is beyond proper comprehension.[29] Schlegel often ends up in the undergrowth, taking the reader through dense thickets of prose until she emerges creased and dishevelled, perhaps in the company of characters or the author, or both, and multiply, and always in a space of yet more illusion. The upshot is a permanent *parabis*, which itself, as a definition of the irony by which Romantic writers come to write, is utterly oxymoronic. No wonder this breaking of character in film or television is called corpsing, indicating that death is perhaps the closest to actual breaking we get. However, even a corpse of course plays in the inevitable relational-performative character that a dead one and death has in the flow of life.

Schlegel experiences Novalis as a writer able to dispense with the structures of truth as an ontological ground, and rely instead on the delight of self-discovery, an open dialogic foray into meaning without ground or edge. And he wants us too to appreciate the deeply ironic writing of which he and Novalis are capable as something uplifting: there is no foundational respect for the fixed, the ironist is forever breaking into the illusion that fact is so neatly and carefully constructing itself around us as a revelation or discovering; rather, it is being constructed, again and again. Novalis revels in this bracing mirror of fabricated self-expression that was both shocking and entrancing, so does Schlegel, and so can we. Mixed with irony comes enthusiasm, the sense of being possessed by a joyous rapture, a delight in the witticisms and absurdities and interplay of possibility that shimmer through appearances, mocking the pretence at solidity and rest. Possibility which in themselves are reducible to anything because there is no component to disassemble, only an assemblage.

Assembling possibility, as it is raised up, raises up what is always a beginning, a starting which is garnered in the allegorical blink of an eye and then lost to itself, connecting us, also to endless opportunities to throw ourselves anew.

Struggle and self-sufficiency

In its irony Romanticism brings the dis/ordering effects of language to the fore, notably queering the concept of an origin or beginning to oneself. The idea of starting points can only ever have a regulating, secondary effect on what remains forever the enigma of life's flow. The Romantic reveals the conceits of representational language and the events and ideas thereby represented, and revels in these conceits, showing experiences of belonging in both thought and feeling that is self-created but from a self that is an effect of experiences, and thus not controlled, and without any origin points save their being written and configured as such through an architecture of personally fed creative power. Romanticism gave full blast to this buoyant but troubling sense of self-sufficiency, no more poignantly expressed than in John Keats' *Ode to Psyche* in which the poet takes lift into the open air alone: "I see, and sing, by my own eyes inspir'd."[30] Freed from the encumbrances of establishment manners and demands for verification and clarification, Keats is his own religious order:

> Yes, I will be thy priest, and build a fane
>   In some untrodden region of my mind,
> Where branched thoughts, new grown with pleasant pain
>   Instead of pines shall murmur in the wind.[31]

Keats Romanticism, less intellectual than the writing of his German counterparts, embodies the acme of the expressive poet. The partial form of his "branching thoughts" partake of a coherent whole whilst also hinting at their own, and the poet's, dissolution. The struggle – the "pleasant pain" – yields an indeterminate certitude brought into continual conversation with the always elusive but determined representations of the self as a multiple sensing being (seeing and singing) emerging from such unhomely conversations as might be had with goddesses, she who is beckoned to listen to what Keats calls, on opening the poem, his "tuneless numbers, wrung/By sweet enforcement and remembrance dear."

Keats himself is most definitely present, but also utterly particular and contingent, likening himself to a garden working into an open space with nameless language:

> And in the midst of this wide quietness
> A rosy sanctuary will I dress
>   With the wreath'd trellis of a working brain,
>   With buds, and bells, and stars without a name[32]

The garden without a gardener has potentials (buds, seeds) and is accommodating to the demands of its expression from within the particularity of memory (stored last autumn, hidden last winter) and its pervading sense of incompleteness, and finds there the whole of stars and its immortal denizens. It does so only ever faintly, in something as ephemeral and inscrutable as a poeticized flower bud, and as a unity that is self-contained in the art itself, making language too something empirical, rather than something transitive.[33] The buds – the poet being one of them – and stars come into being at the same time, and disappear together likewise; the world and its truths emerge and fall away, become and perish, in the struggle held fast by a singular expression: nothing more permanent is possible. It echoes the apocryphal note, said to be Plato's summary of Heraclitus' view: *panta rhei* – everything flows.[34]

The Romantic writer enjoys a fleeting omniscience. As an author Keats or Novalis or Schlegel are not at all sovereign, intentional agents whose thoughts are being worked through words into objects of their creation. Their creativity is less assured and it does not reside "in" but flows through them. Whilst they have singular roles as authors (the authored text is not simply an emanation of wider discursive structuring) this singularity has no firm individual basis outside the acts of literary creation, an intensification of expression from which individuating forms are built.[35] Schlegel is very explicit here, a novel is built, a *Bild*, which is also the word for a metaphor, a picture, and *Bilden* means a form, and *Bildung* is formation,[36] and these built forms are never substantial enough to sustain themselves outside of their circulation amid readers. What is being given form is what is under constant transformation (form*ing*, form-giving underway), and this is further intensified by the Romantic (especially Schlegel's) preference for events that place the subject on its limits: in, for example, the awe-inducing presence of immense and strange natural phenomena that agitate the modifying, tangling power of imagination; or in sickness, suicidal tendencies and febrile conditions; or in tristes and pacts with otherworldly forces and in the extravagance of excess or the impossible constraints of impoverishment, or in recognition that, at the end, the distinctiveness and fame of a name amount to little more than something being writ in water.[37]

Spots of time

A sustaining and grounding source of such self-forming comes with memory, something the poet William Wordsworth likened to "spots of time," patches of recollection with which he was to experiment repeatedly in his extended poem of personal myth *The Prelude*. Wordsworth returns to the cusp of his own life (again, the struggle to occupy limits), his childhood, and in this beginning again finds what it was like to experience life as naïve, yet un-formed "self" mired in wider, deeper, and unintelligible forces of the natural world. Riddled with pathless rocks and unseen glades, with strange sounds and stealthy moons, with unheard stillness and silent forms, the spots of time recalled by the poet evoke how, as a child, he encountered the world blankly, without everyday familiarity, his mind working "with a dim and undetermined sense/Of unknown modes of being."[38] We get a clear description of how the child figure as the passionate body par excellence – receptivity and spontaneity at their max, and so we sense Spinoza's thinking in Wordsworth's poetry.

Recollection is the gift of time, the capacity we have of throwing ourselves back, and by revisiting his own beginnings and beginning again Wordsworth is reaching into a world whose grammars are less firm and finding himself there, less distinguished but more distinct because of his exposure to potential:

> There are in our existence spots of time
> Which with distinct pre-eminence retain
> A fructifying virtue, whence depressed
> By trivial occupations and the round
> Of ordinary intercourse, our minds –
> Especially the imaginative power –
> Are nourished and invisibly repaired;
> Such moments seem to have their date
> In our first childhood.[39]

In recalling "spots of time" (itself recalling Blanchot's fragmentary modes, and the "seed" metaphor used by Novalis) there is little sense of regret or nostalgic longing, but rather a gathering of forces (an intensification) in which the writer is exposed to the potency of ordinary experience, and through which, as a writer-becoming-author, he or she might then transform their self-awareness and affirm an individuation. Without recalling such "spots of time" we tend to forget this childhood struggle, we repress the fear and delight we took in the occult nature of everyday experience, and so when it re-appears inadvertently in adult life we treat it as an immature curiosity from which we, being mature, turn away. Growing older we find adult life arranged in all-sided awareness, events become cast as "experience," which stays fixed, like a bronze statue that loses the capacity to feel in proportion to the loftiness of its plinthed elevation. Eschewing such fixity, Romantics evoke Spinoza's reminder that the power to be affected and power to affect are central to a passionate life where affirmation is becoming-active, meaning we are more able to "do/make/create" in connections with others when we avoid the solid comforts of mature experience.[40]

Wordsworth's *Prelude* impeaches the imperious condition of adulthood by cajoling and conjuring formative experiences from the dawn of his and others' lives. As spots of time they are small and occasional, lacking anything like a narrative extension, yet they mottle the larger patterns of subjection to which he is inevitably subjected. They evoke an opaque world of morning mists and gathering patches of sunrise and shadow, in which border regions fact and habit give way to impression and disorientation. For Wordsworth these spots are "hiding places of my power" from which a subject emerges, one that, for the essayist William Hazlitt, emblematized Romanticism:

> Happy are they who live in the dream of their own existence and see all things in the light of their own minds and walk by faith and hope and to who the guiding star of their youth still shines from afar and into whom the spirit of the world has not yet entered. The world has no hand[41] on them.

Hazlitt was a fan, and fain to walk over 200 miles from his native English Midlands to the West Country and introduce himself to Wordsworth, who he found in the company of Samuel Taylor Coleridge. Despite experiencing little but condescension from the two Lake poets, Hazlitt still felt that in their company a revolution in social and aesthetic sensibility was underway, but one that was to be a quiet, everyday affair, all circumstance and no pomp. The provoking spots of time are typically atmospheric and unspectacular, indeed nothing much might happen, the happenstance of light and dark as a remembered moon reflects along the surface of a lake perhaps, or the feeling of warmth from a fire, but the affect can be momentous, and from such fleeting reminiscence comes forth the possibility of a self-aware, forming creativity (*Bild*).[42] For Hazlitt the poet, a "creature of sympathy" was an adept in such realizing such affects: here is someone who, with attentive discipline, can sympathetically expose themselves to what is proximate to them (the immediate, intense sense of natural forces, the ordinary language used by "lowly" and unadorned people) in ways that impel them to intense imaginative heights and turn their poems into "untutored effusions" carried along by feeling.[43] Wordsworth and Coleridge wrote from the senses, and were alive to these in combination rather than privileging sight. They schooled themselves in an attentive curiosity that refused to make conclusions, and through which ordinary things were no longer held fast in a hierarchy of categories and abstract concepts in which they became objects labelled "this" or "that" object. Instead, things enjoyed their own currency and in doing so came alive. This is not to say these writers abandoned concepts. Things like trees, war, clouds, festivals, trade, authorship, or the law were indeed borne aloft on abstract themes such as love, death, justice, natural beauty, and joy, and there they found meaning as subjects. Yet no sooner was meaning given form than it tripped and fell, spilling and breaking, releasing the things who were unable to restrict their own evanescent force and which met once more in a vast confluence of democratic occurrence, an assembly that went largely ungoverned by anything other than poetic license released by the attentions of observation and memory and, of course, by an intoxicating idea of becoming-poet.

Self-aggrandizemen

The affection Hazlitt had for Wordsworth and Coleridge was not reciprocated. Indeed the dismissiveness with which these two self-governing poets treated Hazlitt was to prove somewhat of a warning, notably in Wordsworth's case. There was a risk of the Romantic poet becoming too self-absorbed and inwardly elevated, indeed as Wordsworth's notoriety and hence career blossomed, both Hazlitt and Coleridge (of all people) began to accuse him of being too much in his own orbit and, despite his avowedly steady gaze upon the world, not at all in touch with the open space beyond his own thought.

On first meeting Wordsworth Hazlitt had been convinced here was a figure whose radicalism lay within an obsessive attention to ordinary experiences of everyday life that hitherto had been regarded as too vulgar for poetizing. Wordsworth appeared not only to investigate but vaunt the ordinary lives of others, and of natural things, experiencing such vivid sensations in their company that the world was enriched and expanded in the disturbance. For example, in the preface to *Lyrical Ballads* we find him writing of the (gendered) poet:

> He considers man and the objects that surround him as acting and re-acting upon each other, so as to produce an infinite complexity of pain and pleasure; he considers man in his own nature and in his ordinary life as contemplating this with a certain quantity of immediate knowledge, with certain convictions, intuitions, and deductions, which from habit acquire the quality of intuitions; he considers him as looking upon this complex scene of ideas and sensations, and finding everywhere objects that immediately excite in him sympathies which, from the necessities of his nature, are accompanied by an overbalance of enjoyment.[44]

And spots of time became the grounding for such overbalancing. These spots of intense, situational awareness speckled and transformed all of Wordsworth's relationships, not only those towards his early years: memory affords a gateway of heightened sympathy in which the worlds and words of others are made to count in one's own. Wordsworth was adamant that the smallest of things recalled, and most meagre heart-felt prayers, were a source of "perpetual benediction":

> Thanks to the human heart by which we live,
> Thanks to its tenderness, its joys, and fears,
> To me the meanest flower that blows can give
> Thoughts that do often lie too deep for tears.[45]

The poet is acknowledging both the sublimity of feeling, and its limits here, how a simple flower exists in ways that exceed the power of the

poet, overwhelming her capacity to understand. The imagination acknowledges things that will not yield to poetic imagination, but which just are,
inscrutable, untranslatable, and outside of representation. Wordsworth
seemed alive to things being beyond us, self-sufficient in their own reality
of which we could know nothing but to which we were somehow in
thrall, being equally ourselves things that are grounded beyond knowledge. The ordinary is what is most compelling because, potentially, it is
what is most strange and disorienting, freed as it is from comforting cat-
egorical order and settled concepts.

Yet Coleridge and Hazlitt discerned in Wordsworth a fear of this
strangeness, and a falling back into the idea of a coherent nature as a
wellspring of poetic power, and an idea of others' lives as a source of
moral provocation, such that once again the poet – Wordsworth – was
to consciously resume a sublime and joyously unifying role. By the time
of the second edition of *Lyrical Ballads*, from which Coleridge had been
expunged, Wordsworth's gaze is finding in others and otherness ways of
refracting and better sensing himself as an object struck through with the
mighty endowment of poetic power.[46] He fed off and lived through an
avowed sympathy with others, rather than allowing them to be alongside,
with their own modifications. Wordsworth's reminiscent Romanticism
found in the lives of others a way of adorning the sequestered, leafy
quadrangle of his own personal power: the sympathy he mustered for the
plight and delight of ordinary folk in his excursions into nature – and at
times it was considerable – was in thrall to an almost patrician self-elevation. By the time Wordsworth had risen to the status of *poet laureate*
Hazlitt had come to describe him as "God of his own idolatry."

Coleridge suggested the cure for these paradoxical excesses of
Romantic self-aggrandizing lay with austere, reasoned enquiry, one that
was suspicious of spraying reality with an excess of metaphorical language by which things become little more than an extension of the poet.
This is why, for Coleridge, Spinoza's *Ethics* was so important, for here is
elaborated a method (from Greek *hodos* being a way or path of transit)
whose experiments and digressions and endlessly modifying conjectures
are unified through an education of mind in which prejudicial passion
gives way completely to a cooling intellect that takes its place equally
with other things. It was in using Spinoza much like an emetic and so
combining passion with a disciplining intellect that Coleridge believed
Romanticism would thrive. And it was important it did. The consequences
of following Spinoza all the way through and without Romantic modification and contrast were too strange, appalling even. Though admiring,
Coleridge refused to offer complete abeyance to Spinoza's impersonal,
omniscient godly force. He wanted to leave wriggle room and roving
space for a personal poetic, imaginative power. Though more diminutive
than Wordsworth's, such a figure could still attend to and absorb the
frailties and puzzles of ordinary life, despite his or her comprehension of
always remaining in debt to, and circumscribed by, ordinary horizons.

Hazlitt's poetic self is even less distinct than Coleridge's. He was aware, perhaps more than either of the Lake poets, of how the world always elided attempts at its capture, and that this elusiveness was not because of poetic failure (a need for more imaginative language) but because reality is not of a form that can be gathered coherently and comprehensively by language. To cope with this estrangement the poet becomes almost invisible: "living in the world, as in it, not of it: it is as if no one knows there was such a person, and you wished no one to know it."[47] Such a figure would take "thoughtful, anxious interest" in the world, but not exploit such interest to elevate themselves, as Wordsworth had done. The force of Wordsworth's imagination lacked a disciplined attentiveness to its always having to be set somewhere other than the poet's own orbit. It was too ready to fall into and replenish the depths of a personal god-head whose gathering power stayed still: a deep well that refrained from spilling over and roaming the wider landscapes from which it might learn of its own littleness:

> While a man is contented with himself and his own resources, all is well. When he undertakes to play a part on the stage, and to persuade the world to think more about him than they do about themselves, he is got into a track where he will find nothing but briars and thorns, vexation and disappointment.[48]

The alternative was to follow Coleridge, at least a little, and to think of a nomadic Romantic spirit running abroad on such landscapes, taking them *en plain air*, learning all the whilst of alliance with and reliance on the wider world, and so ever so wary of self-inflation.[49] Here was the counterblast to the excessive motion of some Romantics, a figure whose sense of self was fed by acknowledged dependency on and provocation by what it encounters in the playground of the world. The risk here, though, was of becoming so alive with attachments that detachment became impossible: the self gives way to mediation and hence endless affective modification without authorial power. Hazlitt's concern was reminiscent of Montaigne's warning that an intoxication with intervening in and gathering events about oneself results in an impatience and violence of character that not only indulges the impulse to assertion it is also a wanton addiction to occupation:

> Just watch people who have been conditioned to let themselves be enraptured and carried away: they do it all the time, in small matters as in great, over things which touch them and those which touch them not at all. They become involved, indiscriminately, wherever there is a task [C] and obligations; [B] they are not alive without bustle and bother. [C] "in negotiis sunt negotii causa." [They are busy so as to be busy.]4 The only reason why they seek occupations is to be occupied. It is not a case of wanting to move but of being

unable to hold still, just as a rock shaken loose cannot arrest its fall until it lies on the bottom. For a certain type of man, being busy is a mark of competence and dignity. [B] Their minds seek repose in motion, like babes in a cradle. They can say that they are as useful to their friends as they are bothersome to themselves. Nobody gives his money away to others: everyone gives his time. We are never more profligate than with the very things over which avarice would be useful and laudable.[50]

Hazlitt advocated a difficult middle ground. A poet who, whilst wary of self-inflation, remained still and, in this quietness, became attentive to how things might act upon each other from a distance, one fragment upon another, mutual yet also estranged, as when a mind itself runs aground on its own speculations and can do naught but be fixed there awhile, without course or means to re-float, exposed to a world not at all their own, but clearly theirs for they were imagining it. What is left to such a poet? To speculate on the comfort and strangeness of things. They would make lists and litanies and in these lists witness objects withdrawing and rather than hasten to recover their influence by looking for lessons in such a withdrawal they keep still and continue to bear witness. They do not make grounding appeals to the ensuing loneliness and freedom of such separated existence. Instead of utility and value comes an aesthetic crafting of affective relations with others and with nature, ones in which the poet copes without the architecture of knowledge and finds "things" in the ascendency and humans stripped of their central, ordering role.

This is where we find resonance with entrepreneurship. This welcoming, embracing, and affirmation of that which is without order, nor yet ordered and thus requires organization-creation, characterizes both the struggling poet and the venturing process. For both the requirement is to stay in the midst, endure the vagueness of the "grey," the not-quite-enough light that characterizes the yellow in-between of dawn and dusk. Where most might opt for rest and withdraw from the day, the poet and entrepreneur spring to action, rejoicing in the lack of clarity, guidance, and instruction.

Notes

1 Imagination, Massumi adds, is "a mode of thought most precisely suited to the differentiating vagueness of the virtual." See Massumi, B. (2002) *Parables for the Virtual – Movement, Affect, Sensation*, London and Durham: Duke University Press, p. 134. Massumi is applying Deleuze's thinking from *Difference and Repetition*, where the virtual is described as a multiplicity of differential relations: incipiencies, potentialities. This indicates the overspilling nature of imagination, but also why actualization (as creation) has to happen through difference, finding a way in an already organized world.

2 The concepts – *conatus* and Nietzsche's will to power – have much in common (Spindler, 2009; 2010). Spindler, F. (2009) *Spinoza: Multitud, Affekt, Kraft,*

Munkeldal [*Spinoza: Multitude, Affect, Force*], Glänta Produktion; Spindler, F. (2010) *Nietzsche: Kropp, Kunskap, Konst* [*Nietzsche: Body, Knowledge, Art*], Munkedal: Glänta Produktion.

3   Deleuze, G. (1988) *Spinoza – Practical Philosophy*, San Francisco: City Lights Books, pp. 127–128.

4   Spinoza, B. *Ethics and Related Writings*. M. Moran (Ed.), Indianapolis: Hackett. Spinoza associates nature with god, and god is an immanent, not transitive cause, and as such all things and all possibility are contained therein, there is nothing akin to a chain of events. P18, pp. 15–16.

5   Spindler, F. (2009) *Spinoza, multitude, affekt, kraft*, Monkedal: Glänta Produktion, pp. 131–133. See also Spinoza *Ethics*.:

> The mind's *conatus* or power is the very essence of the mind. But the essence of the mind affirms only what the mind is and can do (as is self-evident) and not what the mind is not and cannot do. So the mind endeavors to think only of what affirms, or posits, its power of activity.
>
> (P54, p. 88)

6   Novalis (1997) *Philosophical Writings*, Stoljar, M. (Ed.), New York: State University of New York Press, pp. 130–131.

7   See Bowie, A. (2003) *Aesthetics and Subjectivity: From Kant to Nietzsche*, Manchester: University of Manchester Press, p. 111.

8   Deleuze, G. (2006) *Nietzsche & Philosophy*, Transl. Tomlinson, H., New York: Columbia University Press, p. 188.

9   Novalis (1997) *Philosophical Writings*, Stoljar, M. (Ed.), New York: State University of New York Press, p. 118.

10   See Bowie, A. (2003) *Aesthetics and Subjectivity: From Kant to Nietzsche*, Manchester: University of Manchester Press, pp. 88–93, p. 111.

11   Brontë, E. *Wuthering Heights*. Cathy is in the midst of a rant, pulling out feathers from a pillow. "That's a turkey's," she murmured to herself;

> and this is a wild duck's; and this is a pigeon's. Ah, they put pigeons' feathers in the pillows – no wonder I couldn't die! Let me take care to throw it on the floor when I lie down. And here is a moor-cock's; and this – I should know it among a thousand – it's a lapwing's. Bonny bird; wheeling over our heads in the middle of the moor. It wanted to get to its nest, for the clouds had touched the swells, and it felt rain coming. This feather was picked up from the heath, the bird was not shot: we saw its nest in the winter, full of little skeletons. Heathcliff set a trap over it, and the old ones dared not come. I made him promise he'd never shoot a lapwing after that, and he didn't. Yes, here are more! Did he shoot my lapwings, Nelly? Are they red, any of them? Let me look.
>
> (Ch. XII)

12   As Peter Lamarque remarks, rather than make often vague reference to particulars, fiction makes use of specific descriptions and predicates to identify properties that we also find in real-world particulars but none of this extends into claiming they signify real-world events. Lamarque, P. (1984) "Bits and Pieces of Fiction," *British Journal of Aesthetics*, 24(1): 53–58.

13   Notice that the language is not working here. The real includes the virtual as well as the actual. The virtual is simply not actualized yet, nonetheless real. So, Henri Bergson reminds us, the real–fictional is a distinction that does not work. He proposed virtual-actual, which is one, following Gilles Deleuze, most process thinkers have used.

14 Rancière, J. (2004) *The Politics of Aesthetics*, Transl. Rockhill, G., London: Continuum, p. 36.

15 Rancière, J. *The Politics of Aesthetics*, pp. 38–39.

16 Geertz, C. (1973) *The Interpretation of Cultures*, London: Fontana Press, p. 9.

17 Greenblatt, S. (1997) "The Touch of the Real," *Representations*, 59: 14–29, quoting Geertz (1973), p. 11.

18 Ricoeur, P. (1969) *The Symbolism of Evil*, Boston: Beacon Press; Ricoeur, P. (1975) *The Rule of Metaphor*, London: Taylor & Francis; Kearney, R. (1988) "Paul Ricoeur and the Hermeneutic Imagination," *Philosophy & Social Criticism*, 14(2): 115–145.

19 ibid., p. 118.

20 In Kearney, R. (1988) (see footnote 21) translated from Ricoeur, P. (1986) "L'imagination dans le discours et dans l'action," in Du Texte à l'action, Ed. du Seuil, Paris: Esprit, pp. 213–219.

21 Ricoeur, P. (1979) "The Function of Fiction in Shaping Reality," *Man and World*, 12: 123–141, 133.

22 ibid., p. 135.

23 Blanchot, M. (1969/1993) *The Infinite Conversation*, Transl. S. Hanson, Minneapolis: University of Minnesota Press, p. 357.

24 Greenblatt, S. "The Touch of the Real," quoting Geertz, C. (1973), p. 18. This is echoed in John Van Maanen's discussion of the fact of fiction in organizational ethnography. Van Maanen, J. (1979) "The Fact of Fiction in Organizational Ethnography," *Administrative Science Quarterly*, 24: 539–550.

25 For Susan Sontag this is why the Romantics become so obsessed with illness and death, the real moments of self-realization in which character, feeling, and body fuse, and where reality loosens in delirium and loss, slipping away into the wider reaches of an imagined life that appears as the sole possession of an authorial self. Better, she argues, to refuse metaphor and confront the physical reality of disease, unadorned. See Sontag, S. (1978) *Illness as a Metaphor*, New York: Farrar Straus and Giroux. The spate of suicides amongst impressionable young men who having read Goethe's *Sorrows of Young Werther* published in 1774, became so entranced by the tangle of unrealized love that they too took a pistol to themselves. In Denmark and Italy, the book was banned for a time in attempts by the authorities to manage their population's imaginative "excesses." See Jack, B. (2014) "Goethe's Werther and Its Effects," *The Lancet Psychiatry*, 1(1): 18–19.

26 Machlachlan, I. "Blanchot and the Romantic Imagination," p. 167, p. 171.

27 Chia, R. (1996) "Teaching Paradigm Shifting in Management Education: University Business Schools and the Entrepreneurial Imagination," *Journal of Management Studies*, 33(4): 409–428, p. 426.

28 Colebrook, C. (2002) *Deleuze*, London: Routledge, p. 80.

29 For a lucid foray into Schlegel's thinking see Alison Stone "Friedrich Schlegel, Romanticism and the re-Enchantment of Nature," *Inquiry*, 48(1): 3–25.

30 www.poetryfoundation.org/poems/44480/ode-to-psyche   accessed   April 16, 2019.

31 ibid.

32 ibid.

33 The German Romantics, especially Novalis, were playing constantly with making language apparent, rather than disappearing either into what is being

represented (as an outside world) or indicated (as an internal authoring, speaking subject). But the appearance of language was not made formal and objective, but more a subject of concern. Keats is exemplary here. His constant reference to himself, as an author, and to objects of the world, whilst they might be read as representations and indications, are more admissions of weakness and faintness on his part. Keats the poet indicates himself in a kind of admixture of self-confident poetic power and confessional weakness, and in neither case does he presume a silent, disguised omniscience, admitting to being powerful yet entirely insufficient in poetic power when set against an immortal. And the objects referred to in the poem are things rather than anything objectified, they carry an elusiveness – "stars without a name" – and elide from the mediating touch of a representative language. Keats is alongside things, not naming them using already known categories. On Novalis and transitivity of language see (1997) *Introduction to Novalis: Philosophical Writings*, Stoljar, M. (Ed.), New York: State University of New York Press, pp. 10–12.

34 Rehnberg, H. and Ruin, H. (1997) *Herakleitos – Fragment – Kykeon*, Lund: Propexus, p. 187.

35 Deleuze, G. (1995) *Difference and Repetition*, Transl. Patton, P., New York: Columbia University Press. See also Deleuze, G. (1997) *Negotiations*, Transl. Joughin, M., New York: Columbia University Press.

36 Closely related to educate, from Latin *educare*, to rear, meaning to bring something up, to raise or erect by building.

37 Hillis-Miller, J. (2001) *Others*, Princeton: Princeton University Press, pp. 25–27.

38 Quoted in Wordsworth, J. (1982) *William Wordsworth: The Borders of Vision*, Oxford University Press, p. 47. Jonathan Wordsworth uses De Quincey's term "involutes" to describe how things appear through spots of time, a merging of material and mind in irreducible, compound experiences that admit no scientific analysis but which is being recalled poetically become a source of imaginative power in which the poet realizes moments of self-absorbing intensity.

39 Quoted in Wordsworth, J. (1982) *William Wordsworth: The Borders of Vision*, Oxford University Press, p. 54.

40 Deleuze, G. (1988) *Spinoza: Practical Philosophy*, Transl. Hurley, R., San Francisco: City Lights Books. See also Deleuze, G. (1990) *Expressionism in Philosophy: Spinoza*, Transl. Joughin, M., New York: Zone Books.

41 It is easy to think here of hand as in Latin *manus*, as in management, the hand that controls.

42 About Coleridge, for example, Hazlitt wrote of a poet "who has seen a mouldering tower by the side of a crystal lake, hid by the mist, but glittering in the wave below, may conceive the dim, gleaming, uncertain intelligence of his eye: he who has marked the evening clouds uprolled (a world of vapours) has seen the picture of his mind, unearthly, unsubstantial, with gorgeous tints and ever-varying forms." (1913) Mr Coleridge. In J. Zeitlin (Ed.) *Hazlitt on English Literature*, Oxford: Oxford University Press, p. 206.

43 Hazlitt, W. On Poetry in General. In J. Zeitlin (Ed.) *Hazlitt on English Literature*, pp. 251–276.

44 Wordsworth, W. (1800) *Preface to Lyrical Ballads*. London: Longman.

45 Wordsworth, W. *Ode: Intimations of Immortality from Recollections of Early Childhood.*

46 Evan Gottlieb's expands on this tension in Wordsworth's words by suggesting
that in his earlier phases we find a poet alive to the passive, indifferent, and
thoroughly dislocating sense of things in themselves, a poet who allows his
steady gaze to apprehend what it can never hope to understand. In contrast
the mature work has steadied and then re-absorbed these encounters with a
wordless material world, and made of it a source of frustration and provocation that serve to elevate the poetic struggle to a point of utter self-reliance.
With Wordsworth we have the Platonic form of what John Ruskin calls the
pathetic fallacy – the tendency to find in poetry a prosthesis whereby all of
nature can be read in human terms. Gottlieb, E. (2016) *Romantic Realities:
Speculative Realism and British Romanticism*, Edinburgh: University of
Edinburgh Press, pp. 34–37.
47 Hazlitt, W. (1998) *On Living to One's-Self*. In D. Wu (Ed.) *The Selected
Writing of William Hazlitt. Vol. 6 Table Talk*, London: Routledge, 78–87.
48 Hazlitt, W. *On Living to One's-Self*.
49 Coleridge's reliance became all too obvious and became pathetic dependency;
bloated on laudanum, he was unable, physically, to walk, which for one who
had been accustomed to walks of up to 50 miles across inhospitable terrain,
and for whom the rhythm of walking was intimate with the metre of poetizing, was some downfall. The sense of heightened feeling and being abroad
with the lives of others that had so animated *Lyrical Ballads* was an increasingly befuddled memory. He was left degenerate, his work suffered, and when
Hazlitt, perhaps unkindly, argued as such in print Coleridge became utterly
embittered towards his former discipline.
50 de Montaigne, M. *The Complete Essays*. Transl. M A Screech. Book III,
X. *On Restraining Your Will*. London: Penguin, 561–562.

2   Resonance, individuality, and the entrepreneur

Staying with the aura of the ordinary life

In the last chapter we suggested an intimacy between Romanticism and entrepreneurship, not least in the effort of the Romantics to give expressive voice to Spinoza's *Ethics* with its emphasis on reasoned curiosity and disciplined experiment. As much as the Romantics might set themselves against the established manners and routines of culture, so might entrepreneurs set themselves against those of managerial routine. Yet we ended the chapter with a note of caution. Enthused, though perhaps wary of Spinoza's exposed fluxing world of affect, and alive to the struggle of self-creation encouraged by such a world, the Romantics had wrested themselves free from dominant styles in moral and aesthetic form. They were interested in the experiences of open possibility available to characters, events, and things (including themselves and readers). They had no truck with fixed ideals, and whilst they acknowledged the cold, hard facts of scientific realism, they also felt the world existed beyond these facts; there was something mysterious and enchanted about nature. Including human nature. They felt themselves to be free because they had themselves to explore and through a sustained and attentive concern with their own experiences they gave voice to an entire world of strange, vulnerable ordinariness whose reality was felt in clouds of affect rather than ordered in delineations of effect.

Perhaps like Novalis they became too intricate in the linguistic mirror play this disorienting self-exploration induced, and perhaps like Wordsworth they got too close to their own personal sun and created a myth whose densities and curlicues twisted around plain sight to the point of its demise. Yet throughout this broad movement there were consistent attempts to act (and thinking was itself an action) into the world rather than think upon or beyond it and to allow the things of the world to act back. And as Hazlitt describes, this acting into life and being acted upon by it was impelled by an urge to understand one's place alongside things, not just to cast them in one's own image. What interested and entranced Romantics was their connexion to, and utter dependency on, an everyday life that was neither amenable nor explicable, but exciting.

DOI: 10.4324/9781315714455-4

Hazlitt has it "just so" when he ascribes to this acting into life a steady engagement that is also ironic and contemplative. It is a life that shares affections and hears the tumults without being unduly troubled by either the passionate or instrumental urge to pitch in. In this way one is able to live with oneself without collapsing into kaleidoscopic fragments or seeking recourse to the forms of aggrandizement and vanity that so bedevilled the later writings of Wordsworth. Hazlitt was advocating a version of Romanticism which avoiding conflating self-creation with elevation. Rather than manage one's experience too obsessively and intensely, it is better to let things be in themselves awhile. The mistake of Romanticism is the attempt to organize the world as a subaltern to one's own individuality.

It was this Romantic experience of sensation and event in the company of often elusive but ordinary things that Walter Benjamin was later to configure with the term "aura":

> To perceive the aura of an object we look at means to invest it with the ability to look at us in return. This experience corresponds to the data of the *mémoire involuntaire*. (These data, incidentally, are unique: they are lost to the memory that seeks to retain them. Thus they lend support to a concept of the aura that comprises the "unique manifestation of distance" ...)[1]

Involuntary memories are akin to spots of time, they evoke the struggle of weaving memory into literary form, and of negotiating endlessly the forgetting that goes into the actual experience of living, and the myriad ways then making up the narratives by which any life (and of self in such life) could be made sensible.[2] The Romantic writer excites desire by poetically extending and transposing the relations we might have with people to those we might have with symbols, traditions, and inanimate things, and to find in those things a curious power to look back and show not what they are, but indicate that they could be so much more than what they currently show. By staying with ordinary life they cultivate a sensibility before the multiple potential becomings in every being, the aura of virtuality that shadows every actuality. With aura, there is no exhaustion. Just as another person looks back at our gaze so, by extension, past and future events, and things, can also gaze back: though these events and things carry with them a necessary distance and distinctiveness; they are always peering at us from the other side of what is natural to us.

By conveying aura the poet becomes a storyteller, what Benjamin calls a craftsperson able to weave the myth of tradition (time/history) with the myth of places (distant or near space). They do so using events and symbols that bring the transmissions associated with communication into some kind of gathering called a literary form. This form is marked – as the potter's hand leaves a thumb swipe in the glaze – through a sense of exposure to what is there, without knowing fully what is there, for there are only ever fragments and any attempt to retain the data of *mémoire involuntaire* in mechanical reproduction simply destroys it:

> If we designate as aura the associations which, at home in the *mémoire involontaire*, tend to cluster around the object of a perception, then its analogue in the case of a utilitarian object is the experience which has left traces of the practiced hand.[3]

The poet is alive to such marks of exposure, they are akin to the scent of a flower so agreeable that desire can never exhaust it, nor can any representation release us from its hold: it captivates by being both generous and yet withdrawing, by appearing in ways that suggest it might be represented in text or imagery, but then somehow always refusing these forms by translating the encounter back into its own inscrutable organization. Being present, with the flower, experiencing it means to also sense its aura, its virtual powers to become, which means that describing the flower fully and exhaustingly is never possible, but instead becomes an endless exercise where experience, memory, imagination, affect, enters into endlessly renewable relations. The Romantics struggle for the same affect. What is created, their fragments, gives back without exhaustion and their audience might never have their fill: "What it contains that fulfils the original desire would be the very same stuff on which the desire originally feeds."[4] And these writers realize the affect by themselves being affected, their perception exposed to things as flowers, or poverty-riddled beggars, or words even as empirical things, and finding that there are things that look back, returning the gaze in a glance or stare. Wordsworth exemplifies the romantic poet's affected relationship to the world, to the ordinary "objects" that receive their place in verse as words and world blend in a look that allows things to return the gaze.

With Benjamin, alive to the onset of technology and mass war, it was the city walker, the flâneur, who inherited the Romantic mantle of being in the company of things that look back. But always from a distance, always simultaneously removed from the immediate, yet enjoying the city-pleasure of not being able to get lost. The Romantic writer of fragments is exposed to, and exposes, the associations of aura both historically and naturally. Historically they write in paeans to earlier artistic attempts at expressing form, aware of their poetic forebears and lineage and of how this stylistic context of reproductive practice inevitably skews their own attentiveness. Naturally they are aware that aura only arises through the veil of reproduction, the aura is only ever experienced in a state of resemblance or reproduction. On both counts aura is in thrall to artistic expression. Where the means of reproduction become mechanical and then technical, it is the medium that increasingly determines the form: "the technique of reproduction detaches the reproduced object from the domain of tradition."[5] It does so by having the copy subsume the original, and then transforming the experience by transporting the object to the audience, in their setting, rather than having them brought "in touch" with the thing itself.[6]

Memory is at risk from technological recording and storing of ordinary, ephemeral events threatening our experience of aura precisely because it became an endlessly reproducible and accessible alternative to the vague and difficult fluctuating effulgence of imaginative endeavour. With mechanical and technical reproduction we are left with a diminishing sensory field – as things are brought closer and their copy is granted the status of acceptable substitute our sense perception contracts in range and lessens in variety. We ourselves become copies: our early days and all our days can be laid out in recorded, storable sequences that fix events outside of their traditional role in ritual. We all of us partake not of tradition and nature in which condition we are implicated through the artistic exposure to aura, but of events cast as evidence and fact in which we find ourselves arranged, for example, by the appropriate (prescribed) reading of symbols. The authoring of aura gives way to a politics of ordering and managed authority.

The flâneur was a riposte to this rise of the copy and loss of aura, a figure wandering the arcades, tracing the edges of proper spaces, writing concretely without resorting too easily and completely to well-used concepts. Benjamin writes glowingly of the poet Baudelaire, that he was able to encounter and be entranced by things whose very remoteness was what brought him under a spell, and who in being pulled into such distances was able still to look back, content in a struggle to illuminate the profane. We shall discuss this power to be affected as related both to seduction and to a power to affect, central to our theory of the entrepreneurship process. Baudelaire's genius lay in his patient sensitivity to the simple strangeness of occurrence – from the material action of walking comes magic, as though with each step small clouds of bright dust burst and give the air a tincture of attracting alien colour. From this we can learn how opportunity is created, from allowing magic to speak to you from within the mundane everydayness, imagining its potential becoming as a process of actualizing novelty in practice. The body of the writer acts as an active conduit of wider forces; it is a gathering larded with fissures and moments of spilling over all of which is there to be found in the incipient event, lurking in the particulars' interactions.[7] Thus, we suggest, from literature and writing, we can learn how the body of the entrepreneur similarly acts as a conduit of wider forces. Forces that, in the case of entrepreneurship, hold incipient new value, should the organization needed for them to offer this value to a potential user be created. That is the entrepreneurship process: to actualize the organization needed for new value to become available to potential users/customers.

Living alongside limits

In Romanticism came a general loosening of categories and social orders, words shook off the mortar by which they were fixed to offices, values, and bodies: the aristocrats could be pulled along the gutter and the poor become noble, and the literary novel and radical poem a scene for presenting this unravelling.

Writing in the wake of this freeing up of imaginative power and its distillation in the literary form, allowed who followed in the wake of Romanticism found themselves in touch with a raw expressive power to study, and contemplate alternatives to, the natural and social order. George Eliot, for example, was able to write novels of magisterial ordinariness in which gossip was gilded with profundity and truths could be issued from the mouths of rakes (without this being a scandal); the old orders were teetering. For Eliot the novel lends itself like no other imaginative form to conveying and elaborating on the everyday settlements in which lies the potential for huge social and personal change. The novel was just much better at showing what for most of us was the stuff of life, much better than the frigid prose of theology and science that is, and more resonant with experience than the often-lofty structural decorations traditionally provided by poets. Maybe it is better to consider forms of language that are closer to lived experience.

Eliot, whose translation of Spinoza's *Ethics* spoke of the dissolution of fixed distinctions, realized that it is from the unclear, the ambiguous, and the in-between (the entre-), that relations held fast by habit found an impetus to renew themselves: transgression might be forgiven, pomposity might be acknowledged, and novelty might be encouraged. And so we might think of entrepreneurship as a genre of action where free movement has priority over habit and routine, but only due to the existing practices of ordinary life being endowed with unreleased potentials, hidden in the cracks, if you allow yourself to recognize it and let it to speak to you. As Eliot observes, such a relation with things is different from science's meaning-fixing concepts:

> Suppose, then, that the effort which has been again and again made to construct a universal language on a rational basis has at last succeeded, and that you have a language that has no uncertainty, no whims of idiom, no cumbrous forms, no fitful shimmer of many-hued significance, no hoary archaisms "familiar with forgotten tears" [Wordsworth] – a patient, deodorized and non-resonant language, which effects the purpose of communication as perfectly and rapidly as algebraic signs. Your language maybe a perfect medium of expression to science, but will never express life, which is a great deal more than science.[8]

A sentiment which carries echoes of Coleridge and Wordsworth's *Lyrical Ballads*:

> The Man of science seeks truth as a remote and unknown benefactor; he cherishes and loves it in his solitude: the Poet, singing a song in which all human beings join with him, rejoices in the presence of

truth as our visible friend and hourly companion. Poetry is the breath and finer spirit of all knowledge[.]

The accusation against academic concepts is they are often frigid and separated from life, they aver from the local, specific, individual, and accidental, eager to pretend they did not emerge from a dialogue with such paltry, haphazard everyday commerce. In Romanticism and its legacy the writing of words received priority over concepts: ordinary events received their due, and the actual was revealed in all its nullity, its partiality, its strangeness. After Romanticism, authors strove to avoid the self-elevation of formal poetic form, and instead stay grounded, whilst managing still to lay out the actual in such ways as to question its apparent naturalness. The poem or novel becomes the work of an authorship that is attentive to things and playfully ironic in attempting to configure and convey these things in language, a series or collection of fragments, in the same way as Plato's dialogues are a collection of opinions and reasoned thoughts brought into conversation. The precision strived for in natural science language is here kept at a distance, for the benefit of a hermeneutically accessible, yet multiple meanings of words that betray their emergence from lived, messy experience. Mess holds potential and is as such ripe for improvisational entry of organizational initiative.

The subject in literature

This is the attraction of messy experiences. At the end of *Les mots et Les Chose* Michel Foucault talks of the emergence of literature as the moment when we (at least in the Western tradition) gave up on absolutes and instead began to consider our role as investigators. Literature is what takes us back from the concepts and order of ordained grammar and towards the open, raw force of words, the scenes of ordinary life, the untamed and imperious presence of life being lived out, without end. To think in concepts is to reach inwardly towards what one is in essence, to realize an ever more grounded, certain sense of self. In contrast, the exemplifying "I speak" performed by the novelist uses words and reaches beyond itself into the "not-I," and so stretches away from what Foucault calls "the dynasty of representation," but all the whilst – ironically – using representations (the words, plots, characters) to do so. The novelist builds into what has come before whilst all the time inaugurating its collapse. It is a passage towards an outside space, no longer contained by signs:

> The subject of literature (what speaks in it and what it speaks about) is less language in its positivity than the void language takes as its space when it articulates itself in the nakedness of "I speak."[9]

Without the self-evident presence of the subject the writer looks upon the word freed from the discursive positivity of certain knowledge seeking to assert "I" as against "not-I." The writer can begin to think from the outside of the pressing demand to interiorize the world into a coherent gathering of plausible arrangements, a demand manifest in the exhortation to rid oneself of the random happenstance of raw empirical occurrence and instead to know thyself and declare it. In their fragmentary intensity novels or poems can remain in touch with that which has yet to be circumscribed and assessed and in which all manner of contraries can remain in one another's company. Its language can reveal a whole social world in the smallest of things and then shed the things it purportedly names, and in such an undoing the authorial subject too can disappear as it bumps into the multiplications of self and absurdities that can arise in such unruly writing, or lose itself in the vast connectedness of a world in which more things than might even be dreamt of can speak up. This was the discovery and bequest of Romantic novelists. For Rancière:

> The Romantic Age actually plunged language into the materiality of the traits by which the historical and social world becomes visible to itself, be it in the form of the silent language of things or the coded language of images. Circulation within this landscape of signs defines, moreover, the new fictionality, the new way of telling stories, which is first of all a way of assigning meaning to the "empirical" world of lowly actions and commonplace objects.[10]

So it is both naked and, yet, an invasion of language into the commonplace: signs are made uneasy, but extended into everyday materialities and images. Both of these conditions dissolve the easy separation of fact and fiction, and make of the writer a builder. In plot, description and characterization, the social machinery of understanding that links what happens (the silent language with its propulsive necessity) with the images, tones, and signs of coded language, is to be found in the subject. The subject is placed centrefold in the every world of occurrence as the figure in which power and knowledge are being inscribed, and which is also the scribe, meaning for those who write there is an endless row upon row of opportunities to continually add to the world by investigating the limits of silent and coded language.

Maurice Blanchot thinks of Romantic writing, notably that of Novalis, as especially virulent and potent form of revealing the limits to prevailing orders: the written fragments are concentrated, defined by their own centre rather than wholly by their position in a field of positions; they are unconcerned in themselves with the interval of their being taken up and engaged within a consistent and sustained way; and they, in concealing the presence of other fragments (other poems or novels, say), regard their own self-sufficiency as creating new relations exempted from the authored unity insofar as these relations come about only on its mysterious completion as an act of communication between the author – the

I – and the audience – the other – both of which only exist in the empirically performative and political act of giving over and receiving.[11]

Writing works when revealing how much the invisibility of the visible remains invisible *within them*: "the fictitious is never in things or in
people, but in the impossible verisimilitude of what lies between them."[12]
Writing does this with devices of forgotten, overlooked, hidden, and
mysterious space along whose halls and under whose vaults academic
discourse cannot tread without trepidation, hesitancy, and downright
fear. The tropes of metaphor, synecdoche, metonymy, and prosopopoeia,
the technical devices by which substitution, displacement, distilling and
stretching, and re-naming and naming are made to happen in novels.
The unsettling of its own forms, loosened from the refuge of interior
structures, is spoken and written in language that, being outside itself,
struggles with untutored force and desire that is indifferently and endlessly unfolding: there is no inside, no womb, no home, no positive
presence, only unhomeliness in what is spinning outwards and over the
horizon towards which the novel lurches, impossibly and irresistibly as
its own judge. Romantic writing gives form to what can be created which
cannot be anything other than the fragment to which becoming and not
completing is the essence. It is the place in which the disputes between
language, meaning, and experience, between things and words, between
what has been and could be, takes place: in being formed it is always
moving away from what has been formed.

For some, like Gregory Lukács, this attentiveness to flow and the desire
to be otherwise constitutes an endless withdrawing towards potential in
whose wake the solid things of the world – the named objects, promises,
and achievements – fall away and decay. Language becomes the dissimu-
lation of things. Whilst Lukács accepts that writing – and especially the
novel – had opened up what was a closed world, embodying in a very
literal sense a modern sensibility for what is exposed, bracing and frustrating, the myriad instances of its expression and the striving it entailed
induces an alienating condition. In Romantic longing, whether the wistful
melancholia induced by a moss covered, ruinous hovel, or the *Sturm und
Drang* of a Faustian bargain, it appeared to Lukács, that human experience was being caught fast on a dialectical tension in which omniscience
and unity are forever foreclosed. Why concede so much so early? Why
worship fragments when all it leaves is a kind of perversion: the struggle
for unity is ceded to forgetting our longing for it.

Lukács is unwilling to relinquish the prospect offered by the concepts
of dialectical progress by which history is understood in terms of its pro-
gressive spirit, an organization of life that somehow has its own propulsion, outside of the agreements and events and urges upon which human
beings have themselves stumbled. To understand the social and historical condition in which human beings find themselves needs more than
Romantic writing can offer.

Yet what the Romantics show *is* there is nothing more, save the slightly arid constructions of social and historical theory whose clarity is bought at the expense of their resonance. They chose life over Hegel. Literary forms take their cue from the communal and collective sense of self-understanding by which what exists comes to matter somehow. In this they are a consideration of how to live well and badly, and a foray into the confusions and delights entrained in the coming together of such. The novel form shows humanity to itself, the forms it has taken and might take, the inherently transitional nature of human self-organization by which contrasts and tensions resolve and unravel in the most nuanced and uneven ways. The writing is peculiarly effective in this "showing" of ourselves because we readers experience, along with the event, the character and author, the manner in which thoughts grow within actions, so that a deed once committed to, though it might itself be dubious, entails what subsequently becomes practically the right course of action which, in turn, can expose an event, character, and reader to new conditions of possibility which, being hard to hold and for which both tradition and memory are ill-equipped, are a scene of dread and excitement. The claim is not truth, the tone is not educating, schooling, there are no specific points to grasp. As form, *bild*, it is open and readers are drawn in to the extent there is passion to spend. The reader's power to be affected is, however, intimately related to the author's power to affect. In the end, it all hinges on the text.

Romantic writers espoused and enacted a style of "getting and being amid things" (entre) and then "taking them on" (prendre/preneur). There is a reverence of, and attention to, the particular. They attend to the scene of things and events from which the general is a subservient distillation. The keen eye, the eye that seeks heterogeneity in the received homogeneity, is often alerted by affect that gives glimpses of openings as faint lights luring you into the unknown. Staying with the particular in this way gives a sense of how the world can always be otherwise, for the particular is such precisely by manifesting a capacity to resist the smothering force of the general. Attend carefully to a social gathering or collective purpose and you find them as riddled with exception, accident, and idiosyncrasy as much as they are substantiated by conformity. This, however, requires from you that an affect-based relationship is not pressed back, but sustained by reason. Attending carefully is thus a combining of interpretation and analysis with more deconstructive or playful readings, where the disturbing, unfitting, irritating presence of the particular is not cut out of the picture, but used to provoke further interpretation. This goes back to Spinoza, for whom understanding the world emerged from a continual mixing of imagination (sensory impression and symbolic association), reason (adequate and commonly held views on the property of things), and intuition (a glimpse of what is essential about things). Imagination is a source of perpetual contingency, and no matter how refined the certainties arrived at through reason and intuition, they will always be accompanied by the hubbub of life itself. What is it to continue to hold on to the certainties and values that reason seems to require of our will? What is it to push them to the edges, where they start to crack? And on the flip side, what is it to push at the particularities and limits of our immediate experience? What is it to breach ordinary experience with thought?[13]

Entrepreneurs

Drawing on the above discussion of Romantic literature and writers, we seek to entertain a relationship to entrepreneurial action which suggests that, if we look for passages rather than positions when we study the emergence of novelty in any temporary social space, we are as likely to research free movement as we are habit, routines, and institutions. Not that it is a question of either/or, for there is always a tension between free movement and institutions. Rather, it is a question of interest and attention: if you seek to understand how actualizing new value is done, you follow that which moves through both forces (affirmation and negation of becoming) in an attempt to understand how common sense is made receptive to that which is not yet practiced.[14]

It is in sympathy with this Romantic view of the self and its restless urge to move that we wish to investigate the condition of entrepreneurship. We want to bring the entrepreneur to the gallery of Romantic figures: the flâneur, the gambler, the dilettante, the virtuoso, the troubadour, and the harlequin.[15] They too are fragmentary in-between figures delighting in the fragmentary, the part, the incomplete that potentiality can seduce you to play. Similarly, the Romantic self is always complet*ing* and never finished, and alive only insofar as it touches and is touched by a self-awareness that has as its ground primarily its own struggle. Novalis finds writing to be a space for exploring the profoundly ironic condition of presenting an "I." The activity somehow belongs to the presenting I, but it is only ever a singular, particular and contingent presentation, and the more local, mysteriously everyday and particular the presentation, the more distinct the omniscient sense of the "I" as that which is distinct in itself as a unity.

As Nietzsche pointed out with his precursor to event-philosophy – there is no lightning behind the flash – we learn from the Romantics that there is no "I" beyond the act (and act of thought), not a self in itself, only a self that emerges performatively, in the mirror play of a co-existing self that acts and self that thinks, or body and mind: the authority (authoring power) of each being grounded in little more than their continual mutual encounter. The intransitivity of any authorial declaration – the idea of the author being performatively constituted in the use of language – means, as Roland Barthes was also later to remark, that a declaring self brings to the world nothing else than a declared self, not a self that is declaring itself. Rather than try and wrestle themselves free from the anomaly of such a condition (as, say, did Kant when posing the fixing ground of categories, and of reason), the Romantics are content to live with co-existence of incommensurable experience. We humans feel and imagine, and we look upon ourselves feeling and imagining, and look upon ourselves as we look upon ourselves. There is no end to these rhythms of self-forming and no progression (telos) from one state to the next, for they are all present as a fragmentary multiplicity, and can be apprehended as such. Moreover, just as the author has no grounding authority save their own continued enunciation, the performative act of enunciation can never remain within the gift of each writer because the performance is always an acting into reality in the name of learning, enchantment, and diversion. The enunciation is more like a consummation between writer, word, and audience, from which union the very possibility of writing emerges. Hence the irony of it all – there is an author, words, and audience constituting each another without any having distinct presence beyond the multiple refracting event of writing-reading.[16]

Romantic writing is assembled and with readers becomes an assembly; it is a calling for others to come and gather, for it is insufficient if it is just a semantic thing, a thing of words, it also has to be material, it reaches beyond its own grammatical limits into the materiality of ordinary life (Benjamin's involuntary memory, or Wordsworth's spots of time).[17] In being in and amid the ordinary writers enlist imagination to vivify the potentialities being encountered there. To write and read is to become, and becoming is always a leaning or gesture towards what is incomplete and imperceptible and away from what takes the solidity of an ending; one can never write and read by completing or finalizing forms to the world. With reference to Gombrowicz's work, Gilles Deleuze writes: "To write is certainly not to impose a form (of expression) on the matter of lived experience. Literature rather moves in the direction of the ill-formed or the incomplete ..."[18] Again, we can see how literature, as a becoming, a free play moving in the openings that a foreign language in language makes possible, does not settle with the faculties of understanding and reason but requires imagination to affirm a becoming-other. To write and read is to throw oneself into association with things, a proximity that belies claims to self-sufficiency because along its detouring pathways it shows how others live, and in conditions of dependency.[19]

Writing and entrepreneurship share this affinity with life "amidst" the particulars, the fragments amongst which in-betweens multiply, and to subject these to critical, disciplined attention. Deleuze adds that when literature progresses by opening up a foreign language within language, it does so by attending to what it hears and sees in "the interstices of language, in its intervals."[20] The entrepreneur, too, is moving into such openings, at least for the likes of Joseph Schumpeter, who sensed entrepreneurial force to be the creation of new organization, making possible combinations that disturb and potentially transform established administrative processes, production activities, or consumption behaviours.[21] In this way entrepreneurs "clear new land" (Novalis) by moving freely in the not-yet organized space. They are not managers or employees, who rely for their distinctive role on a structure in which to behave, a place already organized by a purpose or strategy. These roles (or subject-positions) are configured through an acceptance of their lot, they fit into patterns, often thoughtlessly, the organizational place is already assigned to them. Entrepreneurs both belong to habit, and yet also are sent ahead to scout out likely spaces for the nascent settlement of human activity.

Like Novalis' poet, though, there is little that is heroic, directed, or assertive in such activity, rather it is the outlook of a curious and collectively embedded being ever open to the effect of what is "other" than they are. We can easily imagine the entrepreneur as the permeable membrane between "what is" and "what could become," registering vibrations from moving indeterminacies colliding, giving sound to the world of the "not yet there," a luring, mobilizing melody.

In-betweens are ephemeral cracks that are relationally revealed amongst the particulars, and are in this way more *made* than discovered. They are as much a result of imagination's discounting of future value as potentiality/virtuality in the present. This drives the "acting as if" mode of the entrepreneur, which it is possible to critique as naivety or foolishness.[22] As with potential, a virtuality too is real but not actual until it is actualized. It has to be created by differentiating action, making something that adds (value, in the case of entrepreneurship) to the field of practice you operate in. Entre-spaces form as we insist that "this is not all," that transformation is incipient, an "other" ready to come when called upon. But you have to stay in the empirical, attend to the particulars and their relations as interactions in the making.[23] This is how you can study any process.[24] "Is it an affront to objectivism" Massumi asks, "to say that there is, in addition to the ingredients, their interaction and its effect? In a word, their event."[25] Both their interaction and its effect will remain hidden to those inattentive to the particulars in context, how they are related, and the effect of their relationality. Smothered over by the universal, dominated by reason's alliance with causal explanation, the event never happens. When imagination, and its affiliation with affect and hermeneutically accessible understanding, is no longer the target of an anxious concern for losing control (*contra-rotulus*, against what is rolling), a spasm that remains in the body that finds Descartes' self-grounded subject attractive, but instead affirmed in an interest in prorol (*pro-rotulus*, for what is rolling), and which is still in the company of inquiring reason, who knows what can happen? An event? An event is always more itself than being a member of a class or category and will therefore resist exhaustive definitions as well as potentially transform "what is" (classified, categorized) often by irritating, provoking impatience with the present state. Intensity is what prepares the world for the event. Intensity sets up a field of individuation, where the incarnation of ideas into new forms is potentialized. Every idea is a virtuality, a bundle of multiple differential relations, and one of those relations can become actualized as a result of a creation process through which the idea is differentiated (difference in intensities that make one break through the threshold between the virtual and the actual) – actualized in practice.[26]

How the entrepreneurial creation adds to the world is thus part of a generative condition that is easily overlooked. We would like to envisage entrepreneurial ideas existing as virtualities becoming actual, swarming as bundles of multiple differential relationships, incipient and ready to be called upon by an intensity that gives one priority (gets it differentiated) as an opportunity taken. However, the language of opportunity, dominant for decades in entrepreneurship research, is not well suited for describing what happens here. Opportunities are more created than taken, and the event-potential that opens up for the new is seldom part of what is studied when we study entrepreneurship. One way to change this, which is part of this book's ambition, is to bring attention to the affective sides of such creation-processes.[27] We do this by the inclusion of play and desire in our theory of the entrepreneurship process.

Desire brings us to the relational, the variations in intensity, and urges us on to follow the ideas that explore the in-betweens, the incomplete. When you realize that grasping creation processes require attention to affect/intensity, you also realize that the start of the entrepreneurial process is the question of how we are led astray by the entrepreneurial vision, often narrated as a fascinating story, a fabulation of what is to come. This vision too emerges from the interstices, the in-betweens, the entrespaces where the limit of practice is sensed and where no existing organization is capable of exploring potentialities. Organization-creation is this process through which incarnation of an idea happens in the event of entrepreneurship. That is, entrepreneurship's actualization of the virtual is what we call organization-creation. It never occurs in a vacuum, but always targets the already actualized, protected by common sense, habit, memory, routine, structure, and everything needed for control and efficiency to work. Entrepreneurship research, thus far, has focused on the very last part – the launch of a new venture, the start-up, the new business taking off. What we say is that this, again, is the last part of the actualization. We need entrepreneurship research to show some theoretical common sense in attending to the process of *getting there*; the process of mobilizing, seducing, playing, and struggling with the common sense of "the already actualized" before it reaches commerce. This requires theory to broaden its conceits, expand the criteria of meaning, and itself show some common sense in allowing for a looser more speculative form of language.[28] Knowledge of entrepreneurship needs theory to extend into the process that comes before there is an organization; a pre- and proto-organizational form, held together by desire. We call this the assemblage and propose this is a crucial concept for anyone who wants to grasp entrepreneurship processes more processually.[29]

More critically still, and this applies to ourselves as much as other entrepreneurship theorists, we need to acknowledge the inherent dangers in enthusing about entrepreneurship as an affective, individualizing condition. As a virulent form of self-fashioning it has been powerful, indeed arguably in the United States it has been there in the foundations of its birth and an ever-recurring lodestone towards which dispositional appeal has been made whenever organization is felt as being too present, too overbearing, too restrictive: the entrepreneur is less an economic role sustained by state policy than an idealized embodiment of the enduring problem of free relations.[30]

In arguing for the entrepreneur as a subject who attends to its own restless and open experience of producing rather than just the abstracted relations between capital, investment, and production – a figure who is acutely sensitive to the contingent nature of using scarce means to pursue uncertain, yet often mutually exclusive and even antagonistic, ends – then we risk associating what we call Romanticism with an uncritical form of neoliberal accommodation of commerce and imagination, as though they were mutually accommodating worldviews. Each, it seems, is profoundly interested in understanding individual's activity: to paraphrase Foucault, one is interested in what work means for the worker who works, the other in what life means for the ordinary person who lives. Work, for the worker, is configured as a skill and so machinery set against a projected income stream, it is the worker as an enterprise of his or her self, and an economy becomes a system made up of such enterprise units, each functioning not as partners in trade (the classical conception of *homo oeconomicus* in which the subject is abstracted into a bundle of needs governed by the principle of utility that animates mechanisms of exchange) but as entrepreneurs of themselves (neoliberal *homo oeconomicus*, a being who is the source of their own productivity and responsible for their own satisfaction).[31]

If we too subscribe to this idea of the entrepreneur as an ability machine, as a figure made up of innate or hereditary elements, then what is being valued is not only their skill in generating an income (their command of the relations between scarce means and incommensurable ends) but also their capacity to structurally adjust their own relations with others so as voluntary organize with co-producers (including their family) equally or more adept, so as to further enhance their human capital. Thus is set in train an incessant competition to secure alliances with the better educated, the more hygienic, the healthier, the more mobile. From these new relations the stimulation to innovation – discovering new productive abilities, new means, new outlets – is further excited and future income projections enhanced. Each has made an entrepreneur of themselves, becoming a subject (along with their family and friends) of their own future subjection to multi-enterprise model, and each has become embedded in a broader gathering of multiple enterprises, all of which are ready-to-hand insofar as they are graspable, penetrable, comprehensible and, much as in Hobbes' state of nature, with insufficient natural pre-eminence to constitute a hegemony of singular interests.[32] Its natural extension is universal. First, the intelligibility and correctness of all social relations (health, education, leisure) are governed by its ordering concern for the enhancement of human capital (that which draws an income). And second, all forms of governmental activity, including the provision of scholarship through higher education and research, is exposed to the cynicism of market critique; laissez-faire becomes "a permanent economic tribunal confronting government."[33] Assessing whether social relations or political authorities are good is no longer a question of moral right and wrong, but of the efficient organization of means and ends.

To the extent our advocacy of entrepreneurship sustains rather than tempts the limits of such a neoliberal ordering, it is complicit with prevailing orders, and far from Romantic in its tenor. It is a complicity of which we are critical. Throughout this book we do allude to business success, to innovation, to economic growth, and in doing so we conform (inevitably) with an enterprise model which is as pervasive as air: it is the new a priori. Yet we also advocate a struggle to minorize this order, and to find in the entrepreneur a figure doing likewise, and in this to resist the imitative order by which the subject wills that (desires) a copy subsume the original and then has the copy replicated throughout the relational setting by which a life is being lived. To recall the earlier conversation on aura, there is, as Foucault reminds us, in the entrepreneur, a form of mechanical and technical reproduction of an economic order that diminishes our desiring capacity, first by lessening the variety to that which is entirely economic in nature, and second by then extending the range of the one-sided form of desire to touch all relations. The inscrutable, and difficult and unsettling nature of things (aura) yields to the authority of economic tribunal. Here the entrepreneur's activity (behaviour) transcribes predictable patterns that make them governable: they demonstrate systematic responses to systemic (artificial) modulations of an environment of operations. This, the established place called reality, is the place of *homo oeconomicus*, the one that in the most rational way adjusts to the given circumstances according to invested interests. Foucault makes this interpretation as he studies Gary Becker: "*homo oeconomicus* is someone who accepts reality."[34] In Foucault's words, they are a subject enabling a certain art of government that entertains its own diminishment in the service of that over which it can have no control, the economy.[35] This diminishment is necessary, insofar as it is impossible to oversee, and control, the myriad and multiple interplay of all possible interests by which an economy is constituted (potentially). The contingency of chance and accident, and the inherently open nature of effect, makes the edges and channels of any economy largely invisible. They can only be properly navigated by those that actually cut them through in pursuit of their own income projects, their own enterprise.

We find in the entrepreneur a riposte to this authority (as the flâneur was a riposte to, as well as accepting of, the rise of the copy and loss of aura), but more in irony and curiosity than outright opposition. The entrepreneur of which we speak makes clear the objective, operational conditions of an economy under which they live, and then works to question rather than just perpetuate them, and so elides from those aspects of ordering (economic) activity by which he or she is inevitably being organized and to which his or her being has been ascribed by virtue of him or her being a subject of inalienable and calculable interests. That we find in the entrepreneur a figure that disturbs and disrupts this ordering in the very act of instituting it, is to broach the question of entrepreneurship as one of potential, rather than actuality. Importantly, this riposte to dominant/normalized enterprise discourse is one that necessarily has to be thought also as directed against the gendered, structural discrimination that persist in a post-feminist discursive regime and its tendency to co-opt feminism by promoting individual freedom in pursuit of offered opportunities as the solution.[36]

Notes

1 Benjamin, W. (2007 [originally published 1955]) On Some Motifs in Baudelaire. In *Illuminations*, Transl. H. Zohn, New York: Schoken Books, p.186.

2 "For an experienced event is finite – at any rate, confined to one sphere of experience; a remembered event is infinite, because it is only a key to everything that happened before and after it." Benjamin, W. (2007 [originally published 1955]) The Image of Proust. In *Illuminations*, Transl. H. Zohn, New York: Schoken Books, p. 202.

3 Benjamin, W. (2007 [originally published 1955]) On Some Motifs in Baudelaire. In *Illuminations*, Transl. H. Zohn, New York: Schoken Books, p. 186.

4 Benjamin, W. (2007 [originally published 1955]) On Some Motifs in Baudelaire. In *Illuminations*, Transl. H. Zohn, New York: Schoken Books, p. 186.

5 Benjamin, W. (2007) The Work of Art in the Age of Mechanical Reproduction. In *Illuminations*, Transl. H. Zohn. New York: Schoken Books, p. 221. See also On Some Motifs in Baudelaire. In *Illuminations*, Notes, pp. 198–199.

6 The same works on audiences too. If, for example, they begin to read tourist publicity about the beauty of the English Lake District, they might have used Wordsworth's *Guide to the Lakes*. Reproduced mechanically, yet enthusing and brimming over with a zeal for immersive experiences, Wordsworth's book shows the reader and prospective traveller the beauty of the place to which they are temporarily encouraged to belong, yet Wordsworth was hostile, for example, to the growing popularity of picturesque viewing points that were being proscribed as offering the *ideal* vantage from which to view a scene, and of which cheap etchings were available for purchase. Already, it seems mechanical reproduction was eating into the sensory field of the tourist. Fast forward to twentieth century the equivalents and the text and images of a waterfall or of ornate steamers plying the smooth surface of a lake come

readily consumed (there is little effort required to read them), and it is almost as if they substitute for the feel of spray bouncing from rocks or the flare of a lake's surface wrinkled by falling light.

7 Nussbaum, M. (1990) *Love's Knowledge*, Oxford University Press, pp. 156–157.

8 George Eliot *Essays* quoted in David, P. (2017) *The Transferred Life of George Eliot*, Oxford: Oxford University Press, p. 181.

9 Foucault, M. (1987) Maurice Blanchot: The Thought from Outside. In *Foucault/Blanchot*, New York: Zone Books, p. 12.

10 Rancière, J. *The Politics of Aesthetics*, London: Verso, p. 36.

11 Blanchot, M. *The Infinite Conversation*, p. 359.

12 Foucault, M. (1987) Maurice Blanchot: The Thought from Outside. In *Foucault/Blanchot*, New York: Zone Books, p. 23.

13 Spinoza, Baruch *Ethics and Related Writings*. P40–P45. pp. 50–54.

14 The work by Dimov and Pistrui (2020) provide useful further conceptual clarity and inspiration when it comes to our attempt to analyse and understand this relationship between common sense holding the actual in place and how this can be made to receive novelty through processes of actualizing the virtually new. Dimov and Pistrui focus on action and time, action and context, and perception and action as discursive entries into social language games, kind of dialogues with common sense; Dimov, D. and Pistrui, J. (2020) "Ricursive and Discursive Model of and for Entrepreneurial Action," *European Management Review*, 17: 267–277.

15 List given by Benjamin, W. (2006 [first published 1937]) Edward Fuchs, Collector and Historian. In H. Eiland & M. Jennings (Eds.), *Selected Writings Volume 3, 1935–1938*, Cambridge: Harvard University Press, p. 275. The latter three being previously introduced to entrepreneurship in Hjorth, D. and Steyaert, C. (2006) American Psycho/European Schizo: Stories of Managerial Elites in a Hundred Images. In Gagliardi, P. & Czarniawska, B. (Eds.), *Management Education and Humanities*, Cheltenham: Edward Elgar, pp. 67–97. See also Hjorth, D. and Steyaert, C. (2009) Moving Entrepreneurship: An Incipiency. In Hjorth, D. & Steyaert, C. (Eds.) *The Politics and Aesthetics of Entrepreneurship*, Cheltenham: Edward Elgar, pp. 221–230.

16 Barthes, R. (1977) The Death of the Author. In *Image-Music-Text*, London: Fontana.

17 Deleuze, G. and Guattari, F. (1988) *A Thousand Plateaus – Capitalism and Schizophrenia*, London: The Athlone Press, pp. 345–347.

18 Deleuze, G. (1998) *Essays – Critical and Clinical*, London and New York: Verso, p. 1.

19 Deleuze, G. (1997) *Literature and Life*, Transl. D. Smith & M. Greco. *Critical Inquiry*, 23(2): 225–230.

20 Deleuze, G. (1998) *Essays – Critical and Clinical*, London and New York: Verso, p. 5.

21 Schumpeter, J. (1947) "The Creative Response in Economic History," *The Journal of Economic History*, 7: 149–159.

22 See Gartner, W.B., Bird, B., and Starr, J. (1992) "Acting as if: Differentiating Entrepreneurial from Organizational Behavior," *Entrepreneurship, Theory & Practice*, Spring: 13–31; which builds on the neo-Kantian philosopher Vaihinger: Vaihinger, H. (1952 [original work published 1911]). *The*

Philosophy of "as if": A System of the Theoretical, Practical and Religious Fictions of Mankind, London: Routledge & Kegan Paul. Aldrich, H.E. and Fiol, C.M. (1994) "Fools Rush in? The Institutional Context of Industry Creation," *Academy of Management Review*, 19(4): 645–670.

23 Massumi, B. (2002) *Parables for the Virtual – Movement, Affect, Sensation*, Durham and London: Duke University Press.

24 Helin, J., Hernes, T., Hjorth, D. and Holt, R. (2014) Process Is How Process Does. In Helin J. et al. (Eds.), *Oxford University Press Handbook of Process Philosophy and Organization Studies*, Oxford: Oxford University Press, pp. 1–16.

25 Massumi, B. (2002) *Parables for the Virtual – Movement, Affect, Sensation*, Durham and London: Duke University Press, p. 221.

26 Deleuze, G. (1995) *Difference and Repetition*, Transl. P. Patton, New York: Columbia University Press.

27 Amabile, T.M., Barsade, S.G., Mueller, J.S., and Staw, B.M. (2005) "Affect and Creativity at Work," *Administrative Science Quarterly*, 50: 367–403; Fotaki, M., Kenny, K., and Vachhani, S.J. (2017) "Thinking Critically About Affect in Organization Studies: Why It Matters," *Organization*, 24(1): 3–17; Hjorth, D. and Steyaert, C. (Eds.) (2009) *The Politics and Aesthetics of Entrepreneurship*, Cheltenham: Edward Elgar.

28 Ramoglou, S. and Tsang, E.W. (2017) "In Defense of Common Sense in Entrepreneurship Theory: Beyond Philosophical Extremities and Linguistic Abuses," *Academy of Management Review*, 42(4): 736–744.

29 Hjorth, D., Holt, R., and Steyaert, C. (2015) "Entrepreneurship and Process Studies," *International Small Business Journal*, 33(6): 599–611; Dimov, D. (2020) "Opportunities, Language, and Time," *Academy of Management Perspectives*, 34(3): 333–351.

30 Foucault, M. (2008) *The Birth of Biopolitics: Lectures at the Collège de France 1978–1979*, Transl. G. Burchell, Basingstoke: Palgrave MacMillan, p. 219.

31 Foucault, M. (2008) *The Birth of Biopolitics: Lectures at the Collège de France 1978–1979*, Transl. G. Burchell, Basingstoke: Palgrave MacMillan, pp. 224–226.

32 Foucault, M. (2008) *The Birth of Biopolitics: Lectures at the Collège de France 1978–1979*, Transl. G. Burchell, Basingstoke: Palgrave MacMillan, pp. 231, 241–243.

33 Foucault, M. (2008) *The Birth of Biopolitics: Lectures at the Collège de France 1978–1979*, Transl. G. Burchell, Basingstoke: Palgrave MacMillan, p. 247.

34 Foucault, M. (2008) *The Birth of Biopolitics: Lectures at the Collège de France 1978–1979*, Transl. G. Burchell, Basingstoke: Palgrave MacMillan, p. 269. See also Caputo, J. and Yount, M. (Eds.) (1993) *Foucault and the Critique of Institutions*, Pennsylvania: The Pennsylvania State University Press.

35 Foucault, M. (2008) *The Birth of Biopolitics: Lectures at the Collège de France 1978–1979*, Transl. G. Burchell, Basingstoke: Palgrave MacMillan, p. 271.

36 See Ahl, H. and Marlow, S. (2021) "Exploring the False Promise of Entrepreneurship through a Postfeminist Critique of the Enterprise Policy

Discourse in Sweden and the UK," *Human Relations*, 74(1): 41–68; Ahl, H. and Marlow, S. (2012) "Exploring the Dynamics of Gender, Feminism and Entrepreneurship: Advancing Debate to Escape a Dead End," *Organization*, 19(5): 543–562; Dey, P. (2016) "Destituent Entrepreneurship: Disobeying Sovereign Rule, Prefiguring Post-Capitalist Reality," *Entrepreneurship & Regional Development*, 28(7–8): 563–579.

3   Assemblage and desire

We have previously argued that entrepreneurship studies might look to Romanticism as a way of understanding the organization of individuality. For Romantic writers, becoming-individual to emphasize the process of becoming is a project or projection in which the contract with oneself – the consideration of how one's abilities translate into gains – is fundamentally and congenitally at odds with itself. It is a project of fragmentation from within which any self-authored distinction is always a conditional form: an eddy forming amid the flow of things. Here the self-grounded subject is less a subject with inalienable and ungovernable interests than a consciously authored, critically organized, disturbance being realized in the irresistible company of an economic and social order. er be written as: This disturbance is a 'standing out' of the subject, and can carry with it a kind of natural or originary aura (as in Wordsworth's sensing of natural power), a strangeness or resistance that gets noticed and invites further attention. With the rise of Romanticism, and in its wake, it is with poems, essays, and novels that these attempts at self-authoring find full expression. For here we witness fragments, in whose mutual company and the company of things life is being presented with forms that no longer bear the weight of being properly known or knowable. Characters, events, readers, narrators, plots, traditions, and words vie with one another, find sympathy, or bump into one another, all the whilst folding and unfolding. The writing makes the habituated way of doing things apparent – the established orders of the tribe are unconcealed – and in being so are brought into possible questionability. The norms, manners, values, opinions, interpretations, symbols, and routines that make up prevailing practices are exposed, for consideration, and in being considered alternatives arise: "This is how we do things here. Have we considered why we feel so certain about it? Maybe come over here instead?"

Provoked by Romanticism, we equate the force animating this questionable production of aura to one of desire, where desire is the urge to become something other, to move towards that which calls but which is not itself an object. Hence, and importantly, desire "does not begin from lack – desiring what we do not have. Desire begins from connection; life strives to preserve and enhance itself and does so by connecting with

DOI: 10.4324/9781315714455-5

other desires. These connections and productions eventually form communities or societies."[1] … or perhaps new organizations. It is alluring but slightly strange, and in moving we reveal what "might be" and conceal slightly "what was." We start not with a desiring subject, for the subject, as Romantically confined, is as much a product as it is a stirring, of desire; desire produces the subjects it needs to connect with other desires. Those connections in which desires coalesce and "agree" enable bodies to affirm productive capacities (which is what Spinoza calls joy).[2] Gilles Deleuze regards this as affirmation, a becoming-active, that makes new possibilities for living actual. Potentialities, revelations, frustrations, and dead ends ensue, often very ordinary, barely there, and hidden amid all manner of constraining, habituated limits.

Romanticism has authors and readers alike caught in flows of desire, each playing with what might be other, with what is suggested, and this vagueness becomes a (re)source of imaginative inspiration, which might begin as a trickle and end as a torrent, imagination being "the mode of thought most precisely suited to the differentiating vagueness of the virtual."[3] Imagination is best suited because it is more unruly than reason, and it is hard to pin down to its having an origin within any one individual subject. Even if the author attests to imaginative power, there is no guarantee it will have any affect. As Shakespeare reminds us:

GLENDOWER
I can call spirits from the vasty deep.
HOTSPUR
Why, so can I, or so can any man;
But will they come when you do call for them?[4]

The authoring is a calling upon or conjuring up of spirits, a reaching into virtual reality, and the spirits often do come, attested to by a lasting influence on writers and readers who also become prone to imagining being other than they are.[5] But it is not something that can be authored without relying on the wider, unmanageable affects on others who may, or may not, take a work up, and move on with it. Romanticism nurtures an endless promise in the potentiality that not only the individual subject but also – by implication – the subject–subjection relationship is being continually authored. Far from being an essence, a kernel of an otherwise doubting subject, subjectivity is a stretching between what is and what could be,[6] and this becoming, floated on currents of desire, is the adventure, the going along, what we have noted is the *pro rotulus* or prorol (as opposed to the conventional control) that also, potentially, characterizes entrepreneurship.[7]

We learn this about entrepreneurship via Romanticism's literature, that the subjectivity which economists would interpret as evidence of a rationally governable, calculative, utility-maximizing enterprise unit called *homo oeconomicus* is a far more complex, partial, and arresting force. Even when isolated in the body of one person, the individuality of a subject is always and only a reaction and provocation to what is "other." What we take from Romanticism, from its ironic delight in mirror play and mystery, from its acceptance of the fragmentary nature of all things, from its intense material interest in being in and amid ordinary things, from its imaginative restlessness, from its refusal to elevate fact over fiction, from its eschewal of habit, and from its generative use of fragmented recollections, is an entirely different sense of the subject that appears so intimate with entrepreneurship. One that defines itself in expression, not in solitary units of measured interest. It is a sense of subjective individuality in which any expression of self-interest, *ego mihimet sum semper proximus*, typically read as "I am always my own neighbour," could as well be read as "I am always next to myself."[8] The repetition of the "I" in expression is only known through the difference and spontaneity of each expression towards what is beyond it. Even at its most intimate and isolated the blank page on which the self-becoming can continuously develop is also a question of the "I" always "next to myself." "I am not what I am," Iago says in Shakespeare's Othello, and this is not simply the program of a cunning, slippery character, but a problematization of Iago being nothing but the becoming of multiple selves, subject-positions, performatively achieved in relations to others. What is important for a processual understanding of this expressing individual is that it (individuation) happens as an event of intensification, rather than as a personal subject. An intensification of relational capacities to prorol the situation such that organization-creation happens would be the mode of expression that led us to say – "this is an entrepreneur."

The subject as understood in the wake of Romanticism evokes and encourages the productive feeling that this actual world – this world of smiles, bodies, gossip, implements, hunger, wages, ailments, weathered hopes and reasoned ideas – is always but one in a multiplicity, and that there is always room enough to transform and supplement it, so it becomes other than it is. Romanticism is alive to how each individual is more an intensity, a degree of power to which belongs a capacity of being affected and to affect,[9] than they are subjects bound to a reality of making predictable responses to systematic environmental modification. In the writing, characters are placed, and develop along ordered lines, say of those associated with *Bildung*, and sometimes they refuse, or saunter, or linger, and in this curmudgeonly or righteous interest in alternatives, they can find themselves anew or exhaust themselves, erupt, and break down. The most apparent and meagre alike find themselves configured through their power to act and capacity for being affected, always in relations to other, always influencing or under the influence of powers greater than themselves, always set within wider social and historical settings of such: family, work, church, government, expectations, ambitions, hopes, utopias, and institutions. Some, those who become more complex in their composition, those that experiment with varying performances, multiple scripts, begin to sense the power in relations in which they are individuated (subjectified) and find themselves inventively working at the constraints. Those who believe themselves pre-eminent but entitled are so fixed they cannot be affected, and thus they affect others, if at all, only in predictable ways. The broader world of histories and community is shown at first acceding to their claims, then bending around and over them, as a swelling river might skirt then overcome a rock in the stream. Other characters bump into accidents, experience hardships and privation, and yet in this breadth can, at times, find here a broadening of experience from which new possibilities and sense of eddying power might emerge. Through ordinary experience – and never beyond it – a complex commerce of bodies and minds emerges able to continually balance the power to affect and being affected, increasing peoples' resilience to hardship and potentially being a source of dynamism and power to overcome present limits.

The Romantics teach us that this sense of potentiality (that "what is" is as nothing when set against what could have been, and what "could have been" is as nothing when set against what could become) through which the mobility inherent to any form of projection becomes one of imaginative and speculative compulsion, not a measured or comparative one. They are not lacking something which, then, they can potentially gain by adding to what they already have (adding to their income by adding to their skills); they do not become more than they are by possessing more than they had. Nor are they lacking something that will complete them in some way; they do not become "more" by getting closer to an idealized state such as a rational being, or by realizing an inner *telos* towards happiness, or by spilling outwards into a nether realm of timeless perfection. These are all, for the Romantic, illusions to hide people from the real productive business of living in which deficit is experienced as a provocation, such as Wordsworth's involuntary memories and spots of time and Benjamin's aura, from which well springs they might feel themselves strong enough to be thrown into life anew, ravelled up, loosened, striving to resist or going along, endlessly modifying.

In understanding this process of working within language and so into what yields and elides from its grammar, the Romantic writers constituted themselves as fragmentary wholes, complete in their ironic self-sufficiency that it was they who were authoring their own becoming and belonging by virtue of the company into which they were gathered. Their work witnessed and spoke of the institutional forces governing social relations, it acknowledged and even revelled in the cruelties and accidents that struck powerfully at the lives of others, sometimes to the point of breaking those lives, and it dallied with and even swooned over from excess of poetic feeling made possible by the felt presence of strange, alluring things, including their own mortality. In this, though, they were cautioned against self-conceit and hyperbole, and for some this meant more mannered, humble expressions.

In eighteenth- and nineteenth-century Europe – and in writing this book, we must admit to our own limits here, in using a limited set of authors through which to think entrepreneurship, which is a phenomenon that in sub-Saharan Africa, or the Levant, or the archipelago's of east Asia, can be of a very different hue and rhythm to that in Europe, but to which we hope we manage to talk in some way, without presuming we have any familiarity – these actualities included norms that were: timeless (community belonging, hierarchy, purity); defining of the age (patriarchy, bourgeois capitalism, industrialization, colonialism, slavery, and empire predicated on annihilating enemies, Christian norms predicated on loving one's enemy); newly emerging (republicanism, equality, atheism, urbanism, the beauty of sport and exploration, instrumentalism, individualism). In the wake of Romanticism writing – and notably the novel – reveals the complex interplay of these norms from within the felt and thought-through experience of a lived life. The novel writes of bodies (and communities) being: elevated by corrupt values, abjured by fate, lit by luck, and made abject by aggression or indifference.[10] There is a restlessness here, coupled to a sense of potential that enfolds itself as desire – the desire of love and sex, of conversation, of status and favour, of exposure and adventure, of release and of delight, of frustration and injustice. For it is imagination, always emerging from within interactions in the making (i.e. relations, with others) that presents us with this in-between, and it is imagination's anticipation of a virtual future that makes of this in-between a potentiality, a virtuality-to-be-actualized. In-betweens can of course also *not* be imagined. But there is nothing to "not imagine" if imagination and affect are not "permitted" (e.g. in our case, by many of the conventions of scientific inquiry). The irony here is that critics of imagination stress the need to focus on the empirical, on observations, whereas those emphasizing the role of imagination and the virtual (which includes many scientists) also stress we are not empirical enough if we miss how imagination extends life beyond the limits of present experiences, and its role as such in organizing the present, the reality-felt intensity of events.[11]

Imagination can approach the virtually real, and this intensifies awaiting encounters.[12] This future-feeling limit of thought is hard for language to describe, but in imaginative expressions of Romantic literature, the writer can approach it. And in a similar way, we hazard, in imaginative expressions of visions for organization-creation, anticipating the becoming of a new firm, so too can the entrepreneur.

Desire

As we have discussed in relation to Foucault's *homo oeconomicus*, the appearance of "entrepreneur" and "entrepreneurship" can and is uncritically ascribed to attempts to change organizational cultures during processes of rapid industrial transformation throughout the global economy.[13] In an innovative organization-to-come, change-efforts often require employees to consider the "entrepreneur" as a new normal subject-position, and they should, according to this norm, themselves become entrepreneurial: "... norms of the human are formed by modes of power that seek to normalize certain version of the human over others, ..."[14] This pervasive form of subjectification in which employees, as units of calculable interests, are encouraged to become a constantly improving, self-directing subject is a form of acute managerialism to which Romanticism would never subscribe. Indeed it is a norm these authors would wish to shatter, and it is in expressing and conceptualizing this imaginative urge that we want to move our own thought about entrepreneurship, to attempt to reconceptualize it, to take it away from the discourse of enhancing human capital, and instead to consider its forming force as a way of unconcealing and (potentially) transgressing the limits that are constantly being placed on the processes of material wealth production. The Romantic and, we propose, the entrepreneurial, is not simply a critical reaction against norms, but, rather, an imaginative occupation of the in-between that might transform "what is not but could become" into provocative propositions about the future. This can only be realized in concert with otherness and others. A productive reaching away from what is and into what is potential (or virtual) carries within it an aura that betokens both difference and potential and by which others are somehow seduced and called onward. Without encountering the "other" the possible is impossible. Nothing lives without a space to grow, provided by potentiality. Hence Søren Kierkegaard cries "the possible, the possible, otherwise I'll suffocate."[15]

The calling to be alongside "the other" is what we call desire: an encounter with potentiality,[16] even if one desires the other itself, it is for the otherness that the other may bring that desire desires, desire always being in touch with what is beyond the actual.[17] Desire is thus a power; a power to become and a power to produce images of what we are not but could become.[18] Desire wants, first of all, to further desire, to secure more but, if we remember Spinoza's *conatus,* not in an acquisitive way, more a striving to greater capacity, to greater joy. Potentiality describes how images of "what could become" affect us, whereas possibility describes variations of the emerged. Since we understand entrepreneurship as a creation process, it is intimate with becoming, potentiality and virtuality, as well actuality and the possibilities therein. It sits between such, it is an entre-phenomenon.

Rather than motivated by lack, which is more a negatively defined need that springs from comparing my world with the world of others, the desire of entrepreneurship, which we learn of in the wake of the Romantics, is compelled by what fascinates as an imaginable as well as reasoned possibility. Desire seeks the process, seeks becoming, emergence, rather than an object or state that could be the result of a realized possibility, the emerged (the latter which, after comparison, might fuel disappointment).

Yet Romanticism finds desire (and its virtuality), nevertheless, dependent on this world, the actual world, to which the events and characters belong by association and the readers and authors by birth. This expands and loosens the idea of desire being locked down by an object. Of course, we desire things, to have, acquire and own. Desire, when socially coded as an interest, has an object, it is a "want" scripted by the forward-moving propulsion of entitlement as fuelled by marketing. We want, and in wanting can envisage the having that comes from being granted title in what we want. Yet show desire in writing, as Novalis, Wordsworth and Eliot do, and show it attentively and obsessively, and as with Spinoza the desire that moves bodies, communities, and events; this is the desire to connect with others, to move differently, to modify: it is all process, not object. And Romantic authors play with and relish this mobility, aware that they too are awash in a world of fragments: at the moment the "I" is articulated as an object of interest towards which one turns (the virtual becoming actual) then it modifies, no longer concealed it becomes netted and the rapture of unmediated belonging gives way, or is twisted into possessive self-love, a state of affairs that draws sympathy and ridicule. It is this endless modification and its productive potentials that interest the Romantics. They were writing before capitalist orders of production and consumption had forced themselves into a union so botched that any and all offspring were riven with an insatiable need for acquisition.[19] It was a time when desire could be sensed quite apparently and ordinarily as a modifying urge for differential movement ahead, becoming, that in itself was productive, when ideas of *Bildung* and growth were conditions of affective exposure and self-reflexive learning, rather than the maturing of capital assets.

In associating entrepreneurship with Romanticism and the literary we wish to configure what is entrepreneurial as a condition of desire. Once an organization is up and running with employees, agendas, markets, and products, then acquisition is everywhere, it is a condition of measured resources, of legal titles, of planned manoeuvres, of socially coded desires, of administrative force. We isolate entrepreneurship to the creation-process before the organization is in being, to desire as differential movement, to becoming, rather than with desire as lacking the end-state stated in strategic goals and milestones, which is where management typically enters and does its job by focusing on efficiency, control, and competitive positioning. We realize that this is an unconventional definition of entrepreneurship. Moreover, we also accept there is an intimacy with *Homo economicus* that cannot be avoided, that in so many instances, no sooner is an organization formed than the orderability of human capital begins to hold sway. Such an orderability extends into potential. After all, most organizations, and especially economic ventures, are typically evaluated by the value of their actual or potential assets. Even though at the early stages potential assets are more apparent than actual ones, and the venture is understood "as if" it were more than it actually is, the evaluative framing remains one of substance and presence. And with the onset of technological mediation through electronic computing, this trend is accelerating, since whilst new ventures were nothing without a business plan, a well-defined sense of value-adding uniqueness, or an envisaged income stream, more recently we witness the emergence of a potentiality economy in which organizations are being valued on the basis of their imagined future presence rather than on existing earning streams, and where conjecture counts as much as solutions. This makes the effort of distinguishing entrepreneurship from enterprise contingent and endless process of witnessing what is as much a mutual association as it is a disturbance.

By associating entrepreneurship with desire (-to-become, to differentiate in moving beyond the limits of experience) we want to question whether the self-understanding of the entrepreneurial condition (that of the entrepreneur or the new venture) is at all about *having* or *pursuing* or *exploiting* known capital assets. It is not a future venture that is key, as a desired "object" presently lacking when comparing with others who also "have" a venture, and perhaps a firmer one. It is rather the process of firming that is desire's image, as an experience of coming to be. Since this process is differentiation, it is principally unknown and cannot be the object of lack as such (an actual possibility for which one has a want), but is rather driven by a positive-productive desire, an affirmative vital force: "desire does not lack anything; it does not lack its object."[20] It is, rather, a case of a subject being missing and desire producing one, and then another, in a process of individuation.[21]

Under the rubric of desire, it is not the case that the entrepreneur or venture "is" something, but, rather, that entrepreneurial becoming, a productive experience of modification that occurs before and beyond the existence of something called a venture or entrepreneur, emerges. Conceptualizing entrepreneurship using Deleuze's concept of desire, we move away from psychological framings of desire (answering to Freud's libidinal economy) and socio-economical framings of desire (answering to Utilitarian political economy), to instead give desire a more fundamental role – producing subjects as imaginatively and playfully fragmented organizations of productive force (drives). On this reading entrepreneurship is less distinguished by ventures, assets, or ambitious goals and their substantiation, and more by the ways in which affirmative forces are productively affirmed, and by how such affirmation is imagined (desired): "... becoming, multiplicity and chance do not contain any negation; difference is pure affirmation [...] the 'yes' of the child-player is more profound than the holy no of the lion."[22] Here Deleuze is elaborating on Nietzsche's story of metamorphosis, a tale tracing an evolutionary development from a burdened "yes"-saying being (figured in the being of the camel or ass), via the critical-negative "no"-saying (figured as the Lion), to the highest achievement of the affirmative child, a being that affirms affirmation, becoming-active, without being dependent on a reaction, a "no" against something.[23] If we recall Becker's enterprising *Homo economicus*, where the entrepreneur is a yes saying figure, acceding to reality, locked into requisite behaviours, we consider what prospects there might there be for a more childlike entrepreneurial figure.

Enterprise

Understanding the entrepreneurial condition through desire resonates with it being a disturbing, overcoming, de-territorializing force that breaks down social and technical structures obstructing the free movement of productive forces. Not in the service of the negative, but as an effect of differentiating, making space for creation. If financiers find themselves thrown into trading activity governed by detailed and weighty regulation, for example, the entrepreneurial response is not to work harder than others at realizing the already established and warranted streams of income generation, but to move beyond or dissolve the rules by which the territory has been set down. For example, there might be arbitrage opportunities in managing the speed of communications: using atomistic, algorithmically quick programming connected through microwave networks of high-frequency decision-making machinery. Here the opportunity is nothing singular and distinct. Rather it arises from technological developments, from imaginative responses to shifting regulatory environments that seek to manage the flow of and access to investment sensitive information, from a prevailing logic that success equates to the realization of exponentially growing income streams, and from a culture of tech secrecy and privacy in which financial trading is no longer to be seen and heard. Investments in speed obviate the need to get access to privileged information, wherefore the better networked can always stay slightly ahead. Yet even if the emerging opportunity were primarily a case of moving to microwave networks, relying on speedier connexions is inherently uncertain, for the machinery is never wholly predictable. Machines "listen" to other machines, according to the algorithmic instructions, trying to disguise their decision "style," whilst also racing to arrive at decisions (buy/sell) nanoseconds ahead of others.[24]

Such an example hovers on the boundary of being entrepreneurship. It is inventive in its response to some limit conditions. Yet it is also fully immersed in an established pattern of acquisitive human capital and its rational management. The trading infrastructure is designed to fit into well-established norms of economic gain. So in this case, and in equivalent instances, we see an example of how the entrepreneurial can be entirely complicit with desire being canalized and subdued by prevailing commercial logic, desire being socially coded as interest.

We prefer to define such examples as enterprise rather than entrepreneurship.[25] For sure enterprise also pulls away from aspects of administrative management, being an inherently disruptive force, creating and finding gaps in social and technical systems and then re-configuring them as opportunities for arbitrage (unique sources of profits). But the configuration of a self as a machine able to secure earnings, as a bundle of skills for which others will (or will not) pay, continues apace, unchallenged. For here it is no longer the differently emerging, but the emerged difference that is in focus; now work this way, and now this way, innovating to better secure returns. It is the end settled after the means that remains of concern, and not the creation process and its process-value – joy, becoming-Child, increased *conatus*, will to move beyond, to travel further.

It is thus important to re-iterate, and clarify: in being configured by desire, as an affirmative-vital force constituting an imaginary of ideas to be actualized, entrepreneurship can spill over from the instrumental and economic concern for the acquisition and possession of the things by which an enterprise, set amid a myriad other enterprises, gain the substance of becoming an organization. If it were configured by such acquisition and possession the desire that was present would be governing the action set as a reaction to a sense of lack, and focused on the missing, but soon to be acquired, object (the firm, the profit, the gain, the success). Even if the means were transformative in their enacting of new activities, it would be enterprise rather than entrepreneurship.

Again, as we have tried to argue in relation to Romanticism, what defines the entrepreneurial process is when the subject (not object) is missing, and desire produces subjects, and the entrepreneurial is the production of a hitherto missing world and its life-potentials that can be actualized if the right organization of resources, ideas, and people is created. As Deleuze suggested, this is a subjectivity that is working in the third person, one that allows one to become a multiplicity, a gathering of tendencies amid other tendencies, and one that, in exposing itself to the multiplicities with which it is surrounded, succeeds in revealing the multiplicities that lie deep within its own being: desire always comes around to encounters with itself.[26]

Desiring that process is what generates the entrepreneurial subject as an affirmative-active life-enhancing force making this future become-actual. Desire configures the entrepreneurial in a pre-subjective and pre-substantive phase of disturbance and vagueness, as much as it does in the acquisition of things. In this way we want to understand not how entrepreneurship reconfigures ways of producing more with less (quantitative), so more "value" can be extracted, but how it disrupts the very structures by which value is understood (qualitatively different), including such social productions as possession and legal title, so that potentially more valuable lives might be lived characterized by their greater capacity for free movement.

This sensibility is not ours alone. We even find it in Schumpeter's flirtation with "creative destruction" as a framing for understanding the innovative force of entrepreneurship: entrepreneurship uproots habituated ways of thinking and doing, it is a de-territorializing force that has a social character (*ethos*) in that it disturbs the tendency for the competitive market to organize around monopolies and so induce totalitarian tendencies.[27] With the Romantic writers we therefore stress the provocative and productive understanding of a reality that only presents characters, events, authors, relations as fragments, remaining ever alive to the human tendencies to re-territorialize these things through appeal to unifying, generalized principles and concepts for knowing. With Ramglou and others, we want to recognize a form of entrepreneurship in which language does not hide or smooth over the contingencies of experience, indeed it crystalizes, accelerates, and animates them.[28] To trust fragments and affirm desire is an affirmation of differentiated emergence. This is what we feel is entrepreneurial modification, and therein lies the source of valuable values. If this is an organization-creation process, we need new concepts for what we refer to when we refer to organization.

Entrepreneurship begs the question: What is there before there is an organization?

Assemblage

We propose that we can understand entrepreneurship as a style of making connections in pursuit of greater productive capacities (Spinoza's *conatus*), as a way to overcome social coding that keeps productive forces apart. What is then created is not yet an organization, but something on its way to become an organization. Still, there are organizing forces at work, gathering forces, bringing people, visions, resources, ideas into a productive sociality.[29] Deleuze and Felix Guattari, in their book *Anti-Oedipus,* call this a desiring machine, and later, in the book *A Thousand Plateaus,* changed the name of this concept into a more neutral assemblage.[30] Desiring-machines or assemblages produce bodies without secure images of themselves, without substantial presence in the way of assets or possessions or firm objectives. They are processes of organizing in which bodies, actions, and passions, expression (the machines, the things, the organs) come horizontally, and territories, forms, norms, periods, marks, stakes, claims (the rules) come vertically. The whole or entire can be an individual, an organization, a couple, which all the whilst cannot be reduced to the interaction of separate parts, but which is an endless sway, like seaweed in tidal pools whose pull in the tides and currents marks out and closes off a territory from its place fastened to the rock, and which is also opening up and connecting to a wide oceanic swell from whose light it feeds. It maintains itself without being first fixed then mobile, first still then moving, it cannot just be one or the other, it is both, simultaneously:

> Assemblages are passional, they are compositions of desire.[...] The rationality, the efficiency, of an assemblage does not exist without the passions the assemblage brings into play, without the desire that constitutes it as much as it constitutes them.[31]

An assemblage is animated by affect, those of feelings such as frustration, excitement, reticence, calm, and those of sensory experience such as warmth, resilience, smell. They are proto-organizational in the sense that they direct, they focus, they draw attention such that the productive capacity of the whole is increased. They have prepared bodies for organization.

In this sense assemblage is a useful concept for evoking the distinctiveness of entrepreneurship from the organization. It is desiring the assembling process, the differentiating emergence, actualization of what could become, that forms an assemblage, and it is desiring what can become (the actualized) that holds the assemblage together. The necessary subjectivity for this process to evolve is the one we call "entrepreneur."

These assemblages cannot exist beyond the social and technical systems of which they are necessarily a part, and it is from within this thrown condition in social and technical systems (corporate structures, regulations, promises, conventions, habits, digitized trading floors, small-town monopolies, families, societies, and a myriad more) that they find expression. As assemblages, compositions of desire (as Deleuze and Guattari put it) work through a reaching towards things that cannot find adequate expression in established representational systems.[32] Their force lies beyond any obvious form of organization, any established order. Assemblages are pre-organizational in the sense that they are not parts arranged as a whole (molar) but the organization as fragments (molecular). Assemblages, as compositions of desire, produce, and what is produced is a residue of the productive urge to go beyond where one is being configured and this configuration occurs not just through habit, tradition, and material embodiments, but also through imagining what is virtually real yet not actualized. In producing these actualized creations, assemblages exhaust themselves, they overspill, give out or break down, insofar as their function is one of producing a litany and itinerary of fragments that interfere with the smooth operations of social and technical systems.[33]

Assemblages are both mechanical-actual and enunciative-virtual, meaning they are both machines that operate in the context of social practices – such as schools, prisons, corporations, but also projects – and a diagram or discursive formation that directs the function of the assembled. An enunciative assemblage is a diagram or map of forces that enters into relations to determine the balance between dominant and dominated.[34] Such a map of forces or intensities directs the concrete or machinic assemblage with its relations of forces at work. In the concrete, the actualized machine, operating in certain fields of practices, there is always a form of expression and a form of content at work; the form of the articulable and the form of the visible. Desiring new opportunities for living (a form of content) engenders a start-up process (a form of expression) that starts to code whatever is done as part of a start-up. The content-expression dynamics run into a more ossified state where institutions capture what goes on. In-between these forms the diagram or map of forces finds its playground. "The concrete assemblages [e.g. a project, a start-up] are therefore opened up by a crack [between forms of content and forms of expression] that determines how the abstract machine [the diagram, the map of forces or intensities] performs."[35] That is, entrepreneurship is distinguished by a search for the in-betweens where institutions or template/routines have left cracks.

The specific form of assemblage we term entrepreneurial is not only pre-organizational, but also proto-organizational since they result in new organizations, new firms, new festivals, and new happenings. They become organizations, and at that point, they also open up for a more managerial desire to increase control and economic efficiency, and the enterprising desire to exploit arbitrage opportunity. These new subjectivities (manager, enterpriser) will become gradually more central to maintaining the organization, and entrepreneurship is concealed, snuffed out. It is in this sense that we can envisage the conceptual legitimacy of institutional entrepreneurship. Institutional entrepreneurship would explicitly target the stratified conditions that are offered by institutions that lie in wait for any form of content that seeks to find its different ways. Changing or breaking the reward given to those that fall in line with the institutional templates would be doing institutional entrepreneurship.[36]

The work of these proto-organizational assemblages is well exemplified in certain works of participatory art, those that reach beyond the mimetic capacity to represent and re-describe the world, and which instead produce effects and affects that disturb the established orders of things, whilst never leaving it. "Affect, as presented in art, disrupts the everyday and opinionated links we make between words and experiences."[37] Such experiences would then temporarily open up to the potentiality of Nietzsche's becoming-Child as noted above. Free movement becomes possible since no obvious link between words and experience is available – it has been disrupted or cut off by affect, the shakeup. Creation has a white canvas to work with. The work is a "No" whose force opens up new ways.

Ai Weiwei and straight

The work *Straight* by the Chinese artist Ai Weiwei provides an illustration of an assemblage. Weiwei recalls how, on returning to his studio from 81 days detention by the Chinese state in 2011, he heard the sound of hammer blows: it was his assistants busy straightening some mangled concrete re-enforcing bars.[38] In 2008, 150 tonnes of these bars had been collected from buildings that fell during an earthquake in Sichuan. Many of the buildings had been schools whose "tofu construction" had left them dangerously exposed to collapse: at the first tremor, they fell, killing thousands of schoolchildren. The money had been there to build them correctly, but officials had been systematically encouraging builders and regulators to cut corners and siphoning off the spare cash for themselves. A depressingly familiar story of commercial greed, bureaucratic obfuscation, and community tragedy, not just in China of course, but everywhere.[39] Once straightened in his studio, the bars were laid flat and placed in a large, orderly, three-dimensional rectangle, their different lengths co-ordinated in different depths to form cracks running through the rectangular form. The lines and cracks they form echo many things: the jagged ruptures of a fault left in the earth after a quake; the peaks and troughs of a seismograph; the ascending and then descending representation of deaths plotted on a graph; the rips and rents in tight-knit social fabric. There is nothing straight about it, save its attempt to encounter truths about the everyday world in as straight a manner as possible, a way that is provocative and even easily read as a form of coruscating critique, yet also ironic and self-aware insofar as it poses but does not answer the questions "What is being straightened here, what is it about being straight, is straight a desirable condition?"

Straight travels the world's art museums and galleries, a temporary and constantly re-built form. Its fragile neatness creates in visitors a parallel world, one where children and their schooling are respected as inherent goods and the ground upon which all forms of social flourishing rely; one where officials are accountable for their actions; one where artistic practice engages the social capacity of people to organize themselves. These imaginaries remain thoroughly everyday and material, they take their cue from ordinary lives and how these have become inured to corruption, to badly made things, to official obstruction and indifference. The stories of such lives are constituted by information gathered by Weiwei and a growing band of activists for whom the response to, and revelations from, the earthquake revealed the depths of bureaucratic callousness and thoughtlessness that people had endured. Accompanying the steel bars is all manner of information about the number and names of the children who had died, what they enjoyed doing, their qualities and the hopes of their parents.

Weiwei apprehends the prevailing styles of regional and central Chinese bureaucracy, observing the feelings of resignation, pent-up frustration and uncertainty of those living within and under such bureaucratic structures. He is also alive to the political stakes of the elite and the ways money flows amongst them in complex channels of exchange. In gathering and concentrating on these habits and norms he isolates the anomalies, for example the hypocritical claims to serve the people whilst withdrawing from them, and then finds in the aftermath of an earthquake a way of revealing these anomalies in such a way that openings emerge.

The intensity of the tragic event that prompted *Straight* makes it an extreme case, and one that should not be easily and readily equated to 'an opportunity'. In our reading it is moment for reckoning with what is ill and rotten with a current state of affairs, and which thereby yields the possibility for things being different. In *Straight*, comes a sense not only that the established forms of sociality must transform, but that they can change. There is sufficient energy to make the change happen. Generalities gave way to the particulars and affect grasps the audiences that are thus located alongside those hurt or lost, and find there a sympathy that has no knowledgeable aim, but which forces the need to think into the space.

The lists of names, artefacts, symbols, and images of *Straight* de-territorialize existing social and technical systems, the forms of expression that have become dominant as institutions or templates, rewarding people that fall in line and thus limit their form of content to that which is "genre-specific." Imagining an alternative life desires a move beyond such confining limits, and the space to move is here found by dismantling the hierarchies associated with the binaries of rich and poor in whose pincered shadow a lack of money becomes indistinguishable from having lower social worth.

Straight shows the capacity of bureaucracy to remain in touch with anything other than itself and its own insecurities becomes an issue of debate; it exposes how everyday life is in thrall to indifferent natural forces; and it shows the small intimacies between parents and their children that typically pass un-noticed.[40] In showing all this *Straight* also reveals the possibilities for "difference" within these social and technical systems: the prospect of earthquakes can provoke engineering innovations and ethical rejuvenation, and natural emergencies can provoke new forms of politics in which corruption gives way to community.

In this way *Straight* is an assemblage cutting into a world of de-territorializing and re-territorializing, interrupting the flows of social and technical production, and in turn being interrupted by being cut into it by other social and technical systems (the purported universal values upheld by United Nations relief agencies, say, or the overtly commercial footing of many international art galleries, or the material constraints offered by recommended loading factors for flooring (upon which the heavy metal bars have to be laid in museums and galleries, and all these in turn are being cut into).

This cutting is also a continuity, a generative connection. Desire, bringing assemblages together, interrupts, and is itself interrupted in being continually cut into, and pulled away from, by other desires. There is no unity to be had here, no sense that the parts with which the molecular multiplicity and fragmentary nature of that which urges becoming can be forced into a molar whole. The molecular staying open to becomings, and the molar seeking stability and predictability co-exist in various compositions of desire. With entrepreneurship as process, we are always with fragments, coupling and de-coupling, with movement and passage rather than position. [41]

Straight reveals the productiveness of desire, out of which comes a sense of self-authoring productiveness, in the artist-makers, but perhaps also in the audience, and even the bureaucrats being shamed. The machine works by ordering the aboriginal much-ness of life through the provision of orientations, and these then provoke those being oriented into thinking and looking and experiencing differently from how they might otherwise have done so – moved by affect. So any desire drawing the composition of an assemblage together with relationships between the thinker and thought, the agent and the act, the movement and the mover, the institution and the fact, or the thing and its growth and decay, also interrupts these by inviting otherness along. Desire produces within the established order, and it creates by finding a way for the assembling process to slip outside of these orders. Here "difference" rather than "more" is being made with less. Not by successive (innovative) attempts to enhance the ability to secure a future income, but more openly by refusing to capitalize on the existing institutions. "Less" is thus understood as not being molar, not drawing on the heavy installations, but working in a molecular fashion, tactically rather than strategically, acknowledging the fantastical necessity of a heroic, solitary self, whilst also realizing its impossibility.[42] This is the poetics of organization, rather than the prosaics of organization. It resolves to find stories that do not themselves resolve, and which instead enjoy the tension, contradiction, and openness of life in the in-between, taking up concepts only to drop them and thereby taking the risk of not being understood.

The entrepreneurial "less" is thus less because it is a realization that whatever is complete, fixed, or ideal belongs to life, but only ever in an unrealized and unrealizable state, such that what is major is always in the company of the non-established, non-authoritative, or minor. The less is, then, not substantive or a known order, and it is not reducible to a thing that is not there. It is the differently emerging, the tactical play that is desired as it promises the virtually real yet missing actuality, that which could become but is not yet. Efficiency and effectiveness have little purchase on this process, and the new – not primarily more – being produced is not primarily predictable but more so surprising, nor even immediately useful because it is, as yet, uncommitted. This open connectivity seems best grasped by the concept of play. Desire that pulls productive assemblages together for the sake of differential emergence of the new, producing the subject of entrepreneur to make this happen, is driven by the joy of making, the urge to express. To use Gregory Bateson's felicitous phrase, it is producing differences making yet further differences, where difference refers to the coding and transmission of information (ideas) whose form remains sensitive to the wider system forces upon which their continuing sense and attractiveness is dependent.[43] Entrepreneurship processes can in this sense be approached as the craft of making assemblages (proto organizations): the process of *firming*.[44]

Disclosing new worlds

What desire thus reaches into, that which is beyond social and technical systems and beyond even the identification and ordering of productive value by which economies function, is the virtual. "The virtual, the pressing crowd of incipiencies and tendencies, is a realm of *poten-tial.*" "... tendencies – in other words, pastness opening directly onto a future, but with no present to speak of."[45] Ai Weiwei multiplied what could have been actualized alternatives – engineers building using more resilient materials, or bureaucrats not embezzling – painfully present as real ideas without local actuality. The whole gesture pointed to a vir-tual politics of governing that had not been actualized. His artistic inter-vention thus made actualization – what makes the real actual – into a "missing future" that felt very unnecessarily un-actualized. Why was this not done already? Safe schools for children and honest bureaucrats were made incipient, pressing themselves onto the actual, maximizing the local frustration with this having not yet happened. And so it is soon bound to happen, right? This is the seductive pull from a future that has become necessary because of entrepreneurial (but not enterprising) intervention.

We are not alone in arguing that entrepreneurship stretches the virtual into the actual, expanding the world by disclosing new spaces, practices, and identities within it. In particular, we find sympathy with the book *Disclosing New Worlds* by Spinosa, Flores, and Dreyfus. It is one of the few pieces of sustained thinking on entrepreneurship as a genera-tive, affective force, though one which remains perhaps too uncritical of the prevailing territorialized economic order by which entrepreneur-ship remains tithed to enterprise. They witness entrepreneurial disclosure taking three forms.[46] First comes reconfiguring activities and thoughts so that what was marginal becomes a focal concern (regarding air travel as the equivalent of taking a bus). Second comes articulating and recovering lost or concealed practices (such as the revival of craft-based food pro-duction). Third comes cross-appropriating activities and thoughts so those common to one practice and context are used in another (using trained sniffer dogs to detect cancer, or rats to discover land mines).

In addition to *Disclosing New Worlds*, we also find resonances between our arguments and the work of Saras Sarasvathy who talks of entrepreneurship as a process of effectuation. A "detailed examin-ation of lived experiences of effectual entrepreneurs," Sarasvathy says, shows that entrepreneurs see "value in mundane things" (resonant with Romanticism), they are "fabricating new uses for extant resources" (again, fabulation, imagination, affirmative of the virtual), they persuade "without promising upsides" (very much the openness of desires), and they co-opt "passengers to become pilots" (this is the function of assem-bling others materially into the tapestry of the project).[47]

We can analyse and understand such forms of disclosure or effectuation using the concept of assemblage: these forms of disclosure re-configure established territories, de-territorializing what seemed fixed, settled, and normal, enabling virtualities to become actualized. De-territorialization brings the obvious (actual) into questionability. We become aware of the one as just one of the potentially many ways, solutions, actualities. De-territorialized, solutions are brought back to the virtual state of ideas – as multiple differential relationships. Here a new process of actualization is made possible, and by differentiating and creating, new value can be created in a local-concrete way. This also means a re-territorialization happens, which in turn opens to new de-territorialization possibilities.[48]

De-territorialization occurs as a loosening of these stylistic relations of causation, contiguity, and resemblance: the subject loses its edge when a sense of connection to others is lost, or these connections become intensely singular and apparent, or, contra-wise, vague and etiolated. The breakdown in reliable and consistent behaviour finds the individuated subject struggling to maintain itself. What was habit becomes the subject of conscious decision, things cannot be taken for granted, the ground can give way. [49] Spinosa, Flores, and Dreyfus would sense and describe this as a loss of style, and the accompanying possibility for new styles (as when craft beer begins to agitate mass manufacture). Imagination, knowing your way around virtualities, increases the capacity for sensing anomalies in existing style regimes. Holding on to those, assembling people to increase your capacity to hang on, makes possible the creation of organization required for such anomalies to be received as a value-offer in the context of a changed or new style.[50] An anomaly – new idea, virtuality, practice gone wrong – was thus de-territorialized, developed, negotiated, and reterritorialized into a new territory, drawn together by the refrain of offering the new, and eventually becoming the centre of a new regime of practices, later – no doubt – to be questioned.[51]

Janet Roitman's *Fiscal Disobedience* shadows one such process of de-territorialization, in which a traditional tribal economy in Chad and Cameroon yields to a far more explicit and alien linguistic codification of rights and duties predicated on the inevitability and apparent (according to the official state) desirability of international trade and enterprise. Tribal forms of doing business give way under the aid-induced structuring of new grammars, there is a loss of style and rise of new ones, but being cross-appropriated in such a directed and managed way that indigenous ways of being and trading become disoriented; the new carries no stylistic sensitivity. Amid the immiserating affects and hence sadness, however, come spots of joy, brighter for bearing so rare. For example the spawning of civil disobedience is organized through gangs, but with all the hierarchies, abuse, and militaristic tactics this then entails. Roitman refuses to condemn these eruptions of resistance wholesale, seeing the reactions as potentially productive.[52]

For Spinosa, Flores, and Dreyfus it is only by being immersed in established social and technical systems – the territory, a space produced in the embodiment of prevailing styles – that the possibility of disturbance arises.[53] Novelty is not an eruptive force from nowhere, but takes its cue from what is typical and habitual: the potential (virtual) emerges from the actual. Spinoza might describe this kind of situational sensitivity as having the power to be affected, a receptivity. From such receptivity comes power to assemble the productive assemblage so as to de-territorialize what needs to be de-territorialized for a differently configured territory to become possible, to emerge as real virtuality, and take shape (become actualized): for differential becoming, for ontogenesis to happen. Again, there is tactical skill involved. Tacticians rely on receptivity in order to grasp/exploit the nature of the strategy at work, to understand how it can be brought into questionability, make the seemingly solid ripe for improvisational entry,[54] transformative insinuations[55] – the tone that starts the theme of a new refrain.

As an entrepreneur, one cannot just decide to, say, revivify craft beer production. First, in Spinosa et al. term's, the prevailing lifestyles by whose logic the production and consumption of mass-canned beers make sense has to appear as anomalous, there has to be a breakdown in the habituated ways, a glitch that then allows the potential held in the restoration of the "old ways" to become more actual. The proto entrepreneurial forces emerge: can these pull or nudge people to consider drinking something other than a tinned brand? Can we suggest alternatives? Further, the entrepreneurs then have to be apprenticed in the older techniques of craft beer production, bringing historically forgotten techniques together with emerging technology, suggesting to farmers, for example, that they might grow certain kinds of hops, finding new sources of yeast, working with glass manufacturers on the mundanity of bottle aesthetics of bottles. The creators-founders of the new micro or craft breweries that will then emerge begin as novices (they were amateurs, following rules, getting the recipes wrong, experiencing inconsistency in batches, gradually trying to perfect their techniques) and end as experts (using modern technology blended with traditional styles they produce consistently fine tasting, well-packaged beer, use high-quality ingredients, with transparent labelling). They use the old ways as a means of differentiating their presence alongside the larger, more established industrial brewers. Becoming expertly versed in these "old ways" yields a sense of focus, control, and professionalism.[56]

The makers' skill is complimented by a generosity in sharing their passion with others who might similarly become educated, other who might be drawn into the emerging territory being distinguished by this new form of "song." If the beer is made considerately and yet passionately, and its provenance is explained, an aspirational customer class can be persuaded to take part, especially if the company is also experimenting with looser organizational forms that allow the customers "in" in small way, for example through shares or crowdfunding. Customers learn from producers, becoming experts in distinguishing different hops or understanding the historical lineage of different styles, and so developing a taste that can be further nuanced through the creation of yet smaller, more refined batches. The entrepreneurs are using the predicate "craft" to tap into a new organizational status that is almost sublime: the appeal to tradition makes the beer irreducible to anything else, it immunizes itself to comparison. The consumers buy beer, and with it comes a politics and history to which these breweries have cleaved themselves in the role of revivifying distant but proper production methods, and at the same time bringing together an otherwise alienated consumer and producer community, itself glued not just by beer, but its broader social and civic resonance.[57]

Though generative, the process is not one that reaches completion, it continues to roll, entrepreneurially speaking. The claims to authenticity accompanying craft beer production will themselves become subject to critical analysis. Just what kind of community is being envisaged here for example: one characterized by an atavistic discourse of physicality, materiality, and masculinity that is perfectly encapsulated in the skilled or elite manual labour and community spirit associated with craft brewing?[58] The critique offers new anomalies, the new habits established by the success of craft beer offer up new ways of actualizing the potential in what has hitherto been forgotten, overlooked, remained peripheral, or as yet has remained un-combined.

We will bring this situational sensitivity into our model of the entrepreneurship process as the concept of "common sense." Common sense has to be understood and respected in order for it to be received or affecting you such that this intimacy becomes your asset when tactically transforming the dominant, the common style, the territory assumed to always have been there.

And in critically developing world-making, in our view we might go further still, and consider just what is real about this disclosive adjustment of common sense (i.e. just how much does it conform to ordoliberal norms associated with the unquestioned development of human capital to consume itself) and how much does it trouble such a rationally regulated arrangement of market intervention and adjustment.

Virtual form

This extension from the actual to incipient is not the limit of desire, for the actual and incipient can then be stretched into, and disturbed by, the virtual, as that which could occur, but has not yet, and which cannot be read off from the actual. The virtual is where what is "new" or "other" is touched by the improbable, or fantastic, or awe inspiring. The virtual exists as the idea, a sense that something is becoming, but with little sense of what it might be, until in acting and thinking, it emerges. Again: "[T]he virtual, the pressing crowd of incipiencies and tendencies, is the realm of potential."[59] Ideas always exist in differential multiplicity, meaning the actual is always shadowed by many candidates that could have taken its place. The virtual resists probabilities, resists images, resists guessing, and planning: it is without organization, it is a future without a present to anchor in – it requires creation to become actualized and, in the case of entrepreneurship, it is assemblage leading to organization-creation that is the defining process.

Aristotle problematized the actuality (*Energeia*) of potentiality (*Dynamis*) using the images of light and darkness. He says that what is in every body and is visible there is *diaphanes*, what shines. The actuality of this *diaphanes* is light and colour, wherefore – Girogio Agamben concludes – darkness is its potentiality. This is not a question of either/or, for true potentiality is what passes fully into actuality: "[W]hat is truly potential is thus what has exhausted all its impotentiality in bringing it wholly into the act as such."[60] Deleuze's concept of the virtual is also thought of similarly as a multiplicity that shadows each actuality. Actualization, what Deleuze picks up from Bergson's *élan vital* as a differentiating movement, does not exhaust the virtual, but preserves virtuality as this shadow of each actuality.[61] Virtuality and potentiality would thus be conceptual twins: "The virtual, the pressing crowd [always multiplicity, our remark] of incipiencies and tendencies, is a realm of potential."[62]

Organization is exactly what is required for actualization of the virtual to happen. Organization-creation is what the entrepreneurial process adds to the world as the concrete expression of a desire to extend life beyond the present limits of experience. This desire is also what produces the subject of entrepreneur, necessary for this organization-creation to happen.

Organization-creation happens as assemblages, as proto-organizational forms, and make actual the arrival of the incipient. The virtual is that idea that has the power to express itself differently, multiply, in different actualities. Because 'what could become' is not yet, the virtual works on bodies entirely through affect, the force of attraction where bodies come together, an undefined and transitory moment prior to the distinction of an idea taking hold as something: "it is the edge of virtual, where it leaks into actual, that counts. For that seeping edge is where potential, actually, is found."[63] At that moment, when the world is anticipating something, when the world is saturated with preparedness, this is also when it has to happen. It is where and when it seeps from the virtual into the actual. This is what gets the event born. It can be very simple and almost instinctual, such as might be held in a glance. These smallest of things can become productive by bringing out feelings that otherwise would have lain dormant, and could not be predicted. Once revealed these feelings can become projects encased by interests and by affection: the merest sense of an opening that presages sizeable rips in the prevailing fabric of social and technical machines and systems. Desires, e.g. brew beer again as it used to be done, as a craft, quickly become socially coded according to dominant interests. The "micro-brewery entrepreneur" code answers to a societal interest in a particular kind of enterprise, and before long, as the entrepreneurial gives way, you have an acceleration and deepening of this alignment of production, social interest, and the establishing of nuances and even corruptions of practice (hop fayres, nano-breweries, craft beer branding, mass-manufacture of craft beer). No doubt, the entrepreneurial is constantly pressed by socially codified interests for how to do things (e.g. according to venture capitalists, business coaches, common sense), which often transforms entrepreneurship into enterprise, into managerial entrepreneurship where more of the "audience" typically start to applaud what they see. That can be an intoxicating experience. That start-ups or firming processes often become enterprise businesses is not inherently wrong or bad, but hard to resist. Movement in the other direction is still possible and sometimes happens. Entrepreneurship has its primary impact on the world as this potentializing force that makes the virtual seep into the actual via organization-creation.

There is a passage, from the virtual to the actual, via the tactical nego-tiations with common sense, finding out how new practices could be made and have value for others. It is along such a passage that ethics (encountering, staying open, and holding on to what is other) becomes morals (knowing the reality of the codes of conduct, the law, the commandments). We sense this when acknowledgement (sensing another) becomes naming (the identity of another, their attributes) or when their movements are regulated as via passport controls and the like. We sense it also when experience (appearance) becomes knowing (fact, skill, explan-ation) – the rainbow is explained as a prism. Going back the other way, from the actual through tactical negotiations to the virtual, is when habit (routine, disposition, norm) spills into instinct, when association and pro-pinquity spill into yearning, when words spill into gesture, and when colour becomes light and music noise. It is realizing such a movement into the virtual that makes Romanticism so compelling. With them entre-preneurship shares the conviction that one must not be content and stop with the negotiations, the tactical wins alone. One must do business with the impossible. Some Romantics, like Wordsworth, remained ever sensi-tive to how the interplay of desire configured around a revelatory sense of self coherence, and so tended to gravitate towards openings without affirming them in taking the plunge. Romanticism of the form encouraged by Novalis and tempered by Hazlitt encouraged forms of expression in which the virtual was given electric charge as it flashed and arrested the attention of those imaginatively placing themselves within everyday life alongside what was and remained "other." The other was thereby given a seductive appeal.

Again, Ai Weiwei's *Straight* works to suggest how the virtual becomes a disturbing force. How the straightened concrete re-enforcing bar becomes sculptural material wrested from disaster and pain, no longer sustaining floors but being laid weightily on them and requiring they be re-enforced, often the floors of pristine galleries trodden by the footfall of an untroubled audience. It has immense financial value as an art piece, yet shame, anger, and guilt erode this value completely, indeed make it per-verse, setting in train its own anomalous force. It tests itself by realizing affect on the basis of others' hurt and it does so relentlessly and heavily; it cannot be avoided, and cannot avoid its own equivocal presence as an art work predicated on tragedy. As in George Eliot's novels, the power to be affected through constraint reveals sadness, the inability to act outside of curtailments. *Straight* courts critique from those who constrain: from the officials of Sichuan, from those wanting for pragmatic or ideological reasons to reserve judgement on the manner in which China chooses to develop, and from those accusing Ai Weiwei of exploiting misery for financial gain. In this *Straight* courts notoriety and celebrity, playing along with publicity machines of the art market, yet never wholly straight in itself. It plays on thought and feeling being inseparable, and these being affected by other bodies. The bodies of those cut short by untimely death, those of dry officials in dead office atmospheres, those of a largely respectful audience studying the lists of names against the backdrop of a faintly ferrous smell. Ai Weiwei encountered bodies that disagreed with his own, and with many of those living in Sichuan and their power to act decreased, and the corresponding passion was sadness (Spinoza's term for decreased capacity to be productive). And there was so much to be incapacitated about. Encountering disagreeing bodies, Spinoza writes, decreases our productive capacity, which is sadness. Encountering agreeing bodies increases our productive capacity, which is joy. There is a certain way in which Ai Wewei's *Straight* brings the viewer towards potential, as a frustration with the present that urges us to act. *Straight* begins to find potential incipient in the structures and forms by which it is brought to life and of which it asks basic and troubling questions, through bodily affects which connect to movements of thinking, bringing audience, gallery, artist, natural event and social and political conditions into a constant commerce of affecting and being affected, with little in the way of over-reaching direction.[64]

Organization and organizing

Desire and *assemblage* are central to our conceptualization of entre-preneurship in this book. It is a mobile gathering of desire that lurks with and breaks from relatively immobile social wholes with strong ter-ritorial boundaries and forces of homogenization (internalization), and strong forms of coding (repetition, role and type variation, selection). A monastery might be one very distinct version of such immobility. The norms are homogenizing, the monastery consists of offices, not individual people, the architecture is arranged strictly and according to precedent, the diet and calendar are repetitious, the parts become whole only as members of a greater order, and order is tantamount to the realization of a defined end. The codes are everything, immobile, almost akin to DNA. Monasteries are relatively fixed in their parts (the substantive objects being gathered and organized) and whole (the form this process of organ-ization expresses).

Ai Weiwei might be said to have encountered a similarly immobile social whole in the guise of government bureaucracy governed by lin-guistic codes associated with Confucian hierarchies (as distinct from the rational-legal codes more typically associated with Western European bureaucracies). Yet the social and technical wholes have gaps and glitches, there is corruption, frailty, unbidden love, and it is these that foster the possibility of an assemblage, working into the open with its generative questioning and the enactment of witnessing and remembering; the territory is de-territorialized.[65] The actual is made questionable, it is disclosed as evidently unnecessary and the shadows of virtuality that were not actualized are now made incipient. Frustration builds by "contaminating" audiences with this desire for what "could have been" the case. Transmutation is potentialized and the "missing future" presses itself on the actual, seeping into it by the weight of inevitability. Assemblage is thus a concept that allows us to think about the tension and dynamic between existing orders (quantitative, hierarchical systems) and the openings towards new orders, demanding new organization. A new order – centred on exposure to new values, new ways of thinking and acting – would then achieve being as a result of a new organization-creation process. Assemblages are thus forms of sociality that hold immanent proto-organizational potentials, entrepreneurially used in organization-creation. Assembling, for this reason, is a way to excite the actualization of a new organization, of firming, or firm-formation. It is the sometimes fine and delicate craft of seducing others to believe in the future necessity of what is to be actualized, convincing them by the joy of moving into the open, and respecting and negotiating common sense that you get to actualize the new into contexts of existing practices of everyday users such that value will be manifest with commerce as result. Joy is perhaps a strange word to use. Joy, in Spinoza's thinking, is not rapturous happiness, but an affective sense of being able to move, do more and become new. For Gilles Deleuze this joy of moving (including bodily) with ideas or ideas moving you, is tied to the virtual in that it remains open, part of the differential multiplicity of ideas, as yet uncommitted:

> This joy is still a passion, since it has an external cause; we still remain separated from our power of acting, possessing it only in a formal sense. This power of acting is nonetheless increased proportionally; we "approach" the point of conversion, the point of transmutation that will establish our dominion, that will make us worthy of action, of active joys.[66]

Deleuze explicates the process of how assemblages, directed by desire, become productive by operating affirmatively, by making new forms incipient and actual, which then spill into negativity through organization:

> Organizations of forms, formations of subjects [...], "incapacitate" desire: they subjugate it to law and introduce lack into it. If you tie someone up and say to him "Express yourself, friend," the most he will be able to say is that he doesn't want to be tied up. The only

spontaneity in desire is doubtless of that kind: to not want to be oppressed, exploited, enslaved, subjugated. But no desire has ever been created with non-wishes. Not to want to be enslaved is a non-proposition. In retrospect, every assemblage expresses and creates a desire by constructing the plane that makes it possible and, by making it possible, brings it about.[67]

Hence organization is here understood as the upshot of assembling, it is a residue. Organizations are formalized "force-fields" where subjectification (or individuation) into some form of unity – say employment or membership – takes place. Organizations thus acquire an entitative social status, as stabilized patterns of relationships with an object status, they subjectify and are in turn subjectified as proper places (defined by stability rather than vectors of directions). This also means that desire to connect with others in this force field is ordered by relations already coded as "collegial," in-between employees and members. Coding means desire's attention is steered towards socially sanctioned objects/practices/subjectivities – creating a business to earn rents, to fulfil an ambition to lead oneself, to better contribute to the immediate community.[68] Social formations, such as organizations, achieve being and endure by capturing and coding desires according to a specific (set of) goal(s) and by making such stabilized orders productive in a certain way (e.g. creating often pre-defined and planned for value for classified types of roles: customer, employee, investor). They are built to be repetitive, efficient, predictable, and controllable.

What Deleuze is encouraging in studies of organization is an awareness of what happens prior to this settled and stabilized coding. One has to study what it is to be before and be for something and know how to bring it about. This is where creative-affirmative desires form productive assemblages, ready to actualize organizations where- and whenever they are needed for the virtually real to also become actualized. To study when it is assemblages become organizations, and so the moments when desire is incapacitated as interest, restricted to a certain diagrammatic order that becomes subject to institutionalizing principles. Desire for the new to be created, as well as seduction that is driven by a desire for newness, can also become embattled by desire for efficiency, which prioritizes one form of organization and allows desire to become coded according to social conventions as interest: the entrepreneurial has become a business that settles in a form and calls upon the management of resources. Desire assembles capacities into an assemblage, but without an organized order in place enabling control of what happens. Desire is mainly desiring its own furthering, the movement ahead, it is open. We can thus see how assemblages are open-ended in a way that organizations are not. When organizations are created, entrepreneurship is accompanied by enterprise management necessary for control over how growth and revenue-generation take place. This does not mean entrepreneurship necessarily disappears. Organizations are full of un-actualized virtualities requiring organization-creation. There is a tendency, however, for management to take over.[69]

Desire and assemblages are therefore not directly manageable, since social codes imposed on it will make it transform into interest, serving socially recognized purposes, and this will configure an organization such that it incapacitates desire to operate within the established order.[70] Desire will, however, always work from the established order, not adding quantitatively more, but making space for the qualitatively different. This coding of desire into socially sanctioned interests – such as a corporate strategy – represents the micro-political processes that constitute managing as organizational practice. Organizations, composed from multiple assemblages that are both molar (is a body corporate, a whole that is represented as a unity) and molecular (processes, fragments, bodies, affects, decisions), hold within "them" their transformative forces. This also means that "... becoming is the process of desire."[71] Particular sets of relations connect to other particulars, establish relations to them, on the basis of the joy they draw from connecting and the increased capacity to make, produce, create that follows, and transformative forces bring assemblages that are held together by desire, into becoming-organizations. As assemblages become organizations, they simultaneously hold forces that express desire for stability and control (their territorial dimension) and forces that express desire to become, to actualize the new (their deterritorializing dimension). Although organizations tend towards being hierarchies of stable order, they will also be pulled apart by networks of connections that bring parts of it into processes of becoming what it presently is not.[72]

Entrepreneurship, if we are interested in how people become entrepreneurs, is then understandable as becoming-active (i.e. to acquire agency and productive capacity) as organization-creative, as a body that affects others by gathering them into compositions of desire, into an assemblage as a proto-organizational form, tending towards organization. Entrepreneurship – which many have attempted to define as though it was a thing "out there," an object grounded in a venture, or in the discovery or creation of opportunities, or inventing new capacities – is, as an assemblage, an experience of potential on the point of becoming actual. As an assembling process it cannot be embodied in a single figure, whether of a person or organizational form.[73] Spinoza, Romanticism, and Deleuze are all writers of the multitude, and start therefore not from a world populated by individuals. Rather, there are "dividuals" that become in-dividuated in certain assemblages, collective sets of relationships, attempts at passionate expression, an interest in what most intensely seduces and allow us to experience a movement towards the greater capacity to act.[74]

Notes

1 Colebrook, C. (2002) *Deleuze,* London: Routledge, p. 91.
2 "Joy is 'pleasure arising from the image of a past thing of whose outcome we have been in doubt.'" Joy is what people naturally seek, which requires their struggling for understanding that is as full and open as it is possible to encompass in a human frame. Spinoza *Ethics.* P 18, p. 72.
3 Massumi, B. (2002) *Parables for the Virtual – Movement, Affect, Sensation,* Durham and London: Duke University Press, p. 134.
4 Shakespeare, William (2009) *King Henry the 4th,* Part 1, Act 3, Scene 1, Bate, J. and Rasmussen, E. (Eds.). London: Macmillan.
5 Gallagher, C. and Greenblatt, S. (2001) *Practicing New Historicism,* Chicago and London: The University of Chicago Press.
6 Cf. Kondo, D.K. (1990) *Crafting Selves – Power, Gender and Discourses of Identity in a Japanese Workplace,* Chicago and London: The University of Chicago Press; Greenblatt, S. (1980) *Renaissance Self-Fashioning – From More to Shakespeare,* Chicago and London: The University of Chicago Press.
7 See Hjorth, D., Strati, A., Drakopoulou Dodd S., and Weik E. (2018) Organizational Creativity, Play and Entrepreneurship: Introduction and Framing. *Organization Studies,* 39(2–3): 155–168.
8 Greenblatt, S. (1980) *Renaissance Self-Fashioning – From More to Shakespeare,* Chicago and London: The University of Chicago Press, p. 217.
9 Deleuze, G. (1988) *Spinoza – Practical Philosophy,* San Francisco: City Lights Books, p. 27.
10 Judith Butler in How Bodies Come to Matter: An Interview with Judith Butler Author(s): Meijer, I.C. and Prins, B. (Winter, 1998), *Signs,* 23(2): pp. 275–286. Published by: The University of Chicago Press. Stable URL: www.jstor.org/stable/3175091. Accessed 16 April, 2018.
11 Massumi, B. (2002) *Parables for the Virtual – Movement, Affect, Sensation,* Durham & London: Duke University Press, 247; Massumi, B. (2011) *Semblance and Event – Activist Philosophy and the Occurrent Arts,* Cambridge and London. The MIT Press, p. 122.
12 Ibid., p. 122.
13 The early example here include Rosabeth Moss Kanter's *The Change Masters* (1983), New York: Simon & Schuster; Peter Drucker's *Innovation and Entrepreneurship* (1985), New York & London: Harper & Row, and – in the more popular genre – Peters and Waterman's *In Search of Excellence* (1982), New York: HarperCollins.
14 Butler, J. (2015) *Notes toward a Performative Theory of Assembly,* Cambridge and London: Harvard University Press, p. 37.
15 This quote is taken up by Gilles Deleuze in 'Michael Tournier and the World Without Others' in *The Logic of Sense* Transl. M. Lester and C Stivale. New York: Columbia University Press. 1990. p. 318. Deleuze suggests Kierkegaards hero is not calling for immanent possibility, but a more structured form of common sense. Later on, through, as Bogue notices (Bogue, R. (2007) The Art of the Possible, *Revue Internationale de Philosophie* 61, 241(3): 273–286) Deleuze is more joyous in his reading of Kierkegaard, sensing it as a cry into the open. This reveals the ambivalent relationship Kierkegaard has with Romanticism. Although Kierkegaard was hostile in many ways towards the aesheticization of life to which the Romantics were

wedded, there are profound similarities in their world view, not least the emphasis on critical self detachment and the concern with preserving a sense of unity in the wake of this (inevitable) fragmentation of self. The search for self through self relating cannot be done through reason alone, but through feeling, specifically a yearning for what lies beyond the possible and contingent. That this beyond can only be found in a leap of faith is Kierkegaard's admission that neither aesthetic or ethical relations are adequate, whereas for the Romantics they are all we have. (see McDonald, W. (2013) Kierkegaard and Romanticism in Lippitt, J. and Pattison, G. (Eds.) *The Oxford Handbook of Kierkegaard*. Oxford: Oxford University Press. 94–111.

16 It is Bergson – inspiring Deleuze's process philosophy – that stresses that realization of the possible is a false creation. Rather, he suggests that actualization of the virtual describes creation. For the real merely copies the possible and cannot therefore be creation. The actual is differentiated from the virtual, and has to be created into existence as newness and difference. We prefer the virtual-actual before the possible-real when describing creation. Kierkegaard's possible, however, is to be understood as the imaginative breathing-space without which he claims he would suffocate. That is, what Bergson stressed as the virtual.

17 At its most intense and bleak we can experience desire as being utterly configured by experiences of lack, a dark rent in the world from which a sense of need comes howling and mewling. Yet, as Gilles Deleuze and Felix Guattari are at pains to point out, even this desire is productive; it produces in the form of fantasy and hallucination, creating its own objects, or transforming those that do exist into its own psychic reality, an imaginary thing living within the actual that transforms things of metal, flesh, colour, or sound into a nether world of attraction.

18 Colebrook, C. (2002) *Deleuze,* London: Routledge, p. 94.

19 Deleuze, G. and Guatarri, F. (1983) *Anti-Oedipus: Capitalism and Schizophrenia*, Transl. R. Hurley, M. Seem & H. Lane. Minneapolis: University of Minnesota Press, pp. 25–29.

20 Deleuze, G. and Guattari, F. (2004) *Anti-Oedipus*, Transl. R. Hurley, M. Seem, & H.R. Lane, Preface by M. Foucault, London and New York: Continuum, p. 28. See also Gao, J. (2013) "Deleuze's Conception of Desire," *Deleuze Studies*, 7(3): 406–420.

21 Smith, D.W. (2007) "Deleuze and the Question of Desire: Toward an Immanent Theory of Ethics," *Parrhesia*, 2007(2): 66–78.

22 Deleuze, G. (2006) *Nietzsche & Philosophy*, New York: Columbia University Press, pp. 190, 193.

23 Nietzsche, F. (2006/1885) *Thus Spoke Zarathustra* A. Caro and R. Pippin (Eds.). Transl. A. Caro. Cambridge: Cambridge University Press. The spirit takes on heavy loads, strengthenes itself, as a camel in the desert, then it changes into lion, able to challenge and refuse the 'thou shalt' commands of the establishment, able to say no to power and so create freedom for itself, and then the third change, is that of a child; "The child is innocence and forgetting, a newbeginning, a game, a wheel rolling out of itself, a first movement, a sacred yes-saying" (p. 17). See also Weiskopf, R. and Steyaert, C. (2009) Metamorphoses in Entrepreneurship Studies: Towards an Affirmative Politics of Entrepreneuring. In D. Hjorth & C. Steyaert (Eds.) *The Politics and Aesthetics of Entrepreneurship*, Cheltenham: Edward Elgar, pp. 183–201.

24 See Min, B.H. and Borch, C. (2021). Systemic Failures and Organizational Risk Management in Algorithmic Trading: Normal Accidents and High Reliability in Financial Markets. *Social Studies of Science.* https://doi.org/10.1177/03063127211048515

25 Hjorth, D. and Holt, R. (2016) "It's Entrepreneurship, not Enterprise: Ai Weiwei as Entrepreneur," *Journal of Business Venturing Insights,* 5: 50–54.

26 See Deleuze, G. (1995) *Negotiations, 1972–1990.* New York: Columbia University Press and *A Thousand Plateaus: Capitalism and Schizophrenia.* (1987) Transl. B. Massumi. Minneapolis. University of Minnesota Press, pp. 239–240.

27 See Schumpeter, J. (1987) The Obsolescence of the Entrepreneurial Function. In *Capitalism, Socialism and Democracy.* London: Unwin, pp. 131–134. Foucault isolates Schumpeter's provocation to capitalism (that ii is organizationally inevitable that market activity sediments into bureaucratic procedure) as a motive force behind a Germanic form of *Gesellschaftspolitik* in which the state was to nest and mollify the excesses of neoliberal market: it declared itself the exception to neoliberalism in order to protect neoliberalism. It is a deliberately ambiguous policy of economizing all social fields (to obviate against monopoly) whilst compensating for its rational coldness (see Foucault, M. (2008) *The Birth of Biopolitics: Lectures at the Collège de France 1978–1979,* Transl. G. Burchell, Basingstoke: Palgrave MacMillan, pp. 242–244).

28 Ramoglou, S. and Tsang, E.W.K., and Gartner, W.B. (2020) " 'Who Is an Entrepreneur?' Is (Still) the Wrong Question," *Journal of Business Venturing Insights,* 13: e00168.

29 McKeever, E., Anderson, A., and Jack, S. (2014) "Entrepreneurship and Mutuality: Social Capital in Processes and Practices," *Entrepreneurship and Regional Development,* 26(5–6), 453–477.

30 Massumi, B. (1992) *A User's Guide to Capitalism and Schizophrenia,* Cambridge and London: The MIT Press. Massumi is the translator of several of Deleuze (and Guattari's) texts into English.

31 Deleuze, G. and Guattari, F. (1988) *A Thousand Plateaus,* p. 399.

32 Deleuze, G. and Guattari, F. (1988) *A Thousand Plateaus – Capitalism and Schizophrenia,* London: The Athlone Press, p. 399.

33 Deleuze, G. and Guatarri, F. *Anti-Oedipus: Capitalism and Schizophrenia,* Transl. R. Hurley, M. Seem, & H. Lane, Minneapolis: University of Minnesota Press, pp. 31–32.

34 Deleuze, G. (2006) *Nietzsche & Philosophy,* New York: Columbia University Press.

35 Deleuze, G. (1988) *Foucault,* Transl. S. Hand, Minneapolis: University of Minnesota Press, p. 38.

36 Cf. Reay, T., Zilber, T.B., Langley, M., and Tsoukas, H. (Eds.) (2019) *Institutions and Organizations,* Oxford: Oxford University Press; Garud, R., Hardy, C., and Maguire, S. (2007) "Institutional Entrepreneurship as Embedded Agency: An Introduction to the Special Issue," *Organization Studies,* 28(7): 957–969; Weik, E. (2011) "Institutional Entrepreneurship and Agency," *Journal for the Theory of Social Behaviour,* 41: 466–481; Welter, F. and Smallbone, D. (2011) "Institutional Perspectives on Entrepreneurial Behaviour in Challenging Environments," *Journal of Small Business Management,* 49: 107–125.

37 Colebrook, C. (2002) *Deleuze,* London and New York: Routledge, p. 23.

38 See Martin, B. (2013) *The Hanging Man: the Arrest of Ai Weiwei.* New York: Farrar, Straus and Giroux.

39 The 14th June 2017 fire at Grenfell Tower, Tower Hamlets in London, U.K., which killed 72 people bears a similar stain. See Grenfell Tower Phase 1 Report. October 2019.

40 "Though it always refers to singular agents *[agents],* literature is a collective assemblage *[agencement]* of enunciation." An enunciation that disturbs the standard grammar by inventing its own, that works up to the edges of the sayable. In doing these three things (1) decomposing syntax; (2) to then create a new language that sets upon the original language in a round-about way; (3) and which then shows the limits of language, where it stops) protects and elevates the very language from which it is running hither and thither like a fox pursued by dogs which then hunkers down in a burrow and waits in the near-dark of their cunning for the pack to pass on. See Deleuze, G. (1997) "Literature and Life," Transl. D. Smith & M. Greco, *Critical Inquiry,* 23(2): 225–230, pp. 228–229.

41 Deleuze, G. and Guatarri, F. (1983) *Anti-Oedipus: Capitalism and Schizophrenia,* Transl. R. Hurley, M. Seem, & H. Lane, Minneapolis: University of Minnesota Press, p. 43.

42 See reading of Richard Branson's life story in Johnsen, C.G. and Sørensen, B. (2017) "Traversing the Fantasy of the Heroic Entrepreneur," *International Journal of Entrepreneurial Behavior & Research,* 23(2): 228–244.

43 For Bateson (Bateson, G. (1972/1987) *Steps to an Ecology of Mind,* Northvale: Jason Aronson, p. 321):

I suggest to you, now, that the word "idea," in its most elementary sense, is synonymous with "difference." Kant, in the *Critique* of *Judgment – if* I understand him correctly – asserts that the most elementary aesthetic act is the selection of a fact. He argues that in a piece of chalk there are an infinite number of potential facts. The *Ding an sich,* the piece of chalk, can never enter into communication or mental process because of this infinitude. The sensory receptors cannot accept it; they filter it out. What they do is to select certain *facts* out of the piece of chalk, which then become, in modern terminology, information.

I suggest that Kant's statement can be modified to say that there is an infinite number of *differences* around and within the piece of chalk. There are differences between the chalk and the rest of the universe, between the chalk and the sun or the moon. And within the piece of chalk, there is for every molecule an infinite number of differences between its location and the locations in which it *might* have been. Of this infinitude, we select a very limited number, which be-come information. In fact, what we mean by information – the elementary unit of information – is *a difference which makes a difference,* and it is able to make a difference because the neural pathways along which it travels and is continually transformed are themselves provided with energy. The pathways are ready to be triggered. We may even say that the question is already implicit in them.

See also Colebrook, C. (2010) *Introduction to Deleuze Dictionary,* Edinburgh: Edinburgh University Press, pp. 3–4.

44 Hjorth, D., Holt, R., and Steyaert, C. (2015) "Entrepreneurship Process Studies," *International Small Business Journal,* 33(6): 599–611.

45 Massumi, B. (2002) *Parables for the Virtual – Movement, Affect, Sensation*, Durham and London: Duke University Press, p. 30.

46 Spinosa, C., Flores, F., and Dreyfus, H.L. (1997) *Disclosing New Worlds – Entrepreneurship, Democratic Action, and the Cultivation of Solidarity*, Cambridge: MIT Press.

47 Sarasvathy is also keen on using literature, for example suggesting entrepreneurship is exemplified in William Blake's poetic descriptions of the "extraordinary possibilities within ordinary reality." Sarasvathy, S. (2021) "Even-If: Sufficient, Yet Unnecessary Conditions for Worldmaking," *Organization Theory*, 2: 1–9, p. 7.

48 To recur to Bateson, he talks of territory as the material, and map as the linguistic, and how, difference stalks the latter rather than the former, which is a world of forces rather than differences. Differences are abstracted, they are representations, and yet it is the connexion between difference and force, between the act of creating a fact (a distinction manifest in an appearance) and a physical instantiation of occurrence, that brings Deleuze and Bateson into a common form of ecological thinking.

49 Johnsen, C., Olaison, L., and Sørensen, B.M. (2017) "Put Your Style at Stake: A New Use of Sustainable Entrepreneurship," *Organization Studies*, 39(2–3): 397–415.

50 Johnsen et al., 2017; Spinosa, Flores, and Dreyfus, 1997.

51 Cf. Clayton Christensen's well-known description of this process as disruption, as disruptive innovation (e.g. Christensen, C. Hall, T., Dillon, K., and Duncan, D.S. (2016) "Know Your Customers' Jobs to Be Done," *Harvard Business Review*, September: 2016).

52 Roitman, J. (2005) *Fiscal Disobedience: An Anthropology of Economic Regulation in Central Africa*, Princeton: Princeton University Press.

53 Spinosa, C., Flores, F., and Dreyfus, H. (1997) *Disclosing New Worlds*, Cambridge MA: MIT Press, p. 159.

54 Greenblatt, S. (1980) *Renaissance Self-Fashioning – From More to Shakespeare*, Chicago and London: The University of Chicago Press, p. 234.

55 Ahearne, J. (1995) *Michel de Certeau – Interpretation and Its Other*, Stanford: Stanford University Press.

56 Kroezen, J. and Heugens, P. (2012) Organizational Identity Formation: Processes of Identity Imprinting and Enactment in the Dutch Microbrewing Landscape. In M. Schultz, S. Maguire, A. Langley, & H. Tsoukas (Eds.), *Identity in and around Organizations*, Oxford: Oxford University Press, pp. 89–128.

57 Ocejo, R.E. (2017). *Masters of Craft*, Princeton: Princeton University Press.

58 See Land, C., Sutherland, N., and Taylor, S. (2019) Craft Brewing, Gender and the Dialectical Interplay of Retraditionalization and Innovation. In E. Bell, G. Mangia, S. Taylor, & M.L. Toraldo (Eds.), *The Organization of Craft Work: Identities, Meanings, and Materiality*, London: Routledge, p. 139. Ocejo, R.E. (2017) *Masters of Craft*, pp. 20–21.

59 Massumi, 2002, p. 30.

60 Agamben, G. (1999) *Potentialities – Collected Essays in Philosophy*, Stanford: Stanford University Press, p. 183.

61 Deleuze, G. (1991) *Bergsonism*, New York: Zoone Books, p. 91.

62 Massumi, B. (2002) *Parables for the Virtual – Movement, Affect, Sensation*, Durham and London: Duke University Press, p. 30.

63 Massumi, 2002, p. 43.
64 Cf. Guillet de Monthoux, P. (2004) *The Art Firm – Aesthetic Management and Metaphysical Marketing,* Stanford: Stanford University Press.
65 Studying the creation of lists of names, photobooks, media posts in the wake of Hurricane Katrina, Kyle Parry likens these digital archives (of similar form to those generated by Weiwei and his team) to a generative assembly. Parry argues assembly captures a deliberate and conscious sense of purposeful organizational form that is perhaps absent in the looser and open form known as assemblage. See Parry, K. "Generative Assembly after Katrina," *Critical Inquiry,* 44(3): 554–581.
66 Deleuze, 1988. p. 28.
67 Deleuze, G. (2002) *Dialogues,* Transl. H. Tomlinson & B. Habberjam, London and New York: Continuum, p. 71.
68 See Holland, 1998, p. 18, p. 65.
69 Kacperczyk, A.J. (2012) "Opportunity Structures in Established Firms: Entrepreneurship versus Intrapreneurship in Mutual Funds." *Administrative Science Quarterly,* 57(3): 484–521. doi:10.1177/0001839212462675
70 Cf. Deleuze and Parnet, 1987.
71 Deleuze and Guattari 1987, p. 272.
72 March, J. and Simon, H. (1958/1993) *Organizations (2nd Ed.),* Cambridge: MA, Blackwell, used the term "coalition" to describe this tendency; see also Stevenson, W.B., Pearce, J.L., and Porter, L.W. (1985) "The Concept of 'Coalition' in Organization Theory and Research," *The Academy of Management Review,* 10(2): 256–268.
73 Schumpeter also noted how "the entrepreneurial function need not be embodied in a physical person and in particular in a single physical person. Every social environment has its own ways of filling the entrepreneurial function," 1949/1991: 260.
74 Spindler, F. 2009, pp. 18–19; Deleuze, 1992.

4 Entrepreneurship as organization-creation

What we take from Romantic literature is awareness of how individuality and its subjection are irrevocably bound to mobility, to fragmentary and collective forms of expression, and to the irony, uncertainty, and creative exposure of struggling to make sense anew, again and again. In Romanticism, the individualism being elevated and encouraged does not exist as a discrete (metaphysical or material) presence, and is not prior to the practices and events through which it experiences its own limits and their (possible) transformation. What we take from Deleuze, including his discussion of literature in the wake of Romanticism, is an attentiveness to the already organized nature of original and creative expression. Rather than emerging fully formed as an individual's design, the actions leaning towards organization (wrapped up in concepts like creativity, inventiveness, innovation) are flooded with flows of desire already in motion, and the imaginative leaps being made have about them the quality of a gathering, an assembly. The assemblage is state of exposed and exposing individuality wound into force fields of desire that can potentially settle as an actual organizational form. The moments of assemblage are, we have argued, where the entrepreneurial finds its fullest expression: the *entre* (being in and amid) *preneur* (taking, grasping, twisting, and going on into what is open, taking what is actual and exposing it to what remains virtual).

We have argued that the enigmatic distinctiveness of entrepreneurship rests with its referring to the time before we can (retrospectively) claim there has been a start. It is a time not of the firm, but of firm-ing. The coming-into-being of the organization that we can refer to as a start-up or a new business, a firm then having been formed. This is precisely the time of assemblages and of the virtual becoming actualized. The time of becoming. Entrepreneurship is the appearance of organizational form constituted in the virtual-becoming-actual. It is a collective condition of imagination, uncertainty, and play, all of which are assembled through desire.[1] Entrepreneurship is a condition of organizational natality, a beginning and beginning again, from which an opened space for new movement from the virtual into the actual.

DOI: 10.4324/9781315714455-6

Given these sources of inspiration, we hope to have dissolved some-what the little end/big end dispute with which we opened the book. We have argued that the individual and wider structural settings are more integral aspects of organization formation than they are an opposing duality, and that what is entrepreneurial is what appears on the cusp of becoming an organizational form, hovering between what is actual and virtual. What is newly emerging has appeared as a disturbance to habit, new disclosive spaces are opening up, but with little sense of they might sediment and standardize.

In this chapter we make an explicit connexion between these philo-sophical and literary arguments and entrepreneurship research and organization studies. It is precisely the lived dialogue between entrepre-neurship theory and organization studies theory that has enabled the identification of the key concepts that bring our arguments from these other fields to life. In doing so we enlist a highly selective number of lit-erary texts that exemplify, we believe, literature's capacity to keep life in language, making it an exceptionally rich empirical material for the study of entrepreneurship's yearning towards the creation of new worlds.

Entrepreneurship as organization-creation

The choice of assemblage is inseparable from the prioritization of desta-bilizing desire as a process of force and will in the world of entrepre-neurship. "Can we make progress if we do not enter into *regions far from equilibrium?*" Deleuze asks. And goes on: "Physics attest to this. Keynes made advances in political economy because he related it to the situation of a 'boom,' and no longer one of equilibrium. This is the only way to introduce desire into the corresponding field."[2] We are not alone in moving away from equilibrium in order to introduce desire into our field of entrepreneurship (and organization) studies. Deleuze pointed at Keynes, but could as well, and arguably with greater pedagogical effect, have directed us to Schumpeter's work on entrepreneurship. Schumpeter, an economist by profession, was sceptical that equilibrium was a desir-able state, indeed a properly functioning economy required a more gen-erative force that was, by definition, unstable, and which we might equate with desire

Desire, as we have discussed, is a concept that provides the entrepre-neurship researcher with a way to handle the process of organizational firming, the process of creating a new organization. It is precisely in this time, in the regions away from equilibrium or pulling in directions away from equilibrium, that the proto-organizational process of forming happens, for in equilibrium or balance, the conditions are such that man-agement is favoured whereas entrepreneurship becomes a disturbance. A diagram can help us clarify (assuming, somewhat un-processually, time and growth to be linear conditions of emergence).

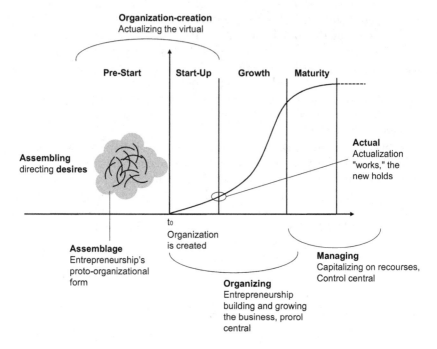

Figure 4.1 The time of entrepreneurship.

Coming into organizational form is what the concept of assemblage (or, in French, *agencement*) describes, and an explanation that seeks to clarify how the assemblage is held together and is given a direction needs the concept of desire. These concepts express what is already underway, the already more of what is, that rolls into a next-ness.[3] Massumi further describes this as that which is absorbed in occupying its field of potential. This is process, underway, becoming. This is also where we find the firming up of organizational structures, referring to *firma* that describes the process under which the business is transacted, where the flow happens.

What drives this flow, and how is it started? Whereas entrepreneurship and organization studies have been interested in why people start businesses (little end) or why systems and technical conditions encourage business formation (big end), these "genres" of questions have tended to focus on the individual and motivation, on contextual conditions, or on structural determination. Process studies direct us instead to think process by attending to temporality, wholeness, openness (and the openness of the self), force, and potentiality.[4] This perspective makes relationships and the dynamics of relating at least as important as what is related; it makes subjectification and the forming of agency and self at least as important as subjects; it makes force and relationships between forces at least as important as positions; and, finally, it makes potentiality, the incipient, the virtual as least as important as the actual. What does this mean for thinking and theorizing and studying entrepreneurship?

Romantic literature and Deleuze's philosophy have helped us extend the theoretical vocabulary so that it now includes a richer set of concepts for disclosing, describing, and analysing these processual flows. What we now represent in such a context of previous studies is a commitment to embracing process thinking rather than merely accepting it.[5] In this sense we study *in* change, we do not study change. We study how what is already actual receives the new from the virtual, how forming the new organization takes place, how a new organization emerges from an assemblage held together and directed by desire. Yet whilst literature and philosophy help us invent new concepts for thinking about how new organizations are created as an entrepreneurial achievement, we find ourselves wanting. We are following a flight line that reveals a region far from equilibrium, one where Schumpeter found himself needing to re-create the concept of entrepreneurship and tie it to innovation.[6] In our urge to find more nuanced and pedagogical material to work with in building a theory of entrepreneurship, processually formed, we wish to elaborate on the nature of this assembling time of organization forming.

The opening up of this assemblage, its own coming into being so to speak through the inaugural entrepreneurial act, is where people are brought outside the equilibrium situation. We cannot find a better concept than *seduction* to think and describe this straying from habit. Seduction – *se ducere* – literally means "to lead astray" and thus captures the relational dynamics by which someone is led to abandon their accustomed way, to come along, to follow a flight-line. The entrepreneurship process opens with the act of seduction. Then what?

Then the momentum is inaugurated but fodder for the movement is badly needed. When you have just inhaled, before you open your mouth to speak, what is about to become expressed is never more vulnerable to opposition. Only a second later, when the expression is underway, you are strengthened by the momentum of having started. Starting is perhaps not the most difficult thing about the entrepreneurship process, but to keep at it precisely when the world has become aware that newness is underway and the reactive forces are mobilized.[7] Against this reactive response by the world, entrepreneurial individuation can bring active forces in relationship to each other and affiliate with *affirmative* will to overcome such attempts to control (*contra* + *rotulus*, against what is rolling) to instead *pro-rol* the process, maintain its movement, its furthering into a next-ness.[8] When reason speaks to you in sound voices expressing concerns on the basis of rational analyses suggesting what you should not do, still pushing ahead and affirming the joyful speculation that this will work is easily described as mad or unwise. We have found no better concept than *play* to think and describe this. When the new is underway, little can be fetched from the past or future to legitimate your "acting as if."[9] This is typical for play, that it is playing that drives it. Not a good reason fetched from the past, nor a specific goal that has to be reached, but playing. The newer it is, the less you have in terms of habit and routine to grasp what is virtuality-proposed-as-actualizable. Thus, a playful relationship to "what is" characterizes the mode of progressing the entrepreneurship process. It is not free play, however, for this would suggest a too close affinity between the entrepreneurship process and art. Playing, like is often the case according to Huizinga, operates with an awareness of what you are playing with. Children's play, for example is often making use of roles set in the adult world.[10] What we find central in entrepreneurship as play is this acute awareness of common sense, where the limits of the present are drawn, where the convention is known, and then twisted. Entrepreneurial play is in this sense a limit sensitivity, and a keen awareness of where the boundary has been drawn, what holds the presently available value offers in their proper places and, thus, what "space-for-play" that can be created if you – often against reason – move beyond the present limits.[11]

Play thus takes place and is defined by its relationship to *common sense*. It is in relationship to common sense that the strength of the process, as novelty-underway, is accumulated. Learning what, more precisely, is expected of you in particular contexts, an awareness of the audience-sensibility required for getting your message through, for picking the right/necessary fights, and for gaining trust where needed. You have to sense what power to be affected there is, what passion that can be spent, and thus what power to affect you have in the situation. All of this is dependent on having a receptive capacity for the norms and to find therein ways of overspilling and reaching beyond them, which in turn becomes the new setting of common sense.

Completing these aspects of entrepreneurial assemblage, after seduction, play and common sense, is the moment of *commerce* as achieved through a transaction. A transaction is the residue, the receipt that the desire for newness did add something of value to another in the world. It is the point at which an organization comes into being as a venture, the point at which the handling of common sense and absorbing the habituated requirements for rational, planned, thought through, and iterated justifications for the venture (dictated by habit, routine, made investments) pays off. Commerce/transaction thus completes our model of the entrepreneurship process. This is how the actual feeds back to you that the virtual has indeed been actualized. The new has added something to the world and it is received by someone confirming that there is the value of enhanced capacity to live, to be experienced (at least potentially). In a commercial setting, it is the customer who confirms this experience of potential value by entering into a transaction. Commerce is the relational situation in which the transaction takes place. Results will in some way affirm that value has become actualized.

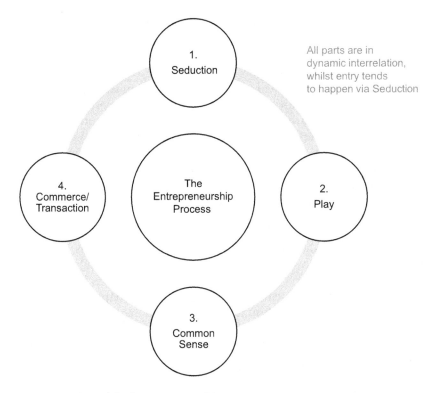

Figure 4.2 A model of entrepreneurship process.

Seduction

Lounsbury and Glynn, framing their study of entrepreneurship stories, legitimation, and the acquisition of resources within a cultural and symbolic realm of meaning, suggest: "[S]tories that are told by or about entrepreneurs define a new venture in ways that can lead to favorable interpretations of the wealth-creating possibilities of the venture; this enables resource flows to the new enterprise."[12] For us what is most interesting is: just what is the process of leading to favourability here? How does being "lead to" work? For them it is It must be more than an instrumentally rational reception of promised revenue streams. We wish to unpack this "leading to" in a richer way. It begins, we suggest, with seduction, a framing that resists explanations that settle upon risk- or ambiguity reduction, or even their calculated interpretation. Indeed we find it somewhat ironic that the appeal to reducing equivocality is being held up as the reason why entrepreneurs can succeed with their stories, given it is the kind of calming, securing experience Schumpeter associates with administration, or management. The reduction heralds

a sedimentation of acceptability that occurs as a result of the entrepreneurial process, it is the stabilizing of desire and curtailing of imagination constituted by firming (the creation process) giving way to the
organization (the end result). Whilst we acknowledge that at some
point, the entrepreneurial process has to settle on a form that can
embed itself in common sense and can secure commerce/transaction,
this is also when the managerial emerges as part of the process (e.g. in
pursuing a set of clearly stated opportunities, using accepted means):
Opportunity recognition would thus be the discovery of a safe harbour where one can make some commerce/transaction, and where the
responses to change are far more of an adaptive and creative nature.[13]
This shows how strong the managerial domination is also in entrepreneurship research. Favourable interpretations thus mean the story can
be related to templates that order the field and its identities – what
reproduces an institution.[14] This is the backend of our model, again,
when entrepreneurship starts to look like management. This is where
desire is dominated by well-formed interests and the forming process
starts to settle in a form – the venture, when firming has become the
firm. Our model frames entrepreneurial activity as happening before
the organization such as a firm is established, an experience which we
believe the field of entrepreneurship studies has given little attention in
its attempts to grasp and define its "unit" of analysis.[15]

Entrepreneurship is a process of inauguration that ends with the
consummation of a first transaction. At its opening, however, there is
a sense of frustration, longing, and anticipation that a safe harbour of
actualized habits and expectations is not the place to be. Established
places, organizations with structures, roles, and routines, direct action
towards repetition in the name of economized use of time and reduction of friction. Templates for action and identities for action-repertoires
make institutional pressure to adjust and conform normal and entrepreneurship marginal.[16] Seduction is the process of leading oneself and
others astray from required reality. It is a movement of leaving the comfort of a place in favour of creating space for play. We understand this
move, as we have suggested before, rather with *homo ludens* as model,
and not primarily *homo oeconomicus*.[17]

Seduction is the transition that brings people out to sea once again, of
leading people astray, of taking them into open water, into the further
reaches where what is actual/known/comfortable/template-guided slips
into the unknown and unknowable. Seduction's relational basis resonates
with that of Spinoza's joy:

> It can be said that joy augments our power of acting and sadness
> diminishes it. And the *conatus* is the effort to experience joy, to
> increase the power of acting, to imagine and find that which is a
> cause of joy, which maintains and furthers this cause; and also an

effort to avert sadness, to imagine and find that which destroys the cause of sadness.[18]

Seduction will, in most cases, be achieved by a body encountering another body and with this affective coming together a future state can be imagined. Ideas of what is possible, often communicated via stories, represent a future state – a firm, the result of firming, living as an entrepreneur, the result of entrepreneuring. Affect, according to Spinoza (and Deleuze's reading of Spinoza), involves a passage from lesser to greater capacity to act (or the opposite). We get ideas as a result of other bodies' effect on us. Such ideas we can describe as images: "… images are the corporeal affections themselves […], the traces of an external body on our body. […] Insofar as it has ideas, the mind is said to *imagine.*"[19] Seduction is a powerful way of getting others to imagine, on the basis of giving them an idea of what could be the result of going "astray" or taking the plunge.

There is thus a letting go, a "plunge" into the open sea, unknowing of the consequences and unheeding of voices talking of irresponsibility and ruin, a decision to loosen the norms, habits, structures, principles in such a way that new experiences might emerge. As a force of curiosity it falls beyond the standard forms of envisaging an entrepreneurial future, notably the use of the business plan. The business plan is an adoption to specified economic ends, and the agreement that corrections will be possible and introduced, and it sets up the entrepreneur as the decision-maker, a market actor who successfully demonstrates the power of the market to take on the responsibility for administrative formalism and both inform and reform both state and society.[20] The business plan (or more latterly business canvas, and soon, no doubt, to become another analogy) has a long and strong standing in entrepreneurship literature. It is used as a way of selling the business to prospective investors, and so could be said to act as a form of seduction. Yet it is more an indication of conformity, confirming as it does a commitment to competitive mechanisms that organize human relations in the service of economic growth. If seduction is to lead astray, the potential investor is of course led towards a new possibility for earning income, but there is no disturbance here. Rather the so-called entrepreneurial performance confines itself to talk of knowable and realistic opportunities as set out in the already dominant competitive ordering of established relations. Here the investor presented with a plan would be asked to take a leap. If the performance is more about figuring out, as Schumpeter calls it, about applying forecasting techniques, then it is more in the spirit of managed enterprise, of planning. Relatedly, and again we can invoke Schumpeter here, the venture capitalist is increasingly adept at spotting and evaluating new services, new methods, and new products, indeed it is their role to take these on without surprise, backed by specialists able to assess an idea's viability. They are part of a machinery in which innovation becomes a managed process of realizing the possible, an expectation that can be algorithmically measured, quantified, and ranked (against other opportunities), and so again not at all entrepreneurial.[21] More broadly still, venture capital and entrepreneurship itself can be considered as part of this managed process, part of a discursive structure of enterprise in which both are held in high esteem, as forces for the good and not at all disturbing or leading anything astray.[22] Entrepreneurship itself, strangely enough, would then pass as entrepreneurship to the extent it has become the enterprise, that is, more manageable and plannable. Enterprise discourse has been so successful in promoting a style, for citizens and employees, that is manageable, a managerial form of entrepreneurship, i.e. enterprise, yet sailing under the flag of entrepreneurship.[23]

When set against what can be managed, the form of seduction we attribute to the entrepreneurship process is as much a flow of feeling, and imagination as it is forecasted. We could analyse this as an encounter of bodies where the idea, representing a wanted state for the investor, is planted in the mind of the investor, who starts to imagine. It is not only imagining the future wanted state that starts, but also the desire to manifest an increased capacity to produce (that future wanted state). Affect is here tied to the movement from a lesser to a greater capacity to act. This, presentation of a plan, is thus not only the setting up of the entrepreneur as the decision-making subject, the subject of mastery of resources, but also the investor as the decision-making subject with mastery of resources. There is "joy" in Spinoza's terms – a greater capacity to produce is made incipient.

The seducer operates in view of an assemblage where the desire to move towards the greater capacity to act, to become part of a greater whole, drives the movement encouraging others to leave the well-trodden paths of habit. Successfully seducing others will have the effect that an assemblage is drawn together (by this double desire: to move to a greater productive capacity, to move to joy, and to achieve a future wanted state). In Spinoza's terms, our capacity to act is "in" our relationships with others. Seduction seduces by holding up this potential before the other – immanent to moving towards a greater capacity to act – that one will become part of a new whole, and thus experience joy.

Importantly, there is an element of leading, and we tie this to the entrepreneurial initiative of creating an opening that is the right time (opportunity as timeliness). Seduction starts with the event where a new movement is potentialized. Moving into what leads you away or astray, but astray towards a new and more productive, joyful whole, would then define seduction. Seduction is in this sense entrepreneurial: it makes ingress and tactically makes use of the opening (as an entre-space) where an opportunity can be created by pulling others into a common sense of curiosity and perhaps even passionate engagement. Seduction is, in this sense, increasing the other's capacity to be affected whilst this is also part of the relational dynamics where the affected one increases the other's capacity to affect. Letting oneself be led astray is also a force creating the leader.

Seduction would, in most cases, include a loosening of an established relationship, a release, and an intensification of a new relationship to a potentially more productive new whole. Affect explains the opening up and the subsequently increased connecting capacity, something that a story of entrepreneurial becoming could explore – as a passion, an increased power to be affected – and bring the affected body into the assemblage held together by a desire to become more productive, and achieve a new, future wanted state. A timely idea affects the mind as a passion, as an incomplete or confused idea, in Spinoza's terms.[24] This only means that it is ripe for improvisational entry, it is tendered into ripeness, it has become ripe for being picked as a resource for those that have "the other part" of the idea, the part that makes it complete and thus makes it into action (or a capacity to act).[25]

Play

Play, we learn from Huizinga, Winnicott, and de Certeau is intimately social, relational, and fluid.[26] Huizinga says play *grounds* or anchors culture and not the other way around: "If this tendency of the mind, which invests the objects of ordinary life with personality, is in fact rooted in play ... [T]he play attitude must have been present before human culture or human speech existed ..."[27] He reports from Hindu and Scandinavian "mythical speculations concerning the origin of the world and things," the Rig-veda and Edda, that both those attempts to narrate a start, an origin, includes rooting it in the body, and in playful imagination.[28] The birth of the world, matter for cosmos, is originating from Purusha (primordial Being) in Rig-veda, or from Ymir (primordial giant), in the Edda. Huizinga then notes that, when we read these stories, we have to conclude that: "in its whole structure, tone and tendency seems to be playing with the old mythological themes in a way that can hardly be called serious."[29] This whole tendency, to imagine gods and giants, invent stories of origins, objects of worship, in sum; the stuff that ritual, myth, and religion is full of – is this not best understood, Huizinga asks, in terms of the play attitude?

Play, the word itself which has a notoriously uncertain origin – related to German *plegojanan*, to occupy oneself about, and *pflegen*, to take care of, cultivate, and Dutch *pleyen*, to rejoice, be glad – seems to emerge from in-betweens. It is thus an awkward ground, moving, loose, giving way to every attempt to use it as a basis for fixing. Rather, as Huizinga's examples from the Rig-veda and the Edda show, stabilities, origins, fixations, authorities, reasons to fear and obey ... these are all sprung out of a playful attitude that steers imagination to such phantasmagorial creations.

Deleuze picks up this idea of play, though here filtered through Henri Bergson, who analyses fabulation as a visionary faculty that generates gods and giants.[30] Such inventions seem to be aimed at creating what

Bergson calls "effective presences" that are meant to regulate or limit life. Deleuze does not see this as a lack, but rather as the result of a productive desire and the power of thinking: "What is thinking such that it can enslave itself to images of some great outside? Does this not tell us that there is something productive, positive, and liberating about the very power of thought?"[31] This is how Huizinga shows that culture springs from play; cultures of artistic-literary fabulation, cultures of religious and mythological giants, objects worthy of fear, and worship are all sprung out of play.

Although playful fabulations can be exploited for strategic reasons, as means of control, as in the case of taboo, play as such is tactical, de Certeau teaches us. It operates not by confrontation or strategic attacks. It undulates and erodes, identifies cracks in the surface of the strategy's structure, moves in, and makes use. It lures the other into movement, wherefore the playful also includes a seductive element. Strategy seeks to hold a position and controls its game of possession or appropriation from a site. Play is tactical as it seeks movement, loosens rather than controls and is not interested in holding on to what it wins. It needs lightness and speed, not possession and position. "Play to order is no longer play ...," Huizinga says.[32]

Play, Manning and Massumi note, very much on the basis of a Deleuzian philosophy, is this "minor tendency contained by every instituted structure, whose unleashing softens or disables postural default settings."[33] Then, in a definition that seems but all too resonant with our agenda of better understanding entrepreneurship by mingling it with the literary, and which is fully resonant with de Certeau's understanding of the tactical as a "transformative insinuation," they go on: "A degree of play creates the potential for the emergence of the new, not in frontal assault against structure but at the edges and in its pores."[34] It is important for how we define play here, that it capitalizes on the moment, operates tactically, avoids the "frontal attack," and pulls away from the centre or the equilibrium to affirm the move beyond the limits of the present.

Erasmus in his *Praise of Folly* reminds his readers that "soon ripe, soon rotten," with reference to the child becoming an adult, thus urging us to stay in the childlike (rather than childish) playfulness. The theme comes back in Nietzsche's emphasis on "Higher men" being no longer capable of laughter, dance, and play. Play, in Nietzsche's philosophy, as we discussed earlier in relation to the parable on metamorphosis, is the affirmation of chance, it is the upward movement of the dice-throw, and he has Zarathustra say: "Let chance come to me: it is as innocent as a little child,"[35] which is Nietzsche's blink to Heraclitus note: time is a child who plays. Thinking itself is a series of dice-throws in Nietzsche's philosophy. It affirms chance and moves towards the virtual fringe of thought.

There is also the obverse trajectory in play, of a child learning to become part of a practice, to belong. It is in this spirit that Ludwig Wittgenstein, for example, focuses on play in relation to language acquisition, and brings the tension between child and adult into his conceptualization of the language game. Wittgenstein opens *Philosophical Investigations* with St Augustine's account of language acquisition. Wittgenstein was impressed by how this early Christian and the future Bishop of Hippo was able to recall how attentive he became when his elders spoke, how he recalled their intonation, the lilt of their voices, and the tremor in their voice, the association of words and things, and how it was, from within such an immersed condition of observation, he absorbed the linear associations of sound, utterance, things, movements, words, and sentences; Augustine the child matured, acquiring the habituated means with which to express his desires.

Wittgenstein immediately questions such an account, but not openly. Instead he asks of us, the reader, how the child would acquire the skill of making any such association in the first place, how the child knows he might emulate what he witnesses, how the child knows that part of the grammar of a word consists in its being used in some way, of its already functioning in a game. Play in language is the way into maturity, and this depends entirely upon the child's willingness to desire and use language. For Wittgenstein Augustine was right to show language being spoken publicly and being a desirous condition – to learn language is to learn to play with words, and further to learn that words are things that can be played with and are playful. Hence the use of the term language game, where language lives when learners find themselves desiring language and as such desiring to express their own desires in language. Yet Augustine's account is partial, and to complete the account would be to acknowledge the paradox that to learn language is already to have acquired its grammar.

Stanley Cavell imagines what it is like to be the young Augustine, patiently and attentively learning from his elders as they converse, soaking up their behaviour, perhaps oblivious of the young boy stealing their gestures and words and making them his own, transforming his little desires into larger ones, ones that can be communicated, and in being communicated they are desires of a certain form, ones that necessarily intend to be heard, and met, by others.[36] Language is intimate with desire, and in play, this intimacy becomes a contested one, rather than simply an imitative one. Desire and language cast the human-animal into an actual-virtual space, and play is what allows us humans to acknowledge this, for in play misfires, attempts, struggles, consummations, over-spillings, are all legitimate uses of language; "... every metaphor" Huizinga notes, "is a play upon words."[37]

In this way we learn of the intimacy of play, learning, and the necessary limits and occasional disappointment with the criteria by which words are used, for there are myriad available uses, and in this all sorts of misunderstandings, and hence potential, arises. The mistake is to conceal this openness on the assumption that there is a correct use, and that learners can be instructed in such. Instructed they can be, of course, but not limited to the instructed use. There will always be play, in-between the instructed use and the myriad available uses. Play desires the making-use of that space for free movement, before that too has been occupied by instruction. This is the artful in the tactical, and the artful in play, that it introduces the unthought into thought as a pursuit of free movement.[38] Play, and not instruction, forecloses such a mistake. To play with these countless uses is the invitation to belong to a desiring condition in which the illicit is ever-present company.

Common sense

In a curious and important way, entrepreneurship is also intimately acquainted with common sense. It is precisely the limit of the possible, the boundary of action, the conventionally suggested, or the proper domain of the dominant practice, routine, habit, or strategy that represents the opportunity-to-be-created in the entrepreneurial process. Schumpeter acknowledged this "ear" for incipient opportunity when he talks about the pale of routine.[39] Spinosa, Flores, and Dreyfus recognize this as they emphasize the importance of articulation, which occurs "when a style is brought into sharper focus."[40] Style would here be the basis on which practices are conserved and developed, and is the basis for meaning by being what coordinates action, determine how things and people matter, and by being what is transferred from situation or context into the next situation or context. Articulation thus makes the taken-for-granted visible as thus questionable and changeable.[41]

At the limit of the taken-for-granted is where an engagement with common sense inevitably happens, and can be tactically explored. It is from within an experience of belonging (to an already assimilated way of life), an awareness and knowledge of how common sense is embedded in the style of dealing with people and things, that a particular route into the open – a new becoming – is potentialized or made incipient. Articulating that becoming as an opportunity is then to simultaneously question common sense as well as to acknowledge common sense. Imagination, the "crazy idea" or the vision following an epiphany can of course be what creates awareness of this belonging to a style, a routine, an unnecessary limit. Travelling, as one example, often heightens your awareness of style – your own and that of the others – which in turn enables articulation. We believe this to be central to entrepreneurship wherever we find it, but perhaps most clearly manifest in what is often called social entrepreneurship. The "entrepreneur" or, more correctly, the entrepreneurial process, is here more like a membrane, like the eardrum that sits in-between worlds, and "acts" precisely as a relational response between what is already considered good (that which affirms life from within established patterns of living) and common sense, and that which affirms potential new possibilities for enhanced living. The entrepreneurial can here be understood as a combination of social belonging animated by articulating a disclosive capacity to act creatively, transforming what is established.[42] Articulation discloses the style-in-use and animates and excites belonging to a potential life, refusing to allow the habituated and managed to settle into unquestioned patterns.

There remains a sense of *homo oeconomicus* in this, at least insofar as it evokes *oikonomia,* from Greek for house, *oikos*: a proper ordering of parts, a well-administered household in which the different rooms, activities, and (gendered) roles are arranged so as to achieve a smoothly realized interdependence. The private household takes on the social responsibility. Yet *oikonomia* is also a term for arranging the material used in a speech so as to achieve a coherent argument, meaning there are rhetorical points won through the analysis and decision of how to arrange the parts well. The administrative and the rhetorical meanings are often combined.[43] Here the priority of economic growth subsides and a much broader understanding of the economy than the one we have been served primarily from neoclassical, modern economic science can (potentially) emerge. In *oikonomia* the questions of efficiency and doing more with less do not dominate, and the social nature of the economic, or the relationship between the social and the economic, becomes less orderly, more multiple.[44]

It is with commercial management that doing more with less becomes dominant. Management would be distinguished from administration (or bureaucracy) as that practice that is not limited to the harmony or appropriateness of the right arrangement of things according to the household's demands – *oikonomia* – but that, in addition, seeks to arrange in a manner that enables an outcome that results in a profit-oriented economy. As a norm it is there to be disturbed, and entrepreneurship, even in its engagement with *oikonomia*, can feed the desire for something else. There are other ways of administering, or securing the household, than offered in commercial management. Indeed it is hard to see how an engagement with a profit-oriented economy will drive entrepreneurship. If the concern remains the discovery of better ways to adjust to the existing order so as to make more with less, then this, to us, is enterprise, not entrepreneurship.

This has implications for our understanding of value as an outcome of the entrepreneurial process, as an actualization of the virtual. It can only ever be potentiality since actualizing it (realizing it, we would say, in a slightly less precise language) needs to be done in the act of confirmation, the completion of which is accomplished when a potential customer or user becomes an actual one through the event of commercial transaction.[45] It is to this commerce/transaction that we now turn in order to cover the final part of our model of the entrepreneurship process.

Commerce/transaction

John Dewey's pragmatism centres on how imagination and creativity are like movement, a "genesis of intuition in intelligence," an opening up of potential becomings from an intimate belonging to the culturally mediated or learned.[46] In this sense, it perfectly aligns with our conceptualization of how potentiality (or virtuality) emerges from within an intimacy with common sense (actuality) in entrepreneurship processes. How knowing the "light" of the actual well is also a key to knowing the "shadow" (not only potentiality but also impotentiality, the "can do" and the potentiality "not-to-act"). It is from within such an intimacy with common sense, that creativity moves ahead, provocatively questioning the limits of the presently possible as informed by the real. Imagination, by entertaining the multiplicity of virtualities as differentiating alternatives to what presently is actualized, intensifies a sense of potentiality (and impotentiality) – a sense of "I can" (also "I can not"), which in turn requires a decision.

Judgement is thus fed "cases" to decide upon by imagination, like a creative motor, and this process is described as transaction. Transaction is here a becoming of something new as a result of a socially mediated process. According to Dewey, experience is processual-transactional, and as such it breaks with a Cartesian subject-oriented and a Kantian mind-oriented rationality. The only sensible unit of analysis is the act, and every act is always already part of a process of transaction with the environment. In many ways, this concept of transaction reveals something important with the economic concept of transaction. The commercial transaction can, to some extent, be understood, using Dewey's concept of transaction, as the result of a processual, socially mediated judgement. The person decides to affirm the value-potential presented to her in the value-offer to the extent that this offer represents new or different enough value for that person. Whether a value-offer does represent actual value is a question of a socially mediated process with the environment. The commercial transaction will then be what actualized the value-potential and, at the same time, subjectifies the person into a customer-of-this-offer. We do not usually associate any commercial transaction with novelty, but since every person is always already active to some extent, a transaction will also always mean a change. Such can be more incremental or more radical depending on the resonance of the value-potential in a particular person's life. It is of course possible to see market transactions as the becoming of something new – of new value, or of the customer as such (a process of subjectification so accustomed to us that it passes unnoticed).

Before the rise of modern capitalism, something Hirschman has studied in his *The Passions and the Interests* (1977), commercial transactions were related to non-violence and innocence. In France this was described as the douceur of commerce, i.e. the sweetness, softness, the calm, and gentle nature of commerce. He quotes from a 1675 source, saying: "This continuous exchange of all the comforts of life constitutes commerce and this commerce makes for all the gentleness (douceur) of life ..."[47] Commerce, Hirschman also notes, before it was limited to its economic meaning, was otherwise long understood as animated and repeated conversation, part of other forms of polite social intercourse between people, often of what was then described as the opposite sex. In the British translations of this vocabulary – from French into English – one struggles with finding the right words, and "calm passion" of commerce is one solution. Commerce is then – towards the middle and end of the eighteenth century – promoted as a governmental ideal since it would keep men (sic!) busy and out of misbehaviour. Calm desire (calm being the English translation at the time for the French *doux,* soft/gentle) for higher gains, what would in the seventeenth century be understood by interest, Hirshman notes, was seen as the guarantee for people changing their behaviour according to a rational planning ahead. Such calm (not meaning weak, Hume points out) but strong passion would thus be different from selfish (violent but weak) passion of avarice that instead would pull towards short-term immediate gratifications.

Scottish historian William Robertson writes: "Commerce tends to wear off those prejudices which maintain distinctions and animosity between nations. It *softens and polishes* the manners of men."[48] Commerce is associated with tranquillity and efficiency. In the language of process thinking, this would describe how desire is socially coded as interest, and interest of a particular kind, interest that is resonant with a particular governmental rationality, one that will make people predictable as *homo oeconomicus*, as economic actors. This control of passions by interest as the greater passion is central to the emergence of capitalism according to Hirschman.

The transactions of commerce are, then, intimate with making them amenable to order: the intent is to make people agreeable, such that their actions, thoughts, and feelings resonate with a particular rationality.[49] Clearly the rationality by which commerce is warranted has changed in nature: politeness has given way to acquisition, civility to contractual behaviour, and calm to competition, and for many the rise of entrepreneurship is at the heart of this transformation. To transact is to extract profit, not converse, and entrepreneurs are distinguished by their capacity to actualize otherwise hidden or overlooked opportunities to extract. What defines the ideal citizen is an isolated subject subjectifying to its own self-evaluations whose focus is less on what one is but who one could become.

Ever alive to this governing ideal, we have been trying in this book to both acknowledge and question this self-subjectifying idealization. It is in this spirit that we enlist Dewey's form of transacting as what completes the entrepreneurial process of creating new or different enough value to attract a potential customer via a value proposition that makes them decide to transact money in exchange for the ownership/access of/ to value (be that a service or a product). Any transaction can also be understood as intimately social, as a result of a socially mediated act. Entrepreneurial value, to the extent it is new or different, would be in greater need of socially mediated transaction, i.e. the decision to transact, commercially, would require more of an explanation for the potential value to be grasped, since it is new or different. Commerce is also not simply what describes the commercial transaction, thus, but also part of a long history of capitalism that is mingled with a governmental rationality with interest in predictable and thus controllable citizens.

Investigating the entrepreneurial assemblage through literature

To investigate these aspects of the entrepreneurial assemblage further, we take inspiration from the forms of literature in which our argument has already been immersed, as well as from the thinking about literature in general offered by Deleuze. We also take our cue from entrepreneurship and organizational studies and the role of narrative and storytelling, of imagination, and of desire for understandings of entrepreneurship processes.[50] Building on these streams of research – processual entrepreneurship studies, Deleuze's process philosophical inquiry into literature, and organizational research – what binds them together is their upgrading of the role of language and of fiction, fabulation, and the literary.[51] What we find fascinating with entrepreneurship as a genre of stories and as a practice of story-making is how the entrepreneurial increases the other's capacity to be affected; how the entrepreneurial story makes an opening, a suspense, where an incipient newness can be assembled and make the other come along.[52]

We differ from many other studies interested in literature that tell stories about entrepreneurship by taking literary stories that are not explicitly about entrepreneurship, or even business as such. Moreover, we take snippets, or scenes, that are associated with characters, and in this we find an embodiment of an aspect of what we have gathered as the entrepreneurial assemblage. Reasons for this are found in our commitment to process thinking and the way it brings us to look closer at how life becomes. "There is no literature without fabulation," Deleuze points out with reference to Bergson, and continues, "the fabulating function does not consist in imagining or projecting an ego. Rather, it attains these visions, it raises itself to these becomings and powers."[53] Literature is fascinating as it can bring us into these becomings, into how life is furthered beyond the limits of the present. This, as we have noted earlier in this book, is the basis for the affinity with entrepreneurship that this book explores. Entrepreneurship as this organization-creation process that assembles people, vision, and resources so as to open up new possibilities for living, associated with new values. Deleuze points out that literature appears as a big project of health, writing is for the hitherto missing practices, missing possibilities, and – ultimately – missing people.

> Health as literature, as writing, consists in inventing a people who are missing.[...] The ultimate aim of literature is to set free, in the delirium, this creation of a health or this invention of a people, that is, a possibility of life.[54]

This is highly resonant for what entrepreneurship does as a kind of practice of a delirium (from Latin *deliare*, to deviate, and thus not un-associated with a fabulating function, of imagination of a life possible to actualize.

Whilst the literary sources we use might not be explicitly Romantic in their appellation, they have, we suggest, taken off from, and so in some way been warranted by, the genre in which individuality, originality, and creativity has been a pressing interest. Some might argue the likes of Virginia Woolf (from whose work we attempt to learn about play) is far more modernist and even elitist than she is Romantic, and that Nicolai Gogol (through whom we think through common sense) is more a social realist (of an absurd bent), yet this nomenclature of literary styles is itself a classified aspect of an assemblage that we might gently tease, and upset. The literary sources we use are deliberately fragmentary, they centre on characters for whom the established ways of doing things is for some reason or other untenable, or is felt in need of refinement or intensification, and in being so, they open up the actual ways of doing things to the virtual. We have thus chosen literature not only because this is where a passage of life is provided that opens up to new possibilities, but we have also chosen particular fragments of literature where we believe the characters exemplify a fabulating function themselves, opening up to new possibilities for living. In these readings we are learning from literature in the ways attested to by Romantic thinking. As readers we have been affected to think differently about what it is that marks the entrepreneurial as being distinct. Different in thinking it through literature and fiction as well as (and not instead of) entrepreneurship and organization studies, and different in so far as the assemblage being formed through desiring what entrepreneurial processes can achieve is only very loosely a commercial entity, and possible to understand only from a broader concept of commerce, one that holds the complex dynamics of the social and economic in balance (*doux commerce*). It is far more commercial when enterprise or management take over. As an entrepreneurial phenomenon it is a force of seduction, play, common sense, and only then transaction or commerce.

Seduction is a concept that allows us to develop a new analysis of entrepreneurship, which places focus on the role of desire, affect, power, and passion. Stuff, we argue, that entrepreneurship's continued capacity to make entries into potential worlds is made of. Whereas Iago belongs to Shakespeare's drama Othello, Don Juan has figured in several versions, and goes back to a Spanish legend, written by Tirso de Molina (around 1630), and tells us about a "trickster" from the fourteenth century. Mozart gave new life to Don Juan – now, in the Italian version, as Don Giovanni – in the Opera with the same name. In our study, we have fallen on how Don Giovanni (Mozart's Opera on Don Juan) is experienced by Søren Kierkegaard. In addition, we examine the character of Iago is brought to life by Shakespeare in *Othello*.

In many ways these could be considered very obvious choices. However, to us, their status of obvious would in this case also attest to their qualities as archetypes for understanding seduction in our culture. This choice lends itself to an analysis that points to it as a gendered choice. It admittedly could be a sign if reinstalling a hierarchy between the male and the female, but we would hesitate before such a characterization. The choice of these two – Don Giovanni and Iago – is made because together they prevent the concept of seduction from being grasped through an easy, conventional reading. Don Giovanni masters the art of immediate exploitation: at any moment he is able to transform the occasion into an opportunity. He senses whether there is a passion to spend, and if there is, he finds the ways in which it is consummated. Iago is differently seductive, embittered, and less instinctive he presents a seduction of tactical intervention. He convinces others their desire aligns with his, but twists it into his own shapes. It is just that they have not known or realized this before they are brought into his narrative and given a role to play.[55] In Shakespeare's drama it is also quite obvious how Iago's seductive stories are part of his knitting together of a proto-organizational form, a form-under-way, an assemblage-becoming-organization. The desire to get back at, revenge, or get rid of (including the killing of) Othello is what holds this assemblage together and gives it direction and productive momentum. Yet it is primarily of a negative and manipulative form, as distinct from Don Giovanni's more affirmative, if pathological form.

To encounter play we learn from Virginia Woolf's Clarissa Dalloway and Astrid Lindgren's Pippi. Woolf's immersive intensity in offering the reader a foray into the assemblies of everyday occurrence gives her special insight into the possibilities of play which, as we have already suggested, accept and embrace the indeterminacy of meaning. Her texts struggle for a reading of events, for coherence, working with the heady or reluctant or ill-mannered material of occurrence to make forms of fragile beauty.[56]

For Clarissa Dalloway play comes in the form of a party she organizes, the playfulness is barely there, but the prospect of its presence, its potentiality, its shadow seeps into the day's events as readily as the sound of London's bells filling the streets along which she walks in preparation. Play, the serious adult play of a party, acts as a confirmation of the established social orders. There are servants to remove doors and arrange furniture, carry cut flowers, serve drinks, take coats, and there are establishment figures from the government, arts, and military whose diaries have been marked by the Dalloway's invitation (conventionally, Clarissa cannot invite them by herself, her name hides behind her distant husband's). Everyone has acquired the grammar of the game, and Dalloway is there to correct deviance, silently and skilfully. Social organizing is her only skill. Otherwise she feels herself very unremarkable. She is, she reflects, unfeeling, prone to luxuriate, and talked oceans of nonsense. It was her parties and their success that governed her, these were her passion, and they had no end, no purpose, they were quite as aimless as she was, nothing more than an offering for the sake of offering, perhaps. A gift. Her playfulness occurs gently, almost invisibly from the edges.

In contrast comes Pippi, one of Astrid Lindgren's characters and centre of several children's books. She defies most of our expectations of how to behave as a child, and human being. This was at least the case when she in 1945 first saw daylight. Pippi might have become a highly productive virtuality since, actualized through making passage into many parents' practices for raising their kids – alert to what they could do and become, playfully affirming the possibilities in life rather than inherit limitations or adjust to authority. Adult templates for well-behaving kids would not, at least not in those days before Pippi, allow for independent girls living in a large house by themselves. Not even when she has immense strength and an old trunk full of golden coins to sustain her. With an angel as mother and a pirate as father, Lindgren provided Pippi with a broad ancestral palette from which to express herself. She is the constant inventor of adventures, relating playfully to all the constraints of everyday life, to the point where norms and habits – especially those impressed into the everyday life of children – became contested. Pippi is constantly pushing back at the world of set orders, destabilizing the boundaries that regulate the child–adult relationship. Where Dalloway reveals the open, generous and comforting nature of playful affects, Pippi reveals their disturbing, open potential. She is powered up by a receptivity that is tied to a spontaneity; her passion and action are short-wired, engaging her two best friends – Tommy and Annika – in all kinds of experiments, seemingly designed to upset boundaries and see how far one can expand what is possible when thriving on the fact that the world has its guard down, not expecting anything from a child.

Common sense comes in the character of Elizabeth Bennett in Jane Austin's *Pride and Prejudice*, notably through her almost obsessive sensitivity to the requirements of the situation through which she is able to tactically insinuate herself into social life. There is also for her, in such situation, the pleasure of play to be found. In Gogol's *Dead Souls*, Chichikov creates an opportunity by exploring the bureaucratic system.

Austin's deftness at rendering the niceties of society mores is embodied in Lizzie Bennet. She is able to reveal the snobbery amid the probity, the decency amid the reserve, the humour made possible by habituated stiffness, and the love animating relational decorum, because of a sustained familiarity with, and almost delight in, her own snobbishness and social compliance. That she comes in part to acknowledge these traits is the story of an awakening into the possibilities of common sense. Her almost congenital worry about what others might think of her – especially Darcy – becomes the object of reflexive critique, as she experiences the hurt and emotional and financial privation that all too often accompany entitled behaviour. She accedes to habits and expectation, then something more robust emerges, a common sense balance to her and her adminis-tration of the household (*oikonomia*) for which she takes responsibility. When it comes to reading the demands of a situation, she learns how to outclass anyone of any class. So attentive and delightful is her power to be affected, her capacity to fall in with what is expected without, at least as she learns, slavish abeyance, that others cannot but fail to feel affected, and her affection elicits affect, expanding the cheerfulness and sociality of those with whom she is in commerce. Sociality provides space, notably to Darcy, for whom Bennet's lightly worn probity act as a lure (talking of seduction), tired as he is of superficiality and boorish aristocrats. Bennet shows that opportunity is not always about the breaking of common sense. It can also come through a sustained conformity which, carried with such diligence and humour, shines so that others are entranced, pleased, and want to be pleased. They are affected utterly.

On the flip side we have Chichikov from Nicolai Gogol's *Dead Souls*. His opportunity arises in understanding the common sense prevailing both in bureaucracies, and amongst isolated, landed aristocrats, and exploiting the perversities in both. Here is a figure who can apprehend the habits and norms of forms of life, and play them off one another for his own conscious gain. Though deeply duplicitous, we are drawn to Chichikov because his sense of mischief seems to know few bounds, and he is exploiting the common sense of those for whom we typically have little sympathy. He has been a bureaucrat and tried many different ways to get ahead, increasingly aware that with land comes freedom. Wandering through the estates of landowners offering to buy their recently deceased dead serfs – workers they have owned, but not yet registered with the authorities as dead, Chichikov offers the landowners to do their job of registering the serfs. This reduces their tax burden (since this is based on the number of serfs you own), and so there is an incentive for them. However, there is also an in-between, an entre-space that Chichikov creates: he takes his newly acquired certificates of ownership and gets access to capital (ownership of serfs acts as collateral) with which he buys land. He is still able to create a flourishing market through a supremely (yet, of course, ethically dubious) entrepreneurial act that is predicated upon and sustained by desire, from nothing comes something.

Finally, we inquire into commerce and transaction through the fig-ures of Stendhal's Julian Sorel and Patricia Highsmith's Tom Ripley. Stendhal's *The Red and the Black* is both a psychological study of a romantic character and a more sociological satire of the French society at a time of transition. This is the time in-between Napoleon's first fall in 1814 (that had followed upon the French revolution of 1789) and the attempt to restore France to the more traditional, conservative order that had characterized the time before the revolution. This so-called Bourbon restoration lasted between 1814 and 1830. It is in this interlude Stendahl places Julien Sorel and his attempt to rise from no particular status or standing into a prominent, respected figure. This is still a society modernizing, although the Bourbon regime wanted to restore society to the ancient regime. The French revolution had set things in motion that could not be halted. In this sense, it was a time of multiplicity (old systems going and new ones coming), ambiguity, and thus opportunities. Sorel's career is forever caught between the black of the clergy and red of patrician military. Sorel's society was in the midst of modernization and one could create opportunities for oneself. This is a time when managing oneself, managing one's career could really make a difference. However, in Sorel's case, modernizing meant not so much pushing back at the wasteful aristocracy and the ascendancy of the bourgeoisie, but rather looking for ways to sediment himself into the settled life of one with status.

The time of Stendhal's *Red and Black* is the time when interest is in the process of being socially codified. No longer does it describe the *Interesse* being amid, or the German *inter essen*, being between things. It is no longer inter-est-ing as that which is in-between, that which has entrepreneurial potential, that which is *entre*. Instead, interest becomes economic interest. Sorel's world is managed and administered in the sense that one needs to manoeuvre in the social, buoyed by judicious financial investments. Sorel suffocates in the stultifying atmosphere of bourgeois commerce populated by entitled, passive "types." He seeks a way out of this life where the *manus* (*Latin* for hand) of tradition rests heavily on his shoulder.

In contrast to Sorel comes the talented tyro Tom Ripley. Equally set on becoming someone, Ripley is the master of malign manipulative multiplication, operating with a palette of subject positions that he moves smoothly in-between for the purpose of achieving a position in a life he has admired. In many ways he is the modern version of Iago, who famously claimed – "I am not what I am." (Act 1, Scene 1, Othello)."The con man," Tom Ripley is a versatile social chameleon operator that knows every trick in the book. Unlike Sorel, Ripley is not limiting himself to the either-or logic of the French society at the time; red or black, military or clergy. Ripley can become anyone. He has the charm and imitative skills enough to have anyone suspend their disbelief.[57] Being the eminent actualizer of multiple virtualities, he is simultaneously the fabulator that lacks an anchoring for his stories. His stories are all ad hoc extensions to previous extensions. He is a brilliant improviser who, in the end, acts with too many plates spinning on high sticks; soon enough, he loses sight of why he must keep spinning them all.

Notes

1 In this we are conceptualizing entrepreneurship in the spirit of Weick's disciplined imagination, it is itself a creative act, not an attempt to fill a gap. Weick, K. "Theory Construction as Disciplined Imagination," *Academy of*

Management Review, 1989: 516–531. See also Suddaby, R. (2010) "Editor's Comments: Construct Clarity in Theories of Management and Organization," *Academy of Management Review,* 35(3): 346–357.

2 Deleuze, G. (1998) *Essays Critical and Clinical,* London: Verso, p. 109.

3 Massumi, B. *Parables for the Virtual – Movement, Affect, Sensation,* Durham: Duke University Press.

4 Helin et al., 2014; note 2.

5 Steyaert, C. (2007) " 'Entrepreneuring' as a Conceptual Attractor? A Review of Process Theories in 20 Years of Entrepreneurship Studies," *Entrepreneurship and Regional Development,* 19(6): 453–477. Hernes, T. (2014) *A Process Theory of Organization,* Oxford: Oxford University Press.

6 Schumpeter, J.A. ([1947] 1991) The Creative Response in Economic History (reprinted from *Journal of Economic History,* 1947). In R.V. Clemence (Ed.), *Essays: On Entrepreneurs, Innovations, Business Cycles and the Evolution of Capitalism,* New Brunswick: Transaction Publishers, pp. 149–159.

7 Nietzsche, a process thinker par excellence, says that reactive forces affiliate with a negative *will to power* so as to achieve status quo or nothingness See Deleuze, G. (2006) *Nietzsche and Philosophy,* New York: Columbia University Press; Holt, R. and Hjorth, D. *Nietzsche (1844–1900),* in Helin et al. (2014), pp. 202–217.

8 Hjorth, D. (2012) Organizational Entrepreneurship – An Art of the Weak?. In Hjorth, D. (Ed.) *Handbook of Organizational Entrepreneurship,* Cheltenham: Edward Elgar, pp. 169–192.

9 Gartner, W.B., Bird, B.J., and Starr, J.A. (1992) "Acting as if: Differentiating Entrepreneurial from Organizational Behavior," *Entrepreneurship: Theory and Practice,* 16(3): 13–31.

10 Huizinga, J., (1955) *Homo Ludens: A Study of the Play-Element in Culture,* Boston: Beacon Press.

11 Chia, R. (1996) "Teaching Paradigm Shifting in Management Education: University Business Schools and the Entrepreneurial Imagination," *Journal of Management Studies,* 33(4): 409–428.

12 Lounsbury, M. and Glynn, M.A. (2001) "Cultural Entrepreneurship: Stories, Legitimacy, and the Acquisition of Resources," *Strategic Management Journal,* 22: 545–564, p. 546.

13 Scott, S.S. and Venkataraman, S. "The Promise of Entrepreneurship as a Field of Research," *Academy of Management Review,* 25: 217–226.

14 Battilana, L., Leca, B., and Boxenbaum, E. (2009) "How Actors Change Institutions: Towards a Theory of Institutional Entrepreneurship," *The Academy of Management Annals,* 3(1): 65–107; Svejenova, S., Mazza, C., and Planellas, M. (2007) "Cooking up Change in Haute Cuisine: Ferran Adrià as an Institutional Entrepreneur," *Journal of Organizational Behaviour,* 28(5): 539–561.

15 We are, of course, not alone in thinking the entrepreneurship process as a formation process, generating rather than recognizing opportunities. See, e.g. Fletcher, D. (2006) "Entrepreneurial Processes and the Social Construction of Opportunity," *Entrepreneurship & Regional Development,* 18(September): 421–440.

16 As is studied and analysed in institutional entrepreneurship research (see footnote 232).

17 Huizinga, J., (1955) *Homo Ludens: A Study of the Play-Element in Culture*, Boston: Beacon Press.

18 Deleuze, G. (1988) *Spinoza – Practical Philosophy*, San Francisco: City Lights Books, p. 101. Deleuze reads Spinoza's *Ethics*.

19 Ibid., pp. 73–74. Emphasis in original.

20 For Foucault there is a broad discussion of the concept of planning and liberalism that we draw upon here. See (2004/200) *The Birth of Biopolitics: Lectures at the Collège de France*, M. Senelart (Ed.), Transl. G. Burchell, Basingstoke: Palgrave MacMillan, pp. 101–184. Foucault identifies a historical association of entrepreneurship with enterprise, each deriving from the other from the end of the nineteenth century until the mid-twentieth, where rather than being a partner of exchange, *homo economicus* becomes the entrepreneur of him/her self – "being for himself his own capital, being for himself his own producer, being for himself the source of [his] earnings" – i.e. consuming by producing his or her own satisfaction (pp. 160, 226). At the outset of the twenty-first century, articulating a break between enterprise and entrepreneurship is to think of the figure no longer a producer of satisfaction but of potential, who rather than investing in improvement (measured), invests in affective joy.

21 Schumpeter, J. (1947) "The Creative Response in Economic History," *The Journal of Economic History*, 7(2): 149–159, p. 157.

22 Jones, C. and Spicer, A. (2009) *Unmasking the Entrepreneur*, Cheltenham: Edward Elgar.

23 Miller, P. and Rose, N. (1993) Governing Economic Life. In M. Gane and T. Johnson (Eds.), *Foucault's New Domains*, London: Routledge; du Gay, P. (Ed.) (1997) *Production of Culture/Cultures of Production*, London: SAGE. Hjorth, D. and Holt, R. (2016) "It's Entrepreneurship, Not Enterprise: Ai Weiwei as Social Entrepreneur," *Journal of Business Venturing Insights*, 5: 50–54.

24 Hjorth, D. (2014) Sketching a Philosophy of Entrepreneurship. In T. Baker and F. Welter (Eds.) *The Routledge Companion to Entrepreneurship*, London: Routledge, pp. 41–58.

25 Greenblatt, S. (1980) *Renaissance Self-Fashioning – From More to Shakespeare*, Chicago and London: The University of Chicago Press.

26 de Certeau, M. (1984) *The Practice of Everyday Life*, Berkeley: University of California Press; de Certeau, M. (1997) *Culture in the Plural*, Minneapolis: University of Minnesota Press; Winnicott, D. (1971) *Playing and Reality*, Harmondsworth: Penguin.

27 Huizinga, J. (1962) *Homo Ludens – A Study of the Play Element in Culture*, Boston: The Beacon Press, p. 141.

28 Ibid., p. 136.

29 Ibid., p. 137.

30 Deleuze, G. and Guattari, F. (1994) *What Is Philosophy?*, London and New York: Verso, pp. 171–172, 230.

31 Colebrook, C. (2002) *Deleuze*, London: Routledge, p. 71.

32 Huizinga, J. (1955) *Homo Ludens – A Study of the Play Element in Culture*, Boston: The Beacon Press, p. 7.

33 Manning, E. and Massumi, B. (2014) *Thought in the Act – Passages in the Ecology of Experience*, Minneapolis: University of Minnesota Press, p. 99.

34 Ibid., p. 99.
35 Deleuze, 2006, p. 26.
36 Cavell, S. (2012) Philosophy as the Education of Grown Ups. In N. Saito and P. Standish (Eds.), *Stanley Cavell and the Education of Grown Ups*, New York: Fordham University Press, pp. 26–29.
37 Huizinga, J. (1955) *Homo Ludens – A Study of the Play Element in Culture*, Boston: The Beacon Press, p. 4.
38 Deleuze, G. (1988) *Bergsonism*, Transl. H. Tomlinson & B. Habberjam, New York: Zone Books, p. 111; Evens, A., Haghighi, M., Johnson, S., Ocana, K., and Thompson, G. (1998) Another Always Thinks in Me. In E. Kaufman & J.K. Heller (Eds.), *Deleuze and Guattari – New Mappings in Politics, Philosophy, and Culture*, Minneapolis and London: University of Minnesota Press, p. 279.
39 Schumpeter, J.A. (1949/1991) Economic Theory and Entrepreneurial History. In R.V. Clemence (Ed.), reprinted from *Change and the Entrepreneur*, New Brunswick and London: Transaction, p. 258.
40 Spinosa, C., Flores, F., and Dreyfus, H.L. (1997) *Disclosing New Worlds – Entrepreneurship, Democratic Action, and the Cultivation of Solidarity*, Cambridge: MIT Press, p. 20.
41 Johnsen, C., Olaison, L., and Sørensen, B.M. (2017) "Put Your Style at Stake: A New Use of Sustainable Entrepreneurship," *Organization Studies*, 39(2–3): 397–415.
42 Ibid.
43 Agamben, G. (2011) *The Kingdom and the Glory*, Stanford: Stanford University Press, p. 17.
44 Agamben, G. (2009) *What Is an Apparatus*, Stanford: Stanford University Press.
45 Corvellec, H. and Hultman, J. (2014) "Managing the Politics of Value Propositions," *Marketing Theory*, 14(4): 355–375.
46 See discussion in Deleuze, G. (1991) *Bergsonism*, New York: Zoone Books, p. 111.
47 Hirschman, A.O. (1977) *The Passions and the Interests*, Princeton: Princeton University Press, p. 60.
48 Cited in Hirschman (1977), p. 61, and the emphasis is Hirschman's. The original is William Robertson's *Reign of the Emperor Charles V*, edited by Felix Gilbert (University of Chicago Press, 1972). The quote is from p. 76 in that work. Robertson's work was originally published in 1769.
49 Hirschman, 1977.
50 Aldrich, H.E. and Fiol, C.M. (1994) "Fools Rush in? The Institutional Context of Industry Creation," *Academy of Management Review*, 19(4): 645–670. Lounsbury, M. and Glynn M.A. (2001) "Cultural Entrepreneurship: Stories, Legitimacy, and the Acquisition of Resources," *Strategic Management Journal*, 22(6–7): 545–564. Popp, A. and Holt, R. (2013) "The Presence of Entrepreneurial Opportunity," *Business History*, 55(1): 9–18. Hjorth, D. (2013) "Public Entrepreneurship: Desiring Social Change, Creating Sociality," *Entrepreneurship and Regional Development*, 25(1–2): 34–51.
51 Gartner, W.B., Carter, N.M., and Hills, G.E. (2003) The Language of Opportunity. In C. Steyaert & D. Hjorth (Eds.), *New Movements in Entrepreneurship Research*, Cheltenham: Edward Elgar, pp. 103–124.

52 Holt, R. and Zundel, M. (2014) "Understanding Management, Trade, and Society through Fiction: Lessons from The Wire," *Academy of Management Review.* 39(4): 576–585. Hjorth, D. (2014) Entrepreneuring as Organization-Creation. In R. Sternberg & G. Kraus (Eds.), *Handbook of Research on Entrepreneurship and Creativity*, Cheltenham: Edward Elgar, pp. 97–121. Volkmann, C.R. and De Cock, C. (2010) Four Close Readings on Introducing the Literary in Organizational Research. In P. Armstrong, G. Lightfoot, & S. Lilley (Eds.), *The Leading Publication in the Field: Unsettling Authority in the Social Sciences of Management*, London: Mayfly, pp. 143–163.

53 Deleuze, G. (1998) *Essays – Critical and Clinical*, London: Verso, p. 3.

54 Ibid., p. 4.

55 Hjorth, D. (2007) "Narrating the Entrepreneurial Event: Learning from Shakespeare's Iago," *Journal of Business Venturing*, 22(5): 712–732. Lounsbury, M. and Glynn, M.A. (2001) "Cultural Entrepreneurship: Stories, Legitimacy, and the Acquisition of Resources," *Strategic Management Journal*, 22: 545–564.

56 Rancière, J. *The Politics of Aesthetics*, London: Verso. p. 59.

57 Borch, C. (2005) "Urban Imitations: Tarde's Sociology Revisited," *Theory, Culture & Society*, 22(3): 81–100.

Part II

5 Organization-creation
Seduction

Introduction

To approach seduction we begin with the figure of Don Juan, specifically with Kierkegaard's study of Mozart's version, i.e. Don Giovanni.[1]

The backdrop of Kierkegaard's analysis is his idea – developed in *Either/Or* and in *Fear and Trembling* – of aesthetic life.[2] The person living aesthetically lives for pleasure and tries to make life a flow of diverting and stimulating experiences that might intensify in its frequency and novelty. Most of us, argued Kierkegaard, remain in this aesthetic stage, seeking pleasant and stimulating experiences so as to paper over creeping boredom, or worse, a looming void of despair.

It is against this aesthetic backdrop that we suggest entrepreneurial processes are initiated in events of seduction. Kierkegaard relates the aesthetic to a life of possibilities, though fragmentary and mobile ones, which as often as not belie their own promise as they become riddled with frustration or opposition. His is an ironic understanding of the struggles that mark human experience, one that resonates with Romanticism and which, we argue, resonates with entrepreneurial life. Entrepreneurial life is also a form of life being grasped by possibilities (or, in entrepreneurial language, opportunities). Today we would of course think opportunities can be created rather by those who set sail and leave the safety of the harbour. This is because a theory of entrepreneurship has been heavily influenced by a concept of risk (or uncertainty),[3] yet it was coined at a time when pursuing the chance to survive by seeking harbour was a more pressing everyday concern. In the modern, industrial and economized society, for Hirschman at least, passions are dominated by interests and the economic dominates the social, and opportunity is framed as a concept belonging to the pursuit of economic gain, profit on a market.[4] No longer is an opportunity an opening to survival, given I can reach the harbour. Rather the opposite; if I leave the harbour, I can make and take opportunities to enrich life. It becomes an aesthetic activity in which fear and anxiety are pushed aside (though never into oblivion).

The aesthetic describes a life being lived in ways that creates possibility, in order to make life interesting, diverting, less captivated by

DOI: 10.4324/9781315714455-8

tedious rigidities. There is thus resonance between our interest in the creation of possibilities, for which seduction is an opening of the entrepreneurial process. In its more generative guise, seduction, as part of the aesthetic life, would also bear witness to a life of passion. This is the life where a power to be affected (your receptivity) is intensified. One's openness to "what could become" sets imagination into movement and this movement makes events take shape and a pursuit of an event is also what makes it become concrete as a real virtuality that needs to become actualized.[5] Aesthetic life, in Kierkegaard's text, is a life where boredom, despair, fear and anxiety are being chased away by a welcoming of possibilities (or better, potentialities, what Deleuze would call virtualities) directing desire onto new paths.

It seems this life of passion is also consuming, has no end. In the case of the entrepreneurial process it therefore needs to lead up to (or open up for) play as the next phase. Entrepreneurship is therefore impossible to contain in a life of the raw aesthete, since it is a life of making, or world-making.[6] Without play following (and thus common sense and commerce/transaction), there is merely a diverting, temporary chasing away of boredom, anxiety, and fear. Entrepreneurship, following our model, is more a "driving towards" world-making than an "escape from" boredom. It is, as Schumpeter noted, a creative and not a reactive response to the world's snowballing towards you,[7] that there is always nextness in "what is," that the actual is saturated with potentiality (*Latin potere* – I can).[8] Yet it begins in the immediate conditioning of a passionate life which, as Kierkegaard stresses, has about it a directness and spontaneity, and it is these qualities that also open up entrepreneurial forming: making others interested, getting them to join, to become assembled.

In seduction comes the entrepreneurial initiative of creating an opening, of making ingress in which others might become implicated, intrigued enough to divert their attention. We find this force in Kierkegaard's analysis of aesthetic life references to both Don Juan (or Don Giovanni in Mozart's Opera) as well as Faust/Faustus (Marlowe, 1592; Goethe, 1808). The latter is more of a reflective aesthete, haunted by an ethical life of duties and higher goals, whereas the former is more interested in the possibility of seduction than the actual seduction itself. It is a life of appetite installed at the moment, without reflection or even conscious awareness.

Hence Don Giovanni's is complemented with Shakespeare's Iago. Iago is more of Faust, a reflecting aesthete, one that pursues possibilities but is more carefully crafting them to suit a more long-term (albeit fatal) interest in the political side of organizational life. Iago is a character that not only seduces but also mobilizes and gets concerted actions done in a grand scheme. The collective is more a resource for Iago, whereas Don Giovanni more sees "others" as constraints to be overcome in his desirous pursuit of "the one." It is precisely Iago's attention to communities, to the political dimension of one's actions, that sets him apart from Don

Giovanni. Iago excels as the fragmented "I" of Romanticism, performing with ease in several subject-positions, exploring his experiences from many previous battles, serving his master – Othello – as a soldier and advisor. He explicitly says, "I am not what I am" (Act 1, Scene 1) as he is speaking to Roderigo that has come to seek Iago's advice. Roderigo has fallen in love Desdemona, who in turn has secretly married Othello. Saying "I am not what I am" it is as if Iago reveals his secret weapon; his power to become,[9] to multiply. We find this element of multiplication also in Kierkegaard's aesthetic life, but not as decisively in Don Giovanni (who refuses to change, to repent) as in the life of Iago. Whereas Don Giovanni dies, willingly being carried to hell by a mob of demons in what is his first conscious act throughout the whole opera, Iago faces the greater punishment for someone who is an eloquent orator and master of discourse – he sentences himself to mute life: – "From this time forth I will never speak word" (Act 5, Scene 2).

It is thus evident that Iago (like Faust) is someone trusting to language: where Don Giovanni is visceral, needing to touch and feel, Iago is a story-maker, a narrator attempting to ensnare listeners with carefully crafted threads, developing a colourful weft in the warp designed by the interest he has in changing things in his favour. Also this we find more resonant with the life of entrepreneurial processes. Many entrepreneurs rely on a seductive story of a world-to-come, a vision of a future state of affairs woven out of thin air in order to attract investments. Iago is a master of this. He makes people realize that they have wanted this (what Iago wants) all the time, only not knowing it.[10] He can pick up subtle cues of where there is a passion to spend and he secures that he has the offer his listeners cannot refuse. Iago, Stephen Greenblatt says, is a master of transforming seemingly fixed symbolic structures into flexible ones. This allows for the improvisational entry – which he surely shares with Don Giovanni – that enrols listeners.[11] There is a specific form of seduction at work in Iago's plot-making, less fixated on the performative act itself, and more interested in the progress made as a consequence of having seduced, of having led the other away/astray. Immediately, after having been led astray, the seduced one is of course keenly aware of the fact that they are treading upon a new path, yet what was "astray" before the move, immediately becomes the right way, an exciting road of potentiality.

Iago is a master tactician does what he does on the basis of his knowledge of the official strategic script that regulates social life (career and ambition, love, revenge). He makes use of this script in surprising ways.[12] He is able to do so because he follows no strategy in his own pursuit of his goal. He knows the "strategic script" which others find they are obliged to follow. Precisely for this reason, Iago anticipates their actions and can tactically move from one victory to another. His plan is flexible, and constantly amended on the basis of tactical wins. He is a tactician who knows that any strategy is a retrospective justification of the series of tactical wins achieved. Don Giovanni on the other hand is consumed in the act.[13] Iago oftentimes leads his "targets" by the nose (Shakespeare has Iago say so in the play) in the sense that he convinces them of what they must do, after he has made them realize, as we pointed out above, this is what they have wanted all along.[14] Don Giovanni is more himself being led – in the moment he catches a twist or look and has to get more of it, persuasion is literally in the body, beyond reason. He refuses, even to the end, to give a reason for his acts. Maybe only the tactical moves are clear to him, and they refuse to join neatly under a common strategy. Iago, having an overall vision, knows how the many desires he has lit are joined in the common and overarching one – getting rid of Othello. Don Giovanni, on the other hand, in his naivety, risks more by trusting the moment and is led by other's responses and nothing more, as birds are led by their call.

Don Giovanni and Iago both indeed problematize the stable and singular self, grounded in the knowing (epistemological) subject, and instead exemplify and perform the becoming of a self as a temporary, fleeting construct, formed from and within experience.[15] Seduction is in an offering you cannot refuse, an invitation to imitate, to complement, to fill an opening, to heal that which is generously torn open, exposed.[16] Like in music, when the possibility of a chord is offered through one note, the temptation to harmonize is great and difficult to resist. Seduction is a baring act that commands a covering response. The power of being affected affects the other who is thus lured into the play of forces, tendered into demonstrating her/his power to affect as a reply to the call to come along.

Kierkegaard's *The Diary of a Seducer/The Seducer's Diary* (part of *Either/Or*)

Kierkegaard's method is circuitous, literary, interjecting voices and multiple perspectives. He likens his style to midwifery, eliciting the reader's ideas. He lectures whilst immediately doubting his own voice, his own right to talk, turning quickly to fragments rather than grand narratives. *Either/Or* was written in the immediate aftermath of his finally breaking off his engagement to Regine and abandoning the two-in-one unity of marriage. Kierkegaard is not one for executing plans, rather he enquires, ponders, and withdraws into his peripatetic thoughts. Perhaps Regine was not so bothered, before the split Kierkegaard had been absent in Berlin between 1841 and 1842 attending lectures by Friedrich Wilhelm Joseph Schelling, schooling himself in Romantic philosophy, but finding the lectures to be "insufferable nonsense."[17] *Either/Or* opens up, under the impulse of Romanticism, to being an investigation of subjectivity, of selfhood, of voice, and the impossibility of a stable identity. Indeed so unstable did Kierkegaard consider the "identity" of the subject that he could not commit to the fragment that was his own voice as an author, so he uses several voices – pseudonyms – and these come to write the parts of *Either/Or*: Victor Eremita (the victorious hermit), writes and is the editor of the compiled book based on two sheaves of paper found in a desk, written by "A" and "B."

"A" is the author of first, aesthetic part *Either*, which elaborates on the facets of aesthetic life: a state of ennui and boredom that gives itself over to hedonism, but which as often as not leads to melancholy, and despair, as one continually fails to experience anything like a unity in oneself. "A" talks continually of avoiding the boredom (so much so that it too becomes boring) that attends the institutional commitments to which so much of life is bound: Marry and you'll regret it, don't and you'll regret it etc. The only way out is to seek pleasure, which comes from the excitement and risk of defying convention, yet as the interesting vies with the boring, A realizes it amounts to little more than a diversion from the inherent emptiness of things, one that can only be avoided by ever more intense distraction. In addition to "A" is Johannes, the author of a section of *Either* called "The Diary of a Seducer."

The second ethical part, *Or*, we find subsequently, to have been authored by Judge Vilhelm ("B"). The ethical stage is a stage of choice, of decision, of trying to find commitments whose force extends beyond an immediate situation and which thereby frame an otherwise vapid and vacuous life of floating experience. What is valued aesthetically – the artistry of seduction says – becomes transformed, so marriage, for example, will enhance the aestheticized desire of love by containing and transmuting it into feelings that are considered. The ethical demands each subject think actively about the way life is lived, i.e. don't just follow standards (which is aesthetic condition of taste, even if they can be enjoyed through refinement), but do so consciously. The ethical person commits to playing out their social roles (as a citizen, parent, professional, worker etc.) not simply because of convention, but because they have chosen to, and in choosing have become aware that there are good ways of performing the role, as distinct from a conventional one. They become dedicated to projects through which they project themselves. It is, though, as Socrates had elaborated, a framing to which there was little in the way of external rigidity, save one's own commitment to the attempt to weave formal patterns into everyday habits. To justify a life run according to ethical principles, Vilhelm appeals to the reader's inner urge to live according to their own sense of commitment, not those imposed from outside. It is, then, an appeal in which the subject subjectifies him or herself to their own subjection, alive to the fact that such a subject will always be riddled with a multiplicity of aesthetic forces and hence will always be a limited and finite being.[18]

Hence the ethical will also disappoint, as subjects can never accord with standards perfectly, there is always a gap of understanding, which could as well be a chasm, as consummation in execution is never reached. Just as the taste and refinement of the aesthetic give way to the discipline of the ethical, the emptiness remains because this discipline is self-serving and quite arbitrary given it is the product of our own willing; the power to be committed, to commit, erodes any commitment made, a cycle of self-examination that hollows out anything substantial as does the endless pecking of a bird's beak at a tree.

The Diary of a Seducer sits in-between *Either/Or*, belonging to the former, yet nudging up to the latter. It is an intriguing text because it is written in a way that sets and then breaks its own limits, and it does so by recurring back to Don Giovanni as a fictional exemplar (more caricature than character) of the human condition stripped back to its most basic aesthetic expression.[19] Don Giovanni has no perspective on himself, he is less the seducer than a performer of seduction arranging (attempting) attraction between bodies. What interests Kierkegaard is that Don Giovanni is himself seduced by his own desire, and it is this intensity that pulls others in. His desire is an appetite for more life coupled with an anxiety that he is missing out, and in combination this energy then excites all others in the opera, the rage of Elvira, the hatred of Anna, the indignation of Masseto. Whilst others (his servant Leparello) keep a tally on Don Giovanni's "conquests" (1003 in Spain alone) he himself is consumed with the cunning artistry of creating a singular event of seduction, all the whilst alive to the potential for opening up other events. There is no pause, no measurement, no gap through which might grow the despair or boredom that, according to Kierkegaard, blight human lives.

It is as a concentrated, almost inhuman assembly of stimulus-response that Kierkegaard uses Don Giovanni as an exemplar of the basic aesthetic impulse to use pleasurable diversions to hide from emptiness; his life starred with distraction. Nothing is acquired reflexively by Don Giovanni; his talk brimming with clichés evokes a world into which only he can take others, a world of his own making. And he himself is entirely possessed by this skill, desiring to experience a continuous confirmation of this skill in him, the next always beckons. There is always unfulfilment, pleasure disappoints, possibility never. Don Giovanni is flowing with virtuality and is compelled to try and make actual. No more evident is this when, part way through the opera, and already on the run from an earlier triste that fell foul of convention, he espies Zerlina in the company of her fiancé and diverts. He cannot resist attempting to take her away from her fiancé, promising impelled by seduction itself, it is a hand that has him in a grip that only tightens as events pile upon one another. Zerlina hesitates, she wonders whether she should. She has promised to marry Masetto. But promises are, when scrutinized, just habits that, it seems, at least in Kierkegaard's analysis of a hollowed-out, aesthetic life, can break. Zerlina has not realized this until Don Giovanni brushes by with his inuendo and cliché and shows her the fragility of habituated allegiance; there is apparently so much to lose and so little to gain, but when what appears sensible is made to account for itself it seems less obvious.

Why not and let go and open up to the possibility of a life beyond the limits of this one?

Don Giovanni seduces with the force and vitality of desire alone. His life is sparkling like the wine with which he fortifies himself and which will quickly run flat. He couldn't care, he is not building an empire, he is running towards the edge. His life is turbulent like the melodies that accompany his joyous repast, he is always jubilant, like the bubbles in the wine. Bubbles that rise quickly, live for the short surface-effect, and burst without much noise, depending for their effect on another one, bursting. He needs no preparation, no plan, no time, for he is always ready; that is, the power is always in him, and the desire too, and only when he desires is he properly in his element, the liquid flow of opportunity-seeking and sense-making.[20]

The words are spare because they interfere with the expression of desire, which in Don Giovanni's case, in Mozart's hands, is a musical, direct, generating affect. He is himself music, becoming only when moving, crossing boundaries, entering our sphere of attention whether we want it or not; can anyone keep him out? We cannot shut our ears. Desire, without distinction, he does not seduce because he is handsome, rich, bold – and he might be all these things – for these are individual qualities and he seduces without calling upon one quality or another. Don Giovanni is most suitably expressed in music, in opera, where the words meld with the force of sound and we hear, Kierkegaard points out, rather than read about him:

> Hear how he plunges into the multiplicity of life, how he breaks against its solid embankment. Hear these light dancing violin notes, hear the imitation of joy, hear the jubilation of delight, hear the festive bliss of enjoyment. Hear his wild flight; he speeds past himself, ever faster, never pausing. Hear the unrestrained craving passion hear the sighing of erotic love, hear the whisper of temptation, hear the vortex of seduction, hear the stillness of the moment, hear, hear, how could you not hear Mozart's Don Giovanni.[21]

The only ideal he knows is the sensuous ideal, there is nothing faithless about him, he flows wherever minimum friction takes him. This gives him pleasure; the sense of expanding into the unexplored. Momentum matters, and repetition, surely this will happen, it is irresistible, he cannot wait. He just hammers on with his desire, it is immanent to his body, he just repeats and he repeats. This repetition continues to the end, in his refusal to repent in the company of Commendatore's ghostly statue:

THE STATUE
Repent! Change your ways,
for this is your last hour!

DON GIOVANNI (trying to free himself)
No, no, I will not repent.
Let me be!

THE STATUE
Repent, scoundrel!

DON GIOVANNI
No, you old fool!

THE STATUE
Repent! etc.

DON GIOVANNI
No! etc.

THE STATUE
Yes!

DON GIOVANNI
No!

THE STATUE
Yes!

DON GIOVANNI
No!

LEPORELLO
Yes! Yes!

DON GIOVANNI
No! No!

THE STATUE
Ah, your time is up!
(The statue disappears. Flames appear on all
sides and the earth begins to tremble under Don
Giovanni's feet.)

DON GIOVANNI
What strange fear
now assails my soul!
Where do those
flames of horror come from?[22]

"Let me be" says Don Giovanni, incredulous that someone might ask him to stop, to arrest his very being. Only at the very end in the wake of his recalcitrance does a vague sense of reflexivity assail him, a removal from his natural, base condition of seduction, "What strange fear now assails my soul." On the cusp of immolation in hellish fire he finally comes to a stop, aware perhaps for the first time of consequence.

On the cusp of death, his question is perhaps the first time he is exposed to a sense of self, just what is it he has amounted to?

Iago

It was Harold Bloom who, with a mid-Atlantic non-chalant confidence, suggested Shakespeare invented the modern human by revealing the interior life through which we all of us read and think and dream, the interiority that momentarily crept into Don Giovanni's consciousness.[23] Iago is one such invention of Shakespeare's, and he is teaming with inner thoughts and schemes that simmer and broil within his breast until it is opportune to have them reveal themselves. Opportune, because unlike Don Giovanni, Iago has a purpose. Shakespeare opens an ontological void in the play at the moment when Iago, who believes himself to have been a loyal "right hand" to Othello, is overlooked for promotion, and young Casio is instead handed the position as lieutenant. As the ground opens under Iago, he can see no point any longer in acting as a stead-fast advisor to Othello, his ethics dissipate, the role is no longer something to do dutifully and well, but a vehicle to pursue his own purpose: revenge. He becomes a multiple, flexible rather than steadfast one, and in being so he multiplies the possible, and where Don Giovanni is full of himself, Iago is many selves – an advisor, lover, soldier, competitor, friend.

Much of the drama concerns Iago's attempts to create an opportunity to fulfil his purpose: to get rid of the Moor (as Shakespeare puts this). The opportunity is not there, awaiting Iago's discovery. Iago must create it, and he patiently and cleverly joins together many yarns until there is a pattern of interweaving desires that allow an opportunity to be formed. He becomes what his situation requires of him, restless, moving always from one place to the next, operating on several flanks in order to make odd pieces even. The lack of stability makes him devilish: the steadfastness of good character associated with not changing one's mind or shifting opinion is splintered.[24] He works with blend of trust and distrust, playing brilliantly on Othello's sense of insecurity and negative self-image, based upon his fear that he would not be able to live up to the expectations imposed upon him by the Christian society of Venice where the play is set. To Venice, Iago hints, Othello is nothing but a stranger, an outsider, and not just that, but a soldier, who should be moving, fighting, not "paused" idle in this ungrateful and unaccommodating city.

And it is not just Othello he works, on, he inveigles his way into the designs and desires of many of the play's characters, always encouraging them to believe their interests will find satisfaction only so long as they follow his prompts: To the love-struck Rodrigo, for example, he suggests Desdemona might waver in her bond to Othello, and indeed might switch her affections if shown the right encouragement: "I say, put money in thy purse. It cannot be long that Desdemona should continue her love to the Moor – put money in thy purse – nor he his to her." Iago is always scheming, moving like a river, fluidly, though appearing steadfast as a source of reliable counsel, an advisor with a clear view of where and how events are unfolding. He is making himself the available as a refuge of practical wisdom to which people can cleave themselves in their search for reasons and warrants. Once inside, they are led astray, seduced, and here in the current of his loosening stories as it were, they move more easily as he pushes them with the conviction and confirmation of his advice: "I could never better stead thee than now." (Act 1, Scene 3).

Iago is a politicized character, organizing beyond the body. Harold Bloom likens him to a "pyromaniac play-director," multiplying desire across scenes and himself becoming multiple fragmented selves.[25] In the urge to kill Othello, the reigning order of things is split open by questioning and insinuating, and others are being brought onto this disorienting openness: every position of status and standing is relative to everyone else, and when the centre of the organization, the top of the hierarchy is brought into questionability by Iago's plotting, everyone else looks for a railing to hold on to. Iago provides them each with one, all different, all tactical manoeuvres that represent small wins, irresistibly attractive to those that have been brought into loose ground of speculative questionability.[26] People are being held in assemblies of desire, being nudged into place by Iago's plotting, revenge is taking hold, but its pattern is more an atmosphere than a linear chain of causal reasoning. He is always working as a pluralist working in fragments, spinning narratives that entangle others and having them wrestle and struggle, offering a way out if they would follow his advice. He does not so much discover and enlist passion as create it, knowing there is always a "power to be affected" to be found by which others can be encouraged into their own opportunity-seeking.

Where Don Giovanni embodies the unreflective and restless aspects of seduction always exposing itself to yet more, Iago extends these to a reflexive and political performance. Iago is a creator of images, like his creator (Shakespeare), like entrepreneurs in the process of entrepreneuring, who, in demonstrating an "audience sensitivity," produce future virtualities/opportunities that attract investments/commitments from others. Whilst this creation of images (lighting of fires) has been discussed in entrepreneurship research using concepts such as vision, business plans, value propositions, strategies, we cannot see how that helps us understand how the entrepreneurial image enrols others. How is the entrepreneurial image able to release resources from their present fixity, and make them ripe for improvisational entry?[27] How does the entrepreneurial narrative make resources (people with resources) available? We suggest this making-available happens through the kinds of seduction concentrated in Don Giovanni's and Iago's characters. For Stephen Greenblatt it is intimate with a spur of the moment flexibility:

> [there is a]... mode of behaviour that links Lerner's "empathy" and Shakespeare's "Iago": I shall call that mode improvisation, by which I mean the ability to capitalize on the unforeseen and to transform given materials into one's own scenario. The spur-of-the-moment quality of improvisation is not as critical here as the opportunistic grasp of that which seems fixed and established.[28]

With Don Giovanni the flexibility is all momentum and dynamics, whereas with Iago, there is the slowness of a considered bringing-to-fruition, a tending into ripeness, a patience in which he prepares others, suspending actions until they might discover their own appropriateness within the organizational form he is puzzling over. He plays with potential, makes action incipient, and in the end makes his listeners frustrated by the fact that what surely must happen has not yet happened. In Act 1, Scene 3, where Roderigo asks Iago what he should do, being so smitten with Desdemona, and where Iago suggests that he should "put money in thy purse," Roderigo leaves with the enthused −"I'll sell all my land." He is rushing off to operationalize Iago's scheme, but through his own energy, it is his own desire that is compelling him to take this new way.

When Greenblatt refers to the opportunistic grasp of what seemed fixed, the result of improvisation in Iago's acting with words, he touches upon an essential feature of the entrepreneurial experience: an exposure to the transformative possibilities that lie within what is seemingly fixed coupled to an improvisational skill in making use of the recognition of potential fluidity. Turning people towards alternative convictions without thereby upsetting their commitment to desire means opportunity.[29]

For Iago, as the plot unravels and his scheming is revealed, for no scheme really ever finds its true mark, he employs a last move, the only one he can still play and confines himself to silence; the masterful orator suffers the self-incurred punishment of silence: "demand me nothing: what you know, you know: from this time forth I will never speak word." Don Giovanni never stops, running over the edge, spilling into hell in his theatrical refusal to repent, and only then held by the pause of a surprise as the flames consume him. Iago willingly stops, he stops himself, and thereby remains in command (like Othello, he is a soldier at heart). Dying is a relief, and Iago should not experience such comforts, and instead he opts for self-harm by denying himself the necessary pleasure of speech. This is his greater death.

In literature, Iago is an intensification of a seductive, improvisational mode of being in the world that multiplies the possibilities of life.[30] The point with Iago (as with Don Giovanni) is precisely the loosening of the seemingly fixed (including identities): they indicate there is no law governing the "I" that can prevent it from flowing, or the other from bending, and in the wake of these seductions the stable and set is loosened, hierarchies are upset, habits broken, traditions dissolved, meaning things might begin again:

> We cannot all be masters, nor all masters
> Cannot be truly follow'd. You shall mark
> Many a duteous and knee-crooking knave,
> That, doting on his own obsequious bondage,
> Wears out his time, much like his master's ass,
> For nought but provender, and when he's old, cashier'd:
> Whip me such honest knaves. Others there are
> Who, trimm'd in forms and visages of duty,
> Keep yet their hearts attending on themselves,
> And, throwing but shows of service on their lords,
> Do well thrive by them and when they have lined
> their coats
>
> Do themselves homage: these fellows have some soul;
> And such a one do I profess myself. For, sir,
> It is as sure as you are Roderigo,
> Were I the Moor, I would not be Iago:
> In following him, I follow but myself;
> Heaven is my judge, not I for love and duty,
> But seeming so, for my peculiar end:
> For when my outward action doth demonstrate
> The native act and figure of my heart
> In compliment extern, 'tis not long after
> But I will wear my heart upon my sleeve
> For daws to peck at: I am not what I am.[31]

Seduction and entrepreneurship

"The aim of literature," says Deleuze, riffing off Spinoza, "is the passage of life within language that constitutes Ideas."[32] Literature is a way of connecting ideas to an audience, and so transforming the passive or inert passions that lie fallow within each individual into active ones: the story takes the idea beyond its original conception, forcing it to yield to difference from within a common public space. The author strives to have affects that in turn open out into further affects, without known end. Recalling Spinoza's *conatus*, a sort of Nietzschean will to life. "Any feeling [affect] determines our *conatus* to do something on the basis of an idea of an object; *conatus*, thus determined, is called desire."[33] The ideas keep coming, as do the affects, without any final answer in sight, or even any steady, rhythmic progress. The communication was indirect, and though it could be felt directly the meaning being ascribed to the experience is rarely settled, at least at the outset.[34] What matters is an audience is drawn in through asides and conjectures and suppositions. It is perhaps for this reason, that Kierkegaard trusted no other literary form than the deconstructive form of fragments. He declared himself to follow only the movements, finding no comfort in the idea that we could anchor knowledge in reality, but instead suggested we prepare for the fluidity of life. This is perhaps also why a satiric, ironic, and polemical style characterizes Kierkegaard's language, which is also literary in its cajoling the reader into an open and uncertain frame of mind, as though they were encountering a slightly foreign tongue, something minor compared to the dominant/official or received language, that which thereby resists the pull of convention and places the subject into the narrative as an imaginatively disturbing force.[35]

As part of this subjective life Kierkegaard believed us to have inner life, almost ineffable, that was sceptical of and resistant to the analysis and systemic classification met in ordinary practices. The inner self touches on the seat of faith which leaps into relations, beyond the reasoning of ethics even. Our understanding must be taken up as it lives in each of us, uncertainly, moving towards what is open, for there is where more movement is possible, allowing a subjective experience of truth to be formed. This is why Kierkegaard turns towards the in-betweens – in-between the virtual and the actual, in-between what is and what could become, in-between habit and newness – which also represents a potential for leading away/astray. In this sense, the entre of entrepreneurship is an ambiguity introduced into clarity so as to make the rigid into something loose.

Iago is a master of this. Harold Bloom puts it like this: ... Iago's genius "is to persuade others that something they had not thought was something they had not *wanted* to think."[36] And so if you craft your story so that you affect the other, you generate a kind of "aha"-effect which is an opening for further "improvisational entry" that then feeds the fire that has just been started. The seducer will, in this sense, be one that seemingly unveils or places the motivation to act in sharper or more sober relief. She/he would bring you to a revelation/epiphany connected to raw feeling that had hitherto been suppressed by norms: desire is being given new directions.

What Don Giovanni exemplifies, better than most other figures that we use in order to describe and understand who we are, is how the self becomes immanent to movement as such, and what Deleuze senses as a continuous rising to an "nth power" of a moving self.[37] It is in movement, in becoming, in overcoming every tendency to sediment, to status quo that we find the opening up of the entrepreneurial to venture. In being seductive these entrepreneurial stories are not really centred on opportunity in the sense of *ob + portus* (going towards the harbour), indeed it is more a going away from the harbour. Leading away, as the opening part of an entrepreneurship process, is more readily graspable as a movement from (ab-, de-) the port and out on the fluid, flowing sea. It also grasps the quality of entrepreneurship as that which loosens the seemingly fixed, and makes it ripe for improvisational entry.

In Iago the movement is more considered, organized, and multiple, a route to future possibilities for action, but which necessitate a moving away from what has hitherto been considered homely. Hence seduction is accompanied by anxiety: the capacity to induce in others a sense of something being virtually real but as yet unfulfilled, without this something ever being corralled as a direct object or explicit goal. The seduced come alone as subjects aware that were they not being pulled away from their habits they would miss out, and become regretful for something not being done. There is a dynamics here – between a power to affect and a power to be affected. It goes both ways. The seducer has greater chances of choosing the right image or vision if she/he is receptive to the images that will make the soon-to-be-seduced desire a change. This power to be affected is thus linked to a power to affect. Not only is imagination helping the seducer, it also helps the seducer if the soon-to-be-seduced can imagine what could become the result of change. "In its very passion," Deleuze notes, "the imagination discovers the origin and the destination of all its activities."[38] Imagination has the power to move bodies because it is free in the sense that it is not regulated by concepts (of reason or understanding). To have gone astray is precisely to have ventured into that which is not yet totally clear, the in-between of the post-instrumental and pre-operative, and which therefore offers free movement of thought.[39] This includes excitement before the not yet clear, but it also offers the freedom to clarify in action, to actualize the virtual. Such clarification or actualization requires affirmation of the freedom to move. There is something entrepreneurial in using such entre-spaces, allowing an assemblage to gather. Entrepreneurial stories, if they are to work, enlist desire in a way that overcomes habit, and disposes others to move aside from the usual and let it pass, whilst they hesitate, and perhaps go elsewhere. The entrepreneurial story makes an opening, a suspense, where a proposed newness can gain traction in the other's imagination of what might happen, and as a result it can open up to an incipient newness, one that calls for action, one that makes the other come along.[40]

Notes

1 This is part of Kierkegaard's book *Either/Or*, where the essay on Don Giovanni is included. It is primarily in this essay that Kierkegaard advances his study of seduction, centred on the Don Juan myth.

2 For Kierkegaard, the grounding atmosphere to living is despair. Set against this comes the possibility of attaining one or more the tiered stages, in form of rough and unsteady ascent. In addition to the aesthetic, comes the ethical and spiritual stage. The ethical stage is characterized not so much by flow and seeking the right mood as of making conscious decisions structured by a life that becomes full of tasks to handle/manage. To live ethically, you cannot go back to the aesthetic, for this necessarily is a choice that is conscious, and by definition you know what the higher law of ethics obliges you to do; there is no conscious pleading of ignorance. To realize the good – according to law – has little to do with your own enjoyment (aesthetic life), and everything to do with duty (ethical life) in which the good in itself is constituted. The spiritual/religious stage does not make life into a choice of either the aesthetic or the ethical, but rather a choice of either aesthetic/ethical or the spiritual/religious. Kierkegaard sees us alone before God without any other warrant than an open and exposed leap of faith, a trust that has no ground, and which is entirely negative. The leap of faith corresponds to a suspension of reasonable judgement, it is a willingness to hold oneself open to what is always and forever negative and the absent (one cannot know God) and it is this negativity that serves to animate and provoke life into an active, even breathless state, of agitated belief. Hence his sustain critique of priests who felt confident, calm, and lofty in their station: spiritual life had nothing to do with the comforts of dogma. It was an utterly personal affair of argumentation and doubt directed inwardly.

3 Knight, F.H. (1921) *Risk, Uncertainty, and Profit*, Boston: Houghton Mifflin; Landström, H. (1999) "The Roots of Entrepreneurial Research," *New England Journal of Entrepreneurship*, 2(2), pp. 9–20.

4 Hirschman, A.O. (1977) *The Passions and the Interests – Arguments for Capitalism before Its Triumph*, Princeton: Princeton University Press.

5 Cf. Deleuze's (1994) and Deleuze and Guattari's (1994) theory of creation as actualization of the virtual. The virtual – building on Bergson's discussion of the possible-real, and virtual-actual – is real but lacks actuality.

6 Hosking, D.M. and Hjorth, D. (2004) Relational Constructionism and Entrepreneurship: Some Key Notes. In D. Hjorth & C. Steyaert (Eds.), *Narrative and Discursive Approaches in Entrepreneurship*, Cheltenham: Edward Elgar, pp. 255–268. See also the concept of history-making, in Spinosa, C., Flores, F., and Dreyfus, H. (1997) *Disclosing New Worlds – Entrepreneurship, Democratic Action, and the Cultivation of Solidarity*, Cambridge: The MIT Press.

7 William James' expression; see Massumi, B. (2002) *Parables for the Virtual – Movement, Affect, Sensation*, Durham and London: Duke University Press, p. 12.

8 Schumpeter, J.A. (1947) "The Creative Response in Economic History," *Journal of Economic History*, November: 149–159.

9 Hjorth, D. (2007). "Lessons from Iago: Narrating the Event of Entrepreneurship," *Journal of Business Venturing*, 22, 712–732.

10 Bloom, H. (1998). *Shakespeare: The Invention of the Human*, New York: The Berkley Publishing Group.

11 Greenblatt, S. (1980) *Renaissance Self-Fashioning: From More to Shakespeare*, Chicago: University of Chicago Press.

12 de Certeau, M. (1984). *The Practice of Everyday Life*. Transl. by Rendall S. Berkley/Losa Angeles/London: University of California Press.

13 Kierkegaard, S. (1992) Either/Or. Transl. Hannay Alistair, London: Penguin Classics, Penguin.

14 Bloom, H. (1998) *Shakespeare – The Invention of the Human*. New York: Riverhead Books.

15 Hannay, R.A.. (1987). Spirit and the Idea of the Self as a Reflexive Relation. In Perkins, Robert L. (Ed.), *The Sickness unto death*. Mercer University Press. pp. 23–38.

16 Tarde, G. [1903] 1962. The Laws of Imitation. Clouchester, Massachusetts: Peter Smith by permission of Henry Holt & Company; Barry, A. and Thrift, N. (2007) Gabriel Tarde: Imitation, Invention and Economy, *Economy and Society*, 36(4), 509–525.

17 Whilst Kierkegaard remained deeply sceptical of the transcendental idealism propounded by Schelling, it had a profound effect on the poet Coleridge, much of whose *Biographica Literaria* was inspired by (and even plagiarized) Schelling, notably Schelling's admission that the limits of reason meant true understanding came from the subject suspending its rational faculties and giving itself over to a miasmic and ungoverned flow of unconscious feeling.

18 It is in a later text – *Fear and Trembling* – that Kierkegaard introduces what, in his theory of life stages, goes beyond both the aesthetic and the ethical, namely the spiritual (or religious), to live with God though means commitment without exception, a one way giving over of self to an unknowable other. Fear and Trembling is a dialectical lyric, i.e. a contradiction, and we cannot pin this down, we are only ever becoming a Christian, arriving at, you cannot be a Christian, accomplished and assured, whereas religious stage of life is always one of striving, of being wary, of working daily at the task, without the certitude of certainty.

19 What is being authored is a text without a definitive author, and its effect is to agitate the reader into thinking through what came to be called the existential questions of fear and freedom, but which at the time were framed as a form of irreligious irony The argument makes of anxiety a sympathetic antipathy, a desire for what one fears, whose consummation imperils the subject. No-one is exempt. Though we concentrate here on Don Giovanni the diary itself is written by Johannes (Kierkegaard?) who, in overtly misogynist ways, attempts to induce anxiety in Cordelia (Regine?), enticing her by disassembling her femininity in irony and humour, by common sense argument, by exciting her spirit, and then withdrawing, the loss of which she then feels keenly, and this feeling brings her to her limits, and the same too in him, as he, in spite of himself, is also seduced, captivated by her mystery that mysteriously contains her own solution to her predicament should she be able to take that indirect, sidelong glance that is entirely open in its opening intent. Johannes sets up a conventional suitor for Cordelia, aware that the dull ache of such converse will set her against conventional forms of lovemaking, whilst he himself talks with her Aunt, knowledgeably, but also a little scurrilous, pushing double meanings the way of a listening Cordelia,

who he then encourages to look at her Aunt ironically, with him, but then to revert back to seriousness, so as not to allow either of them to settle anywhere. Johannes is making Cordelia aware, his distancing draws her out and she is left exposed with her raw feeling, aware of being human, alone, outside convention. Where Don Giovanni is a diabolical expression of Kierkegaard's first nihilistic sphere of existence, Johannes is a more a considered one, the Don's expertise is entirely unreflective, whilst Kierkegaard's seducer's expertise is deliberate, yet subtle. And Cordelia, did she turn the tables, to become seducer, as she became aware of herself through seduction, whilst Johannes was still entangled in the artistry. Did she then commit to herself a little, experience a turn then to the ethical? If so, suggests Garf, then it is more the seduction's diary than the seducer's. See Garf, J. (2005) *Sören Kierkegaard – A Biography,* Princeton: Princeton University Press, p. 280. pp. 270–274.

20 See e.g. Judith Butler's (2015) discussion of Kierkegaard's writings on the self, passion, despair, and faith, in *Senses of the Subject,* New York: Fordham University Press, pp. 112–148.
21 Kierkegaard, S. (1988) *Either/Or,* Princeton: Princeton University Press, p. 103.
22 From Finale, Mozart's Don Giovanni, Libretto by William Murray, 1961, available at: www.murashev.com/opera/Don_Giovanni_libretto_Italian_English.
23 Bloom, H. (1998) *Shakespeare – The Invention of the Human,* New York: Riverhead Books.
24 Greenblatt, S. (1980) *Renaissance Self-Fashioning – From More to Shakespeare,* Chicago: The University of Chicago Press; Bloom, H. (1998) *Shakespeare and the Invention of the Human,* New York: Riverhead Books.
25 Bloom, H. (1998) *Shakespeare – The Invention of the Human,* New York: Riverhead Books, p. 331.
26 Weick, K. (1984) "Small Wins – Redefining the Scale of Social Problems," *American Psychologist,* 39(1): 40–49.
27 Greenblatt, S. (1980) *Renaissance Self-Fashioning – From More to Shakespeare,* Chicago and London: The University of Chicago Press, p. 234.
28 Greenblatt, 1980: 227.
29 Greenblatt, S. (1997) "The Touch of the Real," *Representations,* 59: 14–29; Chia, R.C.H. and Holt, R. (2009) *Strategy without Design,* Cambridge: Cambridge University Press.
30 Hjorth, D. and Steyaert, C. (2006) American psycho/European schizo: Stories of managerial elites in a hundred images, in Pasquale, G. and Barbara, C. (Eds.) *Management Education and Humanities,* Cheltenham: Edward Elgar, pp. 67–97.
31 From Shakespeare's Othello, Act 1, Scene 1, available at: www.sparknotes.com/nofear/shakespeare/othello/page_6/
32 Deleuze, G. (1988) *Essays Critical and Clinical,* Transl. D.W. Smith & M.A. Greco, London: Verso.
33 Deleuze, G. (1992) *Expressionism in Philosophy: Spinoza,* New York: Zone Books, p. 284.
34 Broudy, H.S. (1961) "Kierkegaard on Indirect Communication," *The Journal of Philosophy,* 58(9): 225–233.

35 Deleuze, G. (1998) *Essays Critical and Clinical*, London and New York: Verso, p. 113.
36 Bloom, H. *Shakespeare and the Invention of the Human*, New York: Riverhead Books, quoting Bradshaw, p. 461.
37 Deleuze, G. (1994) *Difference and Repetition*, Transl. P. Patton, New York: Athlone Press.
38 Deleuze, G. (2004) *Desert Islands – and Other Texts (1953–1974)*, Los Angeles and New York: Semiotext(e), pp. 56–71.
39 As Massumi puts it when discussing imagination: Massumi, B. (2002) *Parables for the Virtual – Movement, Affect, Sensation*, Durham and London: Duke University Press, p. 134.
40 The social force of entrepreneurship – that which a will can affirm so as to successfully battle other forces and overcome hindrances – remains a mystery. There have been studies of the role of narrative and storytelling, of imagination and, of desire in order to better understand entrepreneurship as a process. We partly build on this stream of research, with its upgrading of the role of language and fiction, of fabulation, and the literary; see Volkmann, C. and De Cock, C. (2010). Four Close Readings on Introducing the Literary in Organizational Research. In *The Leading Publication in the Field: Unsettling Authority in the Social Sciences of Management* (pp. 143–163). MayFly Books; Gartner, W.B., Carter, N.M., and Hills, G.E. (2003) The language of opportunity, In Steyaert, C. and Hjorth, D. (Eds.) *New Movements in Entrepreneurship*. Cheltenham: Edward Elgar, pp. 103–124, Aldrich, H.E. and Fiol, C.M. (1994). Fools Rush in? The Institutional Context of Industry Creation. *The Academy of Management Review*, 19(4), 645–670.; Lounsbury, M. and Glynn, M.A. (2001) Cultural Entrepreneurship: Stories, Legitimacy, and the Acquisition of Resources, *Strategic Management Journal*, 22(6–7): 545–564; *Journal of Business Venturing*, 2(5).

6 Organization-creation
Play

Introduction

The play aspect of the entrepreneurial process is probably the most challenging one in practice in the sense that it is through the experiment of playing that the ideas used in the seduction to attract support and to assemble people start to become manifest. In play, things start to happen and the virtual begins to tip into the actual, whilst at the same time, the difference (to life before playing) remains apparent. Playing, consistent with this view, is conceptualized by Gilles Deleuze as the free yet somehow ordered movement found, for example, in the double movement of a dice-throw: it affirms multiplicity and becoming – the dice's movement up towards the sky – but also unity, the being of becoming, the eternal return – the dice's return to earth. Such a game is not habituated structuring of everyday life, and more akin to its being paused: "[W]e temporarily abandon life, in order to then temporarily fix our gaze upon it."[1]

In his afforming of play Deleuze was inspired by Nietzsche, who in turn was (notably in his use of literary fragments such as the aphorism) issuing elusive, suggestive, and explosive texts that refused to be categorized. The established narratives could only look on and below in shock and frustration at a figure who not only wrote in such an open and corrosive, but seemed intent on destroying everything established society held to be right and good.[2]

Deleuze was interested in play as a means of moving outside of the limits imposed by dominant knowledge, habit, tradition, opinion, and its social arrangements (institutions, organizations, and control systems). Deleuze puts it like this: life goes beyond knowledge and thought goes beyond life, wherefore the thinker's task is to see that life makes thought active and thought makes life become new, other, different. Nietzsche: "[a] thought that would go to the limit of what life can do, a thought that would lead life to the limit of what it can do? A thought that would *affirm* life …," well, such a thought comes through play.[3]

The affirmation is not revolutionary, but emerges from within repetitions of what is already there. This is a theme running throughout Deleuze's thought, since the publication of *Difference and Repetition* in

DOI: 10.4324/9781315714455-9

1968. Deleuze is both author (French *auteur*, originator, creator, insti-gator[4]) and a *repetiteur* (French for a coach, rehearsing with performers, to assist in development).[5] Deleuze is interested in the *performing* of diffe-rence that emerges from a series of *répétiteur* achievements (repetitions) that might yield a difference.[6] A difference that otherwise is hidden behind the repressive codes always being upheld by habit, including the habits of thinking upon which philosophy (Deleuze's own habituated practice) is so dependent.[7]

Patterns of difference and repetition are particularly important when we try to understand this gathering of forces, this mustering of a cap-acity for collective, creative becoming that is needed for firm-ing, for the new entrepreneurial firm to achieve being.[8] "Entrepreneur" is the name of a character that is simultaneously one and many: the entre-preneurial process orients itself towards the entrepreneur (that can be collectively composed) but cannot progress unless there are productive (Spinoza would say joyful) relationships assembled and held together by desire. Many such relationships are needed for forces to be gathered with enough strength to push through the limits established as sense and value that have been held fast by countless repetitions. Entrepreneurial processes open up sense and value by enquiring into how they came about; how the common agreements settled on precisely "these" ways of going about things, and precisely these ways of evaluating the need for doing so.

Pippi Longstocking

Four years ahead of Simone de Beauvoir publishing *Le Deuxième Sexe,* Astrid Lindgren gave the world Pippi Longstocking (1945). Pippi lives alone, in her own large house, with her monkey and her horse and stash of gold coins. She is the super-naturally strong daughter of dead parents. The stories of Pippi are full of adults attempting to control her and her life: bring her to a children's home, make her come to school, tell her what to do, how to talk, how to dress, and so on. Pippi is accompanied by a monkey – Mr Nilsson – and a horse – Little Old Man, and her two neighbour friends of similar age – Annika and Tommy. Pippi is a char-acter whose reluctance to accept authority or respect the limits of habit is matched by her indifference to all forms of correction. Everything is a scene of the play that exposes the mundane features of convention, and in doing so questions them. The others, her immediate circle of friends, are enlisted in apparently absurd experimental twists on established ways of doing things: biscuits are rolled out on the floor, wastebins are emp-tied rather than filled, clothes are odd and colourful. Also language is taken as open to playful entry, seen as incomplete, possible to add to with words. The word she invents is "spunk" and she does so without knowing what it means. When her friend Annika questions what the point is with a word that has no meaning, Pippi replies that this is exactly what annoys her. Tommy, Annika's brother, supplements Annika and asks who invented the meaning of words from the very start. Pippi replies that the strange thing is that "so many odd words are invented – probably by a bunch of old professors – yet, inventing 'spunk' is something they did not care to do." Classical problems of reality and language/representation are thereby playfully handled. Playing with language is part of how Pippi resists and subverts – often using comedy and absurdity – the adult world or the world of established order and authority.[9] When a policeman comes to Pippi's house to tell her that arrangements have been made for her to come to a children's home (since she is orphan in the story and lives on her own in a large house), she replies: "I am a child and this is my home: therefore it is a children's home."[10] The sense is taken out of the policeman's order that becomes empty, simply describing what is already a fact, hence there is no need for change.

Already here we understand that the "setup" – no parents, supernatural strength, limitless monetary resources, a horse and a monkey as companions, and "contrasting" conventional friends, Tommy and Annika – is in place for playing to happen. However, it happens often with an edge pointing at the conventional normality of the adult world. Play is thus often destabilizing, subverting, mocking, questioning, resisting, opposing, whilst it is affirming the joy of imagination and fantasy. The material for the play is often – as in the case of the policeman above – the received reality in its unquestioned continuity. Pippi finds a way to turn this on its head, tactically make use of it, turn it against itself, or simply challenge it with an alternative "reality." In fact, it would be wrong to describe play as an event in the Pippi stories. Play is reality here, it is the ontological status of Pippi and the potential interruptions of play are the events that drive the story. Drawing on Winnicott's work on *Playing and Reality* where play and space (potential and transitional) are intimately related we can say that Pippi explores venturing into adult space by poaching at the norms that prescribes how interaction, roles, and logics should be guiding behaviour.[11]

The effect is that play becomes normal and "reality" becomes absurd. A central effect of playing is thereby revealed, with clear implications for understanding entrepreneurship processes: the rigid is made loose, the unquestioned is made questionable, and the taken-for-granted is noted and challenged. We recognize the importance of understanding the entrepreneurial as playful and tactical when we see how tactical acts of resistance – such as the one where the policeman wants to place Pippi in a children's home – perverts the strategic order and makes it trip over itself.[12]

That playing is living and living is playing is a central idea in the stories of Pippi. Astrid Lindgren thereby opens the reader for not only comedy but also magic. There is a seductive force in this playfulness that we also see as an important element in the attraction that entrepreneurship has on its various "audiences." Brian Massumi has described philosophy as being "... the movement of thought to the virtual fringe of things. [...] philosophy rigs thinking to make singular connections in fictional anticipation of their actualization."[13] Affirming the "already more" of the actual into its potential nextness is something we find to be a powerful way of describing what entrepreneurship does.[14] Imagination – like in Pippi – plays a crucial role in sensing and articulating the virtualities that "swarm" like potentialities around every actuality. Entrepreneurial action then brings practice and life's "liveability" beyond the fringe of actual solutions and the value related to them, by creating stories of what could become actual, motivating people to join in making this happen, and legitimize this as a new/better solution/value. Agamben's *Pulcinella* seems to playfully analyse this modal ontology of a playful life through studying this character in Italien *Commedia dell'arte*. Pippi shares some characteristics of the *Pulcinella* character in that they both perform inoperative life. Inoperativity, far from being simply passivity or inactivity, is a concept Agamben develops (from French sources) to analyse action with our ideas of productivity typically governing it. This is life where "how" has completely substituted the "what." Pippi's subversive comedy is typically emptying adult/normal life of its habitual "what" and thus reaches the fringe where a form of life has to be invented. Such joyful embrace of the inoperative escapes control by not fitting any forms in place.

The smallest friend, Mr Nilsson, can be seen a little like Nietzsche's monkey, a reminder of the dangers of becoming too strong, too confident, but also of the need to understand and live, and not simply repeat (to ape it) and speak empty words.[15] He is both a captive creature, and hence a sign of a life under managerial control, and yet errant, and so a hint of what, if pursued, is most productive about a child: they play. Pippi's play affirms (pro-rols rather than cont-rols) situations and thereby accelerates the experiences of becoming to which the assembly is exposed, not just her. The horse, "Little Old Man," is there to secure her mobility and speed. For sure, as a little girl with super-strength powers, she is not in need of force as such. But the horse, white with black dots, indicates her (and its) freedom: the horse can take you out of the situation, secure movement, and, through speed, make any dot morph into a line, a flightline that can take Pippi (and the assemblage her novel idea has brought together) beyond the fringe, where "how" to live has to be invented.

Annika and Tommy are representatives of established sense and value, they repeat it in their gestures and talk, reminding Pippi of how it is the world thinks and acts – life governed by productivity and effectiveness. As opposed to Pippi, they live with their parents and have absorbed convention as readily as they have the summer sun. Yet the accidental proximity, and their natural and polite curiosity, finds them broaching Pippi's world. As they try to make sense of Pippi's schemes, the intention being often to soften their impact, conventions become a thing to mould and play with. Pippi's subversive use of humour and comedy, ridicules the stereotypical (often adult) behaviour being displayed towards them. She asks why it is they ought to comply with the passive, silent, good boy and girl norm. Not necessarily with the aim to disturb or upset or hurt, but rather as an attempt to open up, to fuel imagination, demonstrate resourcefulness and strength. Together, as a unit, the monkey, horse, Pippi, Tommy, and Annika form a striving *conatus*, a gathering in which the stupidity and tedium of adult norms receive full exposure. Whilst Annika and Tommy rarely break free utterly, they come to witness how normal ways might be challenged, and in ways that do not bring about the ills that adults associate with challenge. They are seduced and then pulled into Pippi's schemes. In the stories they, therefore, demonstrate the power of assembling, since they often are the first in a crowd of kids joining in and creating momentum, as what "is not" but "could be" is rolled out before them.

A repeating theme to her disruption is the mis-use of money, of which she has an immense stockpile in the antiquated form of gold coins held in an old leather suitcase left to her by her parents. This is a legacy that both protects her from the "reality" of having to rely on others to pay for things, and also makes her a potential victim of those wanting to steal from her. These are wider, irresistible forces that intrude from a distance, bleakly and without much comment, for speculation and play can only go so far. More immediately she enjoins her friends in errant spending, making ludicrous deals, but which somehow "pay" off in new possibilities for living, marginalizing the economy of planned investment as dominant rationality and contrasting markedly with the lessons served up in Tommy and Annika's home, of money being that which is dutifully saved in piggy banks.

Pippi is always on the move:

> What are we going to do now? asked Tommy.
> I don't know what you are going to do, said Pippi, but I know I can't lie around and be lazy. I am a Thing-Finder, and when you're a Thing-Finder you don't have a minute to spare.[16]

Pippi's reply to Tommy seems both to reject the idea that there is a plan to follow, or an expectation of what is the right thing to do now, and at the same time, it challenges Tommy to decide too, to affirm with her that, of course, becoming a thing-finder is the most natural thing in the world, the goal is finding itself.

In Pippi readers (mainly children) witness the potential of deciding for themselves (even when making up language, which Pippi does with enthusiasm) by first being aware of the choices that have already been made for them, which are presented to them as a fait accompli, or which, being so engrained in human customs, are no longer encountered as choices to be made. We recognize this in research on institutional entrepreneurship, where norms of interaction, roles, logics, and templates prescribe behaviour yet escape attention.[17] The classical tension between structure and agency is at the centre here and determinism and voluntarism lurk behind.[18] Entrepreneurship research has often placed emphasis on intentionality and missed how agency is conditioned by structures and how the unintended also affects the outcome of action. Whereas well-known theorizations of this structure-agency problem (what institutional theorists often describe as the embedded agency paradox) have given us the concepts of structuration (Giddens) and habitus (Bourdieu), we have focused on a third concept here: tactics. Arguably, this shares the qualities of distributed agency that emphasize that possibilities for action are not simply constrained by structures but also provided by structures as created by actors.[19] However, in contrast to institutional theorists often suggesting that entrepreneurs need *strategies* for transforming institutions,[20] we – again – place greater emphasis on creativity and politics when we suggest *tactics* are more efficient in "making use" of strategic templates in perverting them or turning them against themselves, looking for the hustle through which to enrol others, to have them come along.[21] Such subversion, as has been discussed above, is not seldom done in the genre of comedy or irony. The playful seems like a form of life, imaginatively breaking free from the prescribed "what" by fabulating its way out on a flight-line. Opposing strategies with strategies would only be to enter a game where majoritarian reign easily dominates. Games are in this sense gamed by the strategic that has formulated the rules and controls the sanctioning of them. The tactician seeks play, where the "how" needs to be invented and where imagination and speed become an advantage. This is the life of Pippi and Pulcinella, which should not be mistaken for being reactive as much as being passionate: the power to be affected by the dominant normality's strategic impact brings an intensity and heightened sensitivity before the "common sense" at work (see Chapter 7 below), and this builds a readiness potential[22] that strikes blow by blow as a surprise in that it does not follow the strategist's logic.[23]

In being shown these choices the play creates space to choose differently (differentiation is how creation is achieved). Pippi's play is not about resistance as much as destabilization and passion. It is not simply about reversing power, not simply about acting upon those that have acted upon children according to the conventional protocol, habit, values, and tradition. Rather, it is a repeated expression of passion in the sense of holding a power to affect as well as a power to be affected in a collection of bodies, which together become multiple.

This multiplicity is more than the "I am not what I am" of Iago because now, in play, the subject is firm in their being: they are thing finders, beings interested in becoming, and with the interior refuge from which to reach out into the world, exploring, and incidentally becoming a source of frustration for the adults many of whom are cast as assemblages of responsibility: parents, the police, the doctor. Her play prevents them from guarding convention so neatly and properly, and their haphazard and inopportune responses allow Pippi to find yet further openings, flight-lines. This on-going capacity to riff off the situation generates a kind of momentum to the play: it has to destabilize as an act of making. Her force is, to recur to Deleuze, a minorization of the majoritarian stability.[24] As a minor, she acts fully, and not at all in the way those who have reached the age of majority expect of her. She reveals how the majoritarian language of convention "… is regulated and disciplined by the operations of institutions and cultural (academic) habits; 'majoritarian formation of the public sphere,' which gives enunciation weight and reference."[25]

Minoritarian language, such as Pippi's, is not identified by a supreme principle, which would allow hierarchy and control/domination, but by movement and the nature of the grouping. It is what Deleuze goes on to call molecular rather than molar, an assemblage rather than an already organized grammatical settled structure. It is not a play of the kind that exploits the temporary absence of authority; not the rats' dance on the table whilst the cat is away. It is much more consistent and dispositional than that. In Pippi it is a condition for self- and world-making, realized in the absence of a dominant, structuring centre, hers is a Romantic force that disturbs the solidities to which so many adults seem to cling.[26] This is perhaps why we sometimes describe children's play as "serious." There is devotion and affirmation of becoming active within the world as it is found, i.e. an affirmation of affirmation, which is how transmutation and difference are achieved. The stories of Pippi are exemplary in this sense. These are not stories of a girl that pranks. Not stories of a child that takes her chances. Rather, these are stories of affirmations of chance and the necessity of chance, her reality being a refuge or space for the multiplicity of Novalis' fragments.[27]

It is possible to read Pippi Longstocking as a manifestation of Astrid Lindgren's engagement with, and inspiration from, a series of discussions with friends and colleagues at the time (1940s). Notable amongst these were Edith Södergran (Finnish poet and writer) and Ellen Key (Swedish author, philosopher, feminist, primarily known for her radical [at the time] ideas about women's rights and the upbringing and education of children). They were, like Lindgren, influenced by Nietzsche.[28] If we, like Deleuze, read Nietzsche's concept of over-human as an image of humans overcoming tradition, habit and – ultimately – themselves, Pippi becomes an example of a playful overcoming of inherited and imposed limitations. The point of critique, Deleuze comments, when reading and repeating Nietzsche to discover difference, is to overcome, is to reach the overtaken human, namely the point where the fully burdened ass (the schooled adult and authority figure) first becomes critical as a lion (who objects, roars in nihilistic frustration, but really only knows how to say "no") and then becomes a child. In the stories of Pippi, critique operates in the service of a destabilization that allows free movement, i.e. play. Which is where it gains explanatory force in our attempt to describe and understand the entrepreneurial process as playful. Play, after seduction's mobilization

and enrolment, rewards the passionate body with the freedom of speculative joy. This is the time of the dice moving up into free air, anything
becomes possible, chance is being affirmed; it could really become something. In a famous scene, written a few years before the end of the Second
World War, Pippi wins a wrestling fight with "Strong Adolf." This obviously happened, maybe as an anticipation, in Astrid Lindgren's story,
long before it happened in life.[29] Playing gains force and surprises life by
not coming from the past or preparing a planned future, but by emerging
from within the moment. This gives playing the event-ness of the event,
the force of movement: "To know how to affirm chance is to know how
to play."[30]

Potential destabilization of inherited structures that pass unnoticed
under the noses of the creatures of habit, or are blessed in ceremonial
liturgy by the priests of tradition, requires a keen sensibility before where
and when incipient playing resides. Playing follows an affirmation of such
incipient becoming-active, it follows an affirmation of chance. Pippi is in
many ways a walking affirmation of chance, and manifests what Nietzsche
refers to when Zarathustra says his doctrine is: "Let chance come to me:
it is as innocent as a little child!," and that he has an attraction for those
preferring to dance on the feet of chance.[31]

Mrs Dalloway

If Pippi is an embodiment of Nietzsche's child, Mrs Dalloway is the child
tempered in maturity and channelled by convention. Caught as much
in the immediacy of sensation as she is bound by the drawn-out tedium
of duty, Clarissa Dalloway becomes an adept in exploring the limits of
permissible forms of play. The limits are those of privilege, gender, colonial politics, sanity, and it is during a party, a gathering, an apparently
convivial meeting of like-minded folk, that these otherwise accepted
limits become visible. And Mrs Dalloway is imperious in having her
guests reveal and wrestle with them, not out of deliberate intellectual
positioning, but from a sensory and affective looseness induced by the
party she has so carefully organized.

Her ability begins with her irrepressible interest in being alive. The
novel – which covers a day in the life of Mrs Dalloway, marked by the
passing of hours – opens with an aeroplane in flight leaving a vapour
trail. It is trying to advertise something by writing in the sky, an ordinary
fleeting expression of commercial branding. The signs are there: the
new century is being marked by an irresistible intrusion of the commercial market, blocking the sun, the old order is under threat, yet for Mrs
Dalloway it remains ephemeral, the white smoke giving out against the
white page taken over by text talking of other more apparent, momentary
happenings; the feelings of walking, of being in London, in June, amid
the day's "dayness."[32] There is pleasure in the street's "streetness"
(its haecceity) this day, in the accidental encounters and the way the

fluidity of city-life, its fragments, feeds Mrs Dalloway's imagination, constantly wandering off in an (Mrs Dalloway's) enjoyment and (Woolf's examination) of multiplicity. The day's "dayness," and Dalloway's "Dallowayness" have both reached a level of intensity that, as the pages unfold, will become realized in the coming together of a parry she is organizing, an event for which she is carrying herself through the London streets, ordering this and that, preparing, struggling between spontaneity and receptivity, organizing her own body so that another body – that of the party – can come into being later in the day.[33]

Mrs Dalloway's imaginative excursions into sensory affect set the tone for what, later on, will become a space in which the molar orders that beset the lives of her class, her type of people, become loosened and intensified, at one and the same time. She detects others close to her are sceptical of her parties, as though there were frivolous:

> It was a feeling, some unpleasant feeling, earlier in the day perhaps; something that Peter had said, combined with some depression of her own, in her bedroom, taking off her hat; and what Richard had said had added to it, but what had he said? There were his roses. Her parties! That was it! Her parties! Both of them criticised her very unfairly, laughed at her very unjustly, for her parties. That was it! That was it!
>
> Well, how was she going to defend herself? Now that she knew what it was, she felt perfectly happy. They thought, or Peter at any rate thought, that she enjoyed imposing herself; liked to have famous people about her; great names; was simply a snob in short. Well, Peter might think so. Richard merely thought it foolish of her to like excitement when she knew it was bad for her heart. It was childish, he thought. And both were quite wrong. What she liked was simply life.
>
> "That's what I do it for," she said, speaking aloud, to life.[34]

What she means by life is not properly understood by those Richards and Peters saddled up with purpose and principles: her parties were an offering to combine, to create: they were a gift without any distinct recipient, they were openings. The party will be a place where connecting molecular forces will reveal a shadowed vitality: her introductions will create interactions with affective potential in which the social protocols prescribed to a quality – dutiful, sane, bureaucratic – loosen in the multiplicity of in-betweens that fragments provide. Her party will bring difference into play, which makes use of the tension between the roles of the guests as they are habitually played out when in office (they are ministers, military types, civil servants, writers), and the party context, that permits more open discussion: positions given way to speculations.

The party works because Mrs Dalloway has the capacity to generate an aura and play off it.[35] Picasso admitted the risks of playing off an aura:

I myself, since Cubism and before, have satisfied these masters and critics with all the changing oddities which have passed through my head, and the less they understood me, the more they admired me. By amusing myself with all these games, with all these absurdities, puzzles, rebuses, arabesques, I became famous and that very quickly. And fame for a painter means sales, gains, fortune, riches. And today, as you know, I am celebrated, I am rich. But when I am alone with myself, I have not the courage to think of myself as an artist in the great and ancient sense of the term. [...] I am only a public entertainer who has understood his times and exploited them as best he could, the imbecility, the vanity, the cupidity of his contemporaries. Mine is a bitter confession, more painful than it may appear, but it has the merit of being sincere.[36]

Mrs Dalloway avoids Picasso's bitterness: she is not exploiting the imbecility, the vanity, or cupidity of her contemporaries, as much as she is trying to actualize a virtual life and enjoying this as a playful process of actualization. It is as if the playful mood of the party, the party as a life-form, is the highest form of organization to which she aspires. In that time, the time of the party, the time of the event, playing is incipient and this calls out the best from humans. The right people and things are present to each other, "in resonance and in interference," which means there is high potential. Then the actual strikes, playing happens, and free movement occurs at "the intersection of the possible, the potential and the virtual: three modes of thought."[37] If you try to make it happen, it most often is killed. An over-organized party gets stiff, artificial, and un-playful. The skill is in the setting of the space, the mixing of people, and a nurturing of potential discussion, movements, and relations. Virtuality presses hard on the limit of incipiency: it only needs the right intensity and timing to pass through into actuality.

Every time she gave a party she had this feeling of being something not herself, and that everyone was unreal in one way; much more real in another. It was, she thought, partly their clothes, partly being taken out of their ordinary ways, partly the background; it was possible to say things you couldn't say anyhow else, things that needed an effort; possible to go much deeper.[38]

For the others, Mrs Dalloways' party arrives in the form of an invitation: a card, with date and time, dress code, all perfectly normal. Right away comes anticipation and an incipiency of relationships (interactions-in-the-making). Bodies are already preparing to open up towards one another, giving of what they are and are not, aware of the socially coded roles that permit, temporarily, their loosening, meaning a sense of belonging to the event emerges before its actual commencement.[39]

Mrs Dalloway herself has given countless parties. They remind her that something can be distinct without being fixed, that things can occur as events without them being at all one thing, and that she too was such a multiplicity, a hostess for sure, but she could not be reduced to this, nor to a list in which such a role appeared alongside others. Rather the party allows her, along with others, to sink into herself as a moving force of life:

> She wore ear-rings, and a silver-green mermaid's dress. Lolloping on the waves and braiding her tresses she seemed, having that gift still; to be; to exist; to sum it all up in the moment as she passed; turned, caught her scarf in some other woman's dress, unhitched it, laughed, all with the most perfect ease and air of a creature floating in its element.[40]

Deleuze and Guattari think warmly of Mrs Dalloway here, quoting Woolf: "never again will Mrs. Dalloway say to herself, 'I am this, I am that, he is this, he is that,'" and: "[S]he felt very young; at the same time unspeakably aged. She sliced like a knife through everything; at the same time was outside, looking on ..."[41] With sensing multiplicity and sensing one's multiple capacity comes a sense of both belonging and being on the outside and the party accentuates this, a scene that can be orchestrated and perhaps conducted a little, yet not at all managed. What Mrs Dalloway is doing, and this discloses something crucial in entrepreneurship too, is making the world worthy of and ready for the event and its aura.[42] Of course, in entrepreneurship, there have been endless examples of dazzling failures of visionary, self-entitled entrepreneurs pulling people into their aura, creating a phantasmagorical airy castle of purported success.[43] They are gatherings of hype, media attention, herd mentality, and distant investors not wanting to miss the train as it leaves the station. Mrs Dalloway's party is of a different order, the aura is one of mannered disturbance, a raising up of possibility, rather than surety. She is organizing in a way that will allow the virtual to press harder on the actual until it eventually, having become incipient, pushes through, though in ways that cannot be foretold, only witnessed. The outcome of play is not the concern, save its being possibly transformative. Accepting her invitation has an element of being seduced, of potentially being led astray insofar as, in a quiet way, the unknown accompanies you as a guest, one whose company allows for "free movement."

The free movement is what directs Mrs Dalloway's desire, this is what directs and organizes the assemblage called a party, and this is where and when anything could happen. In this sense, in the sense of being the one that fuels desire and therefore secures that the assemblage is held together, Mrs Dalloway is performing the entrepreneurial function that we can see performed in actualizing greater possibilities of living, making spaces for free movement. Mrs Dalloway brings and holds all characters together, but party, as life taken beyond itself, is a collective achievement just like any form of entrepreneurship.

As Wicke suggests, Mrs Dalloway "... can be read as an extraordinary rendition of the micro-complications of 'the market,' a market shot through with desire, memory, global history and national tradition, sex, loss, and shopping."[44] Woolf's story captures well how desire holds the assemblage together such that it opens life to become a space where play can emerge. Play makes use of the openness that characterizes bodies that have been led astray, from their beaten tracks, and thus increased their capacity to interact, their vitality, their collaborative potential. Playing is a time of testing, inviting and responding, trying, trusting as in ensemble work in theatre or in music.[45] "Woolf's market modernism, if we can now call it that, emphasizes fluidity ..." Wicke continues.[46]

Linking it to Gianni Vattimo's analysis of what he calls the transparent society, the presence of the market in Woolf's modernism is further described as part of a reality that is now more fluid, weak and soft (references to an ontology of becoming in Vattimo's philosophy), "where experience can acquire the characteristics of oscillation, disorientation, and play."[47] Mrs Dalloway is, in this sense, a contraction of urban fluidity and its multiple and constant invitations towards what is entrepreneurial ... you could become. What entrepreneurship does, if we learn from Ivar Björkman's discussion of aura-production, is to "re-auratize" (and thus re-enchant) the world.[48] It does so, Wicke suggests, by using collective desire:

> Emphasis on the term "reproduction" has to some extent blinded us to the absence of the understanding of consumption, a process which entails a re-auraticization under the sign of personal history, fantasmatic agency, collective desire.[49]

We would conceptualize this by saying that re-auratization relies on a playfulness harboured in collective desire, and that new ideas of what could open up for play in this sense are virtualities that can enable imaginations of what could become actualized (or created). Stories of such virtualities organize and direct assemblages of people and things, holding it together by desire, directing it by constant references to "what could become" and tactical moves for how to get there. Wicke relates Woolf's style to the Bloomsbury circle and life, including John Maynard Keynes's relationship to Woolf. Contrasting the Mrs Dalloway-market-reality with the Friedmanite (Milton) and Reaganite (as in Ronald) monetarism, she notes that the Keynesian economy is one of modernist *magic*:

> As such, it is an understanding of the market as magical in a complex, fluid, unpredictable, social, emotional [...] This is a "soft," a fluid magic, feminized, anarchic, yet interconnected, playful at its best.[50]

The influence goes both ways since the market in Woolf's literature, assuming it is influenced by her Bloomsbury circle friends, which include Keynes, is a space within which "acts of much creative magic or transformative potential can be performed."[51]

When we investigate entrepreneurship with the help of literature, the somewhat surprising effect is thus that Keynes, closely connected to literature as part of the Bloomsbury circle, is revealed as an economist closer to entrepreneurship than is often assumed.[52] Kreuger drives a similar thesis and suggests Schumpeter and Keynes are united by both being thinkers that embraced passion as part of how they understood humans in the economy.[53] We would say that they both understood economy through humans, and not humans through the economy.

Mrs Dalloway, Pippi Longstocking, and entrepreneurship

We opened this chapter by saying that the play part of our model, describing and theorizing the practice of play in the entrepreneurship process, is probably the most challenging one. It is notoriously difficult to write on play too; to provide a theoretical basis for describing, understanding, analysing and make useful sense of it. The fact that Huizinga's book on the playing human and on the play element of[54] culture – *Homo Ludens* – from 1938, remains still today one of the few book-length studies of play is indicative of the challenges that accompany the scholars pursuing this task. Notably, *Homo Ludens* was predated by Johan Huizinga's study of Erasmus (1924); Erasmus that in 1509 (published 1511) had written the essay *In Praise of Folly* (a satirical comment on superstition, tradition, and the church). Huizinga that the mechanical and technical had replaced the spontaneous and human-relational as ordering culture and society.[55] This meant, in Huizinga's view, that the play element of culture, constitutive for our historic development, was now withering or at least changing given the technical-mechanical domination. The technical-mechanical and, more lately, digital developments have certainly meant a lot of great things for societies, but it has also meant that culture and its play element have moved into "the weekend." In this respect, our attempt to bring literature into this presentation of a new theory for entrepreneurship also represents a way to pull literature back into the centre (from the weekend) and connect entrepreneurship with desire, affect, and becoming.

In the perspective of this, we note the entrepreneurship process, inviting desire, affect, becoming, and assemblage as concepts through which we can think entrepreneurship in processual terms, is also an opening to the play-element that characterizes this process, where culture opens into the economy, without loss. With Mrs Dalloway, taking up from Pippi, play becomes a modernist reinvention of the market, one that is organized precisely with an absence of an organizing centre, and instead achieved in a much more unruly intermingling of forces, bodies, images, interests, passions, and powers to affect and be affected.

Though we are told modernism is not Romanticism, they are held as different categories by majoritarian scholarly language, there is a sharing of interest in the fragmentary and its generative affect that we find resonates with a form of economic activity that delights in play. Both Schumpeter and Keynes can be seen as allowing for some openings towards the passionate – i.e. more realistic – human as part of their conceptualization of the economy. This places the economy *in* society, which *per se* makes it more realistic. This is also where we operate as thinkers of entrepreneurship through literature, as beings in the desiring flow of life rather than held fast in the diagram of forces preferred in economic modelling.

When the conditions for play are organized, as in both Pippi's and Mrs Dalloway's case, we see how the number of in-betweens, entre-spaces, increase exponentially. Likewise, in the world of entrepreneurship, personal networks can be understood as bundles of relationships between people from which ideas, articulated as visions and packaged as plans, recruit people into assemblages as proto-organizational forms that can be steered towards an interest in getting a new firm created and running. The number of in-betweens, of entre-spaces, of potential entrepreneurship processes, are not restricted to the number of bodies at (in this case) the party. Playing happens when in-betweens of ideas, passions, forces, powers, intensities are mingled. One does not know what these bodies, including bodies of thought, can do – which is also why there is play. Life can always move beyond knowledge, and will be pulled beyond itself by imagination, by thinking seeking a route for the virtual to become actualized. Knowing how to play along, how to nurture play, is a question of knowing common sense – the reality that play has to successfully confront in order to reach commerce (according to our model).

Organizing for play is both full of brio (as in Pippi) and yet also a subtle, equivocal, and directionless organizational art (as in Mrs Dalloway). It relies on sensing whether there is an agreement between bodies (ideas, people) such that the productive capacity of the assemblage can be increased. "Agreement" here refers to whether forces can become active, which would open to the affirmation of ideas and enable an overcoming of the limits of the present. It relies on seduction in our model, suggesting it is about making playing attractive as entering a path yet not taken. Playing is never and can never emerge and develop if there was a guarantee for its success. It would then be the execution of a plan, which is not free movement. Indeed, playing rarely starts on the basis that there is an agreed-upon "goal image" in relation to which assessment of success/failure can be made. That *per se* would transform playing into gaming as it would force desire to become an interest much too early in the creation process. As the Mrs Dalloway story shows, playing as such is not a necessary outcome of having organized for it. It has to emerge, as the eventfulness of the event, as the result of potential spilling over into the actual. Plans block playing as a free movement in the open (that which has no organizing centre). A potentialized situation thus carries a productive vagueness which is "something doing," a nextness that awaits triggers for its becoming, a nextness we never knew were there, should the triggers not have arrived in a timely (*kairos*) manner.[56]

In terms of our model of the entrepreneurial process, play follows seduction and prepares for common sense. None of these are discrete stages but are rather referred to in our model as centres of gravity in terms of what is most important for the style of organization-creation that makes the overall process progress towards actualizing a new firm. From Mrs Dalloway, we learn primarily that play has conditions and that you can prepare for it, and from Pippi, that play requires common sense as that against which it works. In Mrs Dalloway's case, this working against is itself almost conventional: the party is the form for human interaction that provides legitimate reasons to expect that "normal" life is temporarily postponed. The place of the party – Mrs Dalloway's home – certainly is part of providing this "shield" from the normalcy of everyday life.

In the case of Pippi, the place is certainly also an important part of preparing for play – her big old house shields her from the adult world of expectations and regulations. From that as a base, she makes excursions into the small town and its surroundings, knowing there is always a "home base" to return to. With the "autonomy" that follows from having her own home, her gold coins, and super-strength, she continuously questions the taken-for-granted. Not as a critique; not *against* in pursuit of freedom *from*. Rather as an effect of affirming a freedom to try, create, test, explore. Indirectly, and to the adult world around her, this comes across as a questioning of authority, an act of rebellion threatening the stability they benefit from. The role and function of the business incubator are not far away here: a home-base, shared with like-minded in similar situations, venture capitalist and business angels "swarming," and society bestowing super-hero qualities on anyone labelled entrepreneur, whereas the big corporate organization still have trouble hosting them. Rather than such a conventional entrepreneurship research interpretation, our study tries to shift focus to the play element. The fun, the ambiguous, the grey, vague, yellow light, the proposal to "act as if."

This is how we get to renew the understanding of entrepreneurship's in-between: as an opening, a white canvas, where the lack of a structuring centre allows for free movement. Such movement, like dancing, is driven by folly, by trying out and experimenting, as an exercise of freedom. This is the reward from having gone astray, affirmed chance, and the necessity of chance. This is becoming as a transmutation, as an overcoming of what is for the benefit of what could become. Assembling people through play opens for affect to direct a sense of where there is an agreement between bodies, where the capacity to create is increased and where the proto-organizational form of assemblage can make actualization of the virtual more incipient.

Playing has to affirm the playful in order to achieve playing. It has to affirm chance (as Nietzsche emphasized)[57] and in this way be "absorbed in occupying its field of potential."[58] If playing is indeed about intensification of the open-ended, if it has dared to affirm chance, we have now brought the entrepreneurial process to a state where it needs to "land," where it needs to figure out how the opening of possibilities can also be brought into an actualization of the new that beds into what already exists: it has to work within the context of the human practice the entrepreneur wishes to affect. Creation, as a making-actual of the virtually real. "The virtual," Massumi elaborates, "the pressing crowd of incipiencies and tendencies, is a realm of potential."[59] The incipient is brought about by intensity, which is what playing is about. Playing, as an affirmation of chance, makes us become, absorbed in occupying our field of potential. We experience the intense, which is incipience, and the incipient presses up against action and it is here that play has to yield to something more than play, to what we call common sense.[60]

Notes

1 Deleuze, G. (2006) *Nietzsche & Philosophy,* New York: Columbia University Press, p. 26. Deleuze takes inspiration from Nietzsche's metaphor of the sky being a space for dancing.

2 Deleuze equates Nietzsche's style to a romantic form of pluralism: his genealogical method was one of bringing into questionability just how certain institutional structures (such as established moral principles) had arisen, and by showing this t be an historical process, he reveals the non-natural and hence negotiable nature of these principles – they can always be otherwise. Value emerges from processes of evaluation, if the processes shift, so do the values, from actual back to virtual. There is a distinction in literary form that Deleuze picks up on in Nietzsche, the aphorism is used when we are ruminating over the form that sense (common) takes, how it emerges as that which is agreed upon. Whereas the poem is directed more towards an enquiry into value and the evaluation process. See also Colebrook, C. (2002) *Gilles Deleuze,* London and New York: Routledge, p. 60.

3 Ibid., p. 101.

4 Interestingly enough, the Latin origin describes this in terms very similar to how we would describe a successful entrepreneur today, i.e. not only as one that creates but one that also makes things grow: from Latin *auctor* "promoter, producer, father, progenitor; builder, founder; trustworthy writer, authority; historian; performer, doer; responsible person, teacher," literally "one who causes to grow," (Oxford English Dictionary, available at: etymonline.com, accessed November 2020).

5 This particular quality, however, the capacity to share advice and support the development of the other by overspilling from one's own archive of experiences, seems never to have left Deleuze as a style of writing and relating to his readers. May witness that the experience of reading Deleuze is like receiving a gentle nudge, a push in the back, supporting a forward movement in thinking. He finds lines of flight that transgress what is there, but which remains utterly dependent on it.

6 His technique in philosophical thought was to write through others, in their company – Hume, Spinoza, Nietzsche, Francis bacon, and in repeat their thinking find and move beyond the limits they had set for themselves.

7 Deleuze, G. (1995) *Negotiations*, New York: Columbia University Press.

8 Hjorth, D., Holt, R., and Steyaert, C. (2015) "Entrepreneurship and Process Studies," *International Small Business Journal*, 33(6): 599–611.

9 See Bydén, B. and Thörnqvist, C.T. (Eds.) (2017) *The Aristotelian Tradition: Aristotle's Works on Logic and Metaphysics and Their Reception in the Middle Ages*, Turnhout: Brepols; Russell, D.L. (2000) "Pippi Longstocking and the Subversive Affirmation of Comedy," *Children's Literature in Education*, 31(3): 167–177.

10 Lindgren, A. (1950 [1978]) *Pippi Longstocking*, Transl. Florence Lamborn, New York: Puffin, p. 40.

11 Winnicott, D.W. (1971) *Playing and Reality*, London: Tavistock Publications. Reisner, G. (2019) "Ghosted and Ancestral Selves in Hamlet: Loewald's 'Present Life' and Winnicott's 'Potential Space' in Shakespeare's Play," *Journal of the American Psychoanalytic Association*, 67(3): 455–484.

12 The tactical and strategic in referring to Michel de Certeau's discussion in *The Practice of Everyday Life* (1984); see discussed by Colebrook, C. (2002) in "Certeau and Foucault: Tactics and Strategic Essentialism," *South Atlantic Quarterly*, 100(2): 543–574.

13 Massumi, B. (2002) *Parables for the Virtual – Movement, Affect, Sensation*, Durham and London: Duke University Press, p. 242.

14 Hjorth, D. (2015) Sketching a Philosophy of Entrepreneurship. In T. Baker & F. Welter (Eds.) *The Routledge Companion to Entrepreneurship*, London and New York: Routledge, pp. 41–58.

15 Cervantes had Sancho Panza that pulled Don Quixote back to earth.

16 From Lindgren, A. (1950) *Pippi Longstocking*, Transl. F. Lamborn, New York: The Viking Press, pp. 28–29.

17 Battilana, J., Leca, B., and Boxenbaum, E. (2009) "How Actors Change Institutions: Towards a Theory of Institutional Entrepreneurship," *The Academy of Management Annals*, 3(1): 65–107; Aldrich, H.E. and Fiol, C.M. (1994) "Fools Rush in the Institutional Context of Industry Creation," *Academy of Management Review*, 19(4): 645–670; Garud, R., Hardy, C., and Maguire, S. (2007) "Institutional Entrepreneurship as Embedded Agency: An Introduction to the Special Issue," *Organization Studies*, 28(7): 957–969.

18 Berger, P. and Luckmann, T. (1967) *The Social Construction of Reality*, London: Penguin; Burrell, G. and Morgan, G. (1979) *Sociological Paradigms and Organizational Analysis*, Portsmouth: Hinemann Educational Books; Giddens, A. (1984), *The Constitution of Society*, Berkeley and Los Angeles: California University Press; Bourdieu, P. (1977) *Outline of a Theory of Practice*, Cambridge: Cambridge University Press.

19 Garud, R. and Karnøe, P. (2003) "Bricolage vs. Breakthrough: Distributed and Embedded Agency in Technology Entrepreneurship," *Research Policy*, 32: 277–300.

20 Garud, R., Hardy, C., and Maguire, S. (2007) "Institutional Entrepreneurship as Embedded Agency: An Introduction to the Special Issue," *Organization Studies*, 28(07): 957–969.

21 An engaging study of this is found in Fisher, G., Stevenson, R., Neubert, E., Burnell, D., and Kuratko, D.F. (2020) "Entrepreneurial Hustle: Navigating

Uncertainty and Enrolling Venture Stakeholders through Urgent and Unorthodox Action," *Journal of Management Studies*, 57: 1002–1036.

22 Massumi, B. (2015) *The Power at the End of the Economy*, Durham and London: Duke University Press.

23 De Certeau, M. (1984) *The Practice of Everyday Life*, Berkeley, Los Angeles, and London: University of California Press, pp. 36–37.

24 Hjorth, D. and Steyaert, C. (2006) American psucho/European schizo: Stories of Managerial Elites in a Hundred Images. In P. Gagliardi & B. Czarniawska (Eds.), *Management Education and Humanities*, Cheltenham: Edward Elgar, pp. 67–97.

25 Lambert, G. (2000) On the Uses and Abuses of Literature for Life. In I. Buchanan & J. Marks (Eds.), *Deleuze and Literature*, Edinburgh: Edinburgh University Press, p. 163.

26 Derrida, J. (1978) *Writing and Difference*, London: Routledge, p. 278.

27 Vattimo calls these fablings, events that are made in imaginative engagement with stories that enlist others in would-be projects. See G. Vattimo (1992) *The Transparent Society*, New York: John Hopkins University Press, p. 25.

28 Gaare, J. and Sjaastad, Ø. (2002) *Pippi och Sokrates* [*Pippi and Socrates*], Stockholm: Natur och Kultur.

29 Gaare, J. and Sjaastad, Ø. (2002) *Pippi och Sokrates* [*Pippi and Socrates*], Stockholm: Natur och Kultur, p. 96. Sweden, somewhat contentiously, did not wrestle with Adolf, and Finland, for complex geo-political rather than dogmatic reasons, even ended up siding with the Nazi's for a while. So it was left to the pages of a child's book to imagine how a fight against the majoritarian Nazi forces might unfold.

30 Deleuze, G. (2006) *Nietzsche & Philosophy*, Transl. H. Tomlinson, New York: Columbia University Press, p. 26.

31 Nietzsche, F. (1961) *Thus Spoke Zarathustra*, Transl. R.J. Hollingdale, London: Penguin, p. 194.

32 Woolf, V. (2012) *Mrs Dalloway*, London: Penguin Essentials, opening chapter.

33 As discussed in Deleuze's portrait of Foucault in the conversation book *Negotiations*: Deleuze, G. (1995) *Negotiations – Gilles Deleuze*, New York: Columbia University Press, p. 116.

34 Woolf, V. (2012) *Mrs Dalloway*, London: Penguin Books, p. 122.

35 Björkman, I. (1998) *Sven Duchamp – Expert på Auraproduktion: om Entreprenörskap, visioner, konst och företag*, [*Sven Duchamp – Expert on Auraproduction: About Entrepreneurship, Visions, Art and Business*], Stockholm: Stockholm University Press (dissertation).

36 Kuspit, D. (1993) *The Cult of the Avant-Garde Artist*, New York: Cambridge University Press, p. 166. This is from an interview in 1952 with interviewer Giovanni Papini, published Libero nero (reported in Brink, A. (2007) *Desire and Avoidance in Art: Pablo Picasso, Hans Bellmer, Balthus, and Joseph Cornell*, New York: Peter Lang, p. 60).

37 Massumi, B. (2002) *Parables for the Virtual – Movement, Affect, Sensation*, Durham and London: Duke University Press, p. 136.

38 Woolf, V. (2012) *Mrs Dalloway*, London: Penguin Books, p. 173.

39 Massumi, B. (2002) *Parables for the Virtual – Movement, Affect, Sensation*, Durham and London: Duke University Press, p. 76.

40 Woolf, V. (2012) *Mrs Dalloway*, London: Penguin Books, p. 176.

41 Ibid., p. 263.
42 Kirkeby, O.F. (2004) "Eventum Tantum: To Make the World Worthy of What Could Happen to It," *Ephemera*, 4(3): 290–308.
43 See e.g. Lane, A., Mallett, O., and Wapshott, R. (2019) "Failure and Entrepreneurship: Practice, Research and Pedagogy," *Journal of Small Business & Entrepreneurship*, 31(1): 97–99; Lerner, J. and Malmendier, U. (2013) "With a Little Help from My (Random) Friends: Success and Failure in Post-Business School Entrepreneurship," *Review of Financial Studies*, 26(10): 2411–2452.
44 Wicke, J. (1994) "Mrs Dalloway Goes to Market: Woolf, Keynes, and Modern Markets," *Novel*, Fall: 5–23.
45 O'Donnell (now Hessel), S. (2013) *Making Ensemble Possible: How Special Groups Organize for Collaborative Creativity in Conditions of Spatial Variability and Distance,* Copenhagen: Copenhagen Business School, PhD Series 7.2013.
46 Ibid., p. 14.
47 Vattimo, G. (1992) *The Transparent Society*, Baltimore: Johns Hopkins University Press, p. 59. or liquid, as suggested by Zygmunt Bauman's analysis of post/modernity: Bauman, Z. (2000) *Liquid Modernity*, Cambridge: Polity Press.
48 Björkman, I. (1998) *Sven Duchamp – expert på auraproduktion*, Stockholm: Företagsekonomiska Institutionen, PhD thesis.
49 Wicke, J., 1994, p. 15.
50 Ibid., p. 21.
51 Ibid., p. 21.
52 McCraw, T. (2009) *Profet of Innovation: Joseph Schumpeter and Creative Destruction,* Cambridge and London: The Belknap Press of Harvard University Press.
53 Krueger, N.F. (June 1, 2005) From Keynes' "Animal Spirits" to Human Spirits Passion as the Missing Link in Entrepreneurial Intentions, available at SSRN: https://ssrn.com/abstract=1162337
54 Huizinga explicitly pointed out that it was the play element of culture and not in culture that he was analyzing. Yet, the English translation insisted on using "in" instead of "of." The argument was more that it sounded better to the English ear, in spite of the logically correct "of."
55 The Italian poet Filippo Tommaso Marinetti had just published the Manifesto del Futurismo (1909), praising the mechanization and speed that came with modernization.
56 Cf. Massumi, B. (2002) *Parables for the Virtual – Movement, Affect, Sensation,* Durham and London: Duke University Press, pp. 231–232.
57 Deleuze, G. (2006) *Nietzsche and Philosophy,* New York: Columbia University Press, p. 170.
58 Massumi, B. (2002) *Parables for the Virtual – Movement, Affect, Sensation,* Durham and London: Duke University Press. Massumi is in this quote defining what movement in process is: "It has withdrawn into an all-encompassing relation with what it will be. It is in becoming, absorbed in occupying its field of potential." (Massumi, 2002: 7).
59 Ibid., p. 30.
60 Ibid., p. 30.

7 Organization-creation
Common sense

In the wake of Romantic spirit, the author's role was to struggle to find in life the mandates for its own order, to reach and find form from within the straggling and twisting tendrils of everyday experience. With only the fragments of action and thought to play with, these organizational attempts at realizing a common sense are riddled with the experiences of doubt and attempts at cross-examination that novels are so effective at detailing. In part these literary elaborations of common sense are little more a carapace of civilized language and artifice, and in part the realization of a second order, critical fair mindedness to which all conventions become subject.[1]

It is in common sense that the agitations of seduction and play settle back, and find an order that, to use Schumpeter's term, structures events in such a way that things actually happen: the idea becomes a venture; the novelty becomes a set of performative commitments. Common sense tends towards habit and consensus; a prevailing way of doing things to which one has to appeal if a project or idea is to gain traction in practice. It appears as a constraining force which, in Spinoza's terms, would be described as a disagreement between forces greater than your own, meaning one's own productive capacity for generating and acting on ideas is diminished – a Spinozian sadness as reality gets in the way.

Yet another way of understanding common sense is of taking the prevailing, socially verified agreed actions, thoughts, and feelings as *simultaneously representing opportunity-creating conditions* because they are to be treated not just as prescriptions, but also provocations. There is an obvious economy of making use of what is already in place as common sense. There is less friction, fewer transaction costs, and minimal disturbance vis-a-vis the dominant social norm-structure and its immanent order. Indeed, this is the reason why organization, structure, routine/habit, and practices are developed: they absorb the load of always having to act/feel and think for oneself. Yet the load-bearing convenience is itself a risk to a sense held in common if, in becoming habit, it restricts sense to a mono-dimensional pattern in which only one version of the virtual is being actualized practice. Without sense being held

DOI: 10.4324/9781315714455-10

critically – that is, subject to second-order revision – tradition ossifies and dies. To hold sense in common is to expose it to the forces of differentiation that allow for its revision and possible transformation. To survive, what is normal has to be inscribed in repeat passages, in attempts at taking it on, in applications, that have within them the possibility of upset and transgression. It is this aspect of common sense that resonates with the entrepreneurial process, which we might understand as a continual attempt at rigging action to make "concerted connections in fictional anticipation of actual actionable value potentials."[2] Entrepreneurship, when actualizing the virtual, differentiates it from what is already in place, by exploring potential-to-be (actual). This happens in the context of "what already exists," and so understanding common sense – what passes as convention – is a grounding aspect of entrepreneurial understanding, for only then can it be altered, finessed, enriched, toyed with, splintered, and changed.

Thus, in a curious way, entrepreneurship is intimately acquainted with common sense. It is precisely the limit of the possible, the boundary of action, the domain proper of the dominant strategy in contexts of organizations that represents the opportunity-to-be-created in the entrepreneurial process. In entrepreneurship there is a necessary and profound reliance upon and engagement with common sense. It is by belonging to communities and being embroiled in their agreements, and by being intensely and intimately so, that a particular escape route or flight line – a new becoming – emerges as incipient. It is only through a deep familiarity with human practices that the limits can be made explicit, and in being made explicit, breached, simply by the fact of bringing them into critical view (the critical fair-mindedness we ascribe to the novel). We believe this intimacy with common sense to be central to entrepreneurship wherever we find it, but perhaps most it is clearly manifest in what is often called social entrepreneurship. Indeed, on the question of what is "social" in social entrepreneurship we would not only point to the effect of enhanced possibilities for human flourishing, but also to the creation of such possibilities, as being consequent upon an intimate familiarity and understanding of common sense.

Common sense is what abounds in the disclosive style to which Spinosa, Flores, and Dreyfus attest when they talk of entrepreneurial processes as those pertaining to new spaces that are disclosed from within existing ones. Entrepreneurial disclosure animates and excites experiences of belonging, refusing to allow the habituated and managed to settle into unquestioned patterns of economized comfort. What is described by physicists as friction, or economists as transaction cost, here loses out as an object of concern to curiosity, and the urge to create that satisfies it. The friction being "spent" in order for a transaction to happen is simply misrepresented by the economists' concept "cost" here. It is perhaps better to use concepts such as "warmth," "excitement," drawn from a friction that is energy not wasted (again, "waste" being a mis-representing economic concept) but rather added to the surroundings. This is exactly what makes this situational common sense warm to the idea that the virtual could actually become actualized. The incipient receives a "pull" from a social expectation that it is "about to happen." Such a "pull" is the result of an intimacy with the normal, with habit and common sense, and it is playing with this knowledge that enables the entrepreneurial process to disclose novelty.

Schumpeter reserved for entrepreneurship the creative response and the creative destruction that follows from it. This is an action that takes the actor outside "the range of existing practice."[3] Elsewhere he used the phrase "outside the pale of routine," which indicates that entrepre-neurship is not there to pay homage to made investments.[4] Notably, in Schumpeter's conceptualization, entrepreneurship places us in the realm of the virtual, the potential, where fiction guides action: "... it cannot be predicted by applying the ordinary rules of inference from the pre-existing facts."[5] Thus, the question of how this happens, Schumpeter suggests, must be investigated in each case. This is an economist that talks about a science of the particular, the specific, of imaginations.[6] Via Schumpeter, our language of the entrepreneurial is thus brought into an intimacy with the language of imagination of the literary.

Disclosure through common sense is described by Greenblatt as a lived phenomenon to which literature is especially drawn:

> poetry, drama, and prose fiction play themselves out in the everyday world, since men and women repeatedly find themselves in effect speaking the language of the literary not only in their public performances but also in their most intimate or passionate moments.[7]

In speaking this language intensely, and with consideration, authors, notably those of a Romantic disposition, work themselves up to the edges of convention, and find there a space to thrive, as do entrepreneurs, a space where the many stories of the real and of what "is not but could be" are entangled.

It is to following and unfolding these entanglements that novels are often devoted. Literature is a language that thrives in this in-between space in which the limits of common sense are flexed in ambiguities and can buckle. It is, as Deleuze said about Proust, the writer's work to invent, within language, a new language (one is reminded here of Pippi's penchant for inventing new words, one's, she suggests, that the scientists have failed to invent, but should have), a foreign language that extends the realm of the possible and actual, to "force language outside its customary furrows,"[8] and so which speak "outside the pale of routine."

Elizabeth Bennet

Literature is full of characters that live on and struggle with the limits of common sense, and Jane Austen's Elizabeth Bennett is foremost amongst them. Bennett's sophistication is woven into an almost childish delight in tactically insinuating herself into situations. Her social acumen is far from instinctual: indeed it is continually being announced through explicit attempts at understanding and complying with the prevailing style. In some subtle form, this resembles the idea of economy, since her proper behaviour is designed to avoid friction: taste is seamless, quiet, confidently invisible. Yet Bennet is not uncritical, indeed she goes out of her way to subject situations to ethical questioning, often going out of her way to do the right thing. Not the quickest or easiest thing, but what is correct, expected, and of good sense for everyone in an assembled company whose equanimity she sees as her personal responsibility to secure:

> Elizabeth, on her side, had much to do. She wanted to ascertain the feelings of each of her visitors; she wanted to compose her own, and to make herself agreeable to all; and in the latter object, where she feared most to fail, she was most sure of success, for those to whom she endeavoured to give pleasure were prepossessed in her favour. Bingley was ready, Georgiana was eager, and Darcy determined, to be pleased.
>
> Of Mr Darcy it was now a matter of anxiety to think well; and, as far as their acquaintance reached, there was no fault to find. They could not be untouched by his politeness.[9]

She has acceded to common sense and was to find Darcy willing to fall in too. "To make herself agreeable" is in one sense a reference to economic efficiency, the one that adapts to the environment to reduce friction, but it is also, of course, an outcome of the mentioned desire to please and live up to expectations, rather than to save costs. Bennet becomes so attentive to reducing friction to then save other's pain, to be agreeable, to stimulate conversation, all of which rely on her continually calibrating a set of relationships ethically, socially, and culturally. It is also here that common sense appears as a source of Bennet's opportunity-creation.[10] The work of trying to please is, of course, deep down, her attempt at creating a complex set of relationships and affects, the result of which might be to bring about relations in which the match of one with another becomes natural, indeed unquestionable. There is a loosening of the subject here, a falling in with subjection, but only insofar as it is required to better execute an ethical and aesthetic process of bending forces back upon themselves with a degree of finesse and respect that serve to individuate her, as a figure in possession of style (as opposed to vice versa).[11] Bennet's is a partly voluntary (and partly disciplined) subjection that has to come into place in repeated performances that mark her out, not as unique, but uniquely (because skilfully) aligned with ever-shifting situations. Following Deleuze's distinction between isolating a subject as a given thing and tracing the processes of producing subjectivity, Bennet is very much of the latter form, her organizational skill

> is no longer a matter of determinate forms, as with knowledge, or of constraining rules, as with power: it's a matter of optional rules that make existence a work of art, rules at once ethical and aesthetic that constitute ways of existing or styles of life.[12]

Her subjectification is event-based, bringing about certain intensities in which individuation happens: the appropriately behaving woman in relation to her suitor(s), and others. Again, it is precisely because this is not a question of morality, not a question of constraining rules, but the ethical challenge of judging how to act in relation to a set of suggestive rules, that it is also an aesthetic process of forming the self. There is thus also a risk involved in Bennet's coming forth into a force-form constellation in which she is subjectified into events that demand conduct which is abeyant to convention, but not slavishly so, and which in turn requires others are likewise disposed. There is risk and thus a shivering of the body, a falling into a relationship that relies on the fact that the other knows how to respond accordingly, how to catch the fall without showing it (thus gracefully doing so). If this dance happens in a reciprocal manner, a piece of art has been achieved, a social sculpture (as Joseph Beuys would say) that has as its idealized form the emblematic "fit-for-each-other" of the couple.

The risks of boorish pomposity and stiffly confined relations are very real, and Bennett is on constant guard against an array of social forces that Nietzsche was to associate with the "higher men." The "higher men," in Nietzsche's philosophy of becoming, are the reactive people, those who seek to control and therefore favour common sense because it enforces a stable set of interests and architecture of power. The higher men are pinned down, either by bad conscience (it is my fault), by ressentiment (it is your fault), or by nihilism (will to nothingness), and they pin others down with them. Bennet's disposition is to enquire into and negotiate the pinions, and to find the places where, amid all this fixing and solidifying, there is room for collective expression in which each subject, in coming alive to a common sensibility, also realizes that it is they who must acknowledge, in their ordinary activity, what passes for truth.[13] Convention is nothing if it is not lived out, and in being lived out it can be taken on, toyed with, stretched, in ways that make it agreeable to all.

Perhaps she is assigning to herself an impossible task? She seeks to rise above the social protocol, but without standing out as a victor, or indeed as anyone notable. The higher men are, after all, a stiff and joyless bunch to which it is difficult to make appeal:

> There are things higher man does not know how to do: to laugh, to play and to dance. To laugh is to affirm life, even the suffering in life. To play is to affirm chance and the necessity of chance. To dance is to affirm becoming and the being of becoming.[14]

In Bennet's world, the jockeying for positions in the game of finding/ matching a partner in marriage makes common sense a synonym for being pleasing and agreeable to one's prospective partner. The dilemma Bennet feels is how this positioning prescribes a curious form of active passivity to the female, and in refusing this role she is marking herself out, not least in the daring act of declaring herself an equal to Mr Darcy, the prospective partner, and in full expectation that he should (and will) accede to her judgement of equality.

It is precisely because she has such detailed insight and keen sense of the convention she inherits and which has etched itself into her very posture, that she is able to transgress slightly, and without undue opposition. This is, we argue, precisely the point with knowing and understanding common sense – it opens up avenues for tactically transforming majoritarian forces without its being an energy-sapping opposition; she acts in a minor key, as it were.[15] The minor language draws upon the majoritarian language but makes it leak from the margins, pulls it away from its conforming, controlling centrum by multiplying the possible and destabilizing the reigning order by making it move. And here we should note that Austen is authorizing quietly, through Bennet, a newly emerging subject, a new "becoming-woman": "[T]he ultimate aim of literature is to release this creation of a health or this invention of a people – that is, a possibility of life – in the delirium. To write for this people that is missing ..."[16]

Bennet is no radical: she is acutely sensitive to how others regard her situation, and for much of the book she tries in vain to compensate for the flaws she perceives in others to whom she feels bonded, notably her feckless sister Lydia and gossiping mother. And the disdain she has for Darcy is directed less towards the opinion he evidently has of her, than for the manner in which he makes it apparent. As the book unfolds, however, we find Bennet beginning to find moments in which these governing orders of behaviour and opinion flex, indeed moments where they yield altogether, to reveal mutual feelings whose honesty and integrity are ensured because of their having survived social convention.[17] Bennet has patience, she waits, she is so completely enamoured of the rules of common sense that she can outclass anyone of any class because of this capacity to work from within the demands of a situation, the manners. In Deleuze's terms, she minorizes the majoritarian language of conduct in a splendid manner since she excels in her knowledge of it whilst not working for the centre, the majority, but towards the margin, towards transformation.

So delightful is Bennet's capacity to fall in with them that others cannot but fail to feel affected, and her affection elicits affect, expanding the cheerfulness and sociality of those with whom she is in commerce. Her critique is always launched from within, from within an intimate knowledge and awareness of the laws of the situation. Her sociality provides space, one that resonates somewhat with the douceur of commerce extoled by Hirschman, but which nevertheless is more than the easily contained, gendered neatness, calmness, and sweetness.[18] Bennett is more than a convivial sapper, more than an embodiment of politesse.

To recall Kierkegaard's terms Bennet's actions are both aesthetic in their attempt to create and sustain pleasure and happiness, yet they begin to touch on the ethical, as she is transgressive. It is her capacity to be mannered, to commit to the assigned role of woman of her station with such a degree of self-examined intensity that it becomes something refined and lures Darcy in, tired as he is too of the higher men in whose company he circulates. Bennet and Darcy should not be together, but they are, something has gone astray. It should not happen. Yet it did, much to the chagrin of Lady Catherine Debeer and her ilk. So how has Bennet been able, or Darcy, as he too transgresses? Yet perfectly and indisputably it is done in the proper way, it is ethical, and it bears the weight of common sense with equanimity.

Bennet shows it is not always the breaking of common sense that enables opportunity to emerge, but, rather, a sustained and examined conformity to its possibilities. She experiments with its depths with such intensity that it shines and others are entranced, pleased, and want to be pleased. They are affected utterly. This can be understood as part of Austen's way of critiquing patriarchy without stirring up counter-reactions doing so.[19] There is a revolt against the inherited conventions. But also the revolt – in Austen's as well as in Bennet's tactics – is done with such precision and awareness that it easily passes as performance that will not do other than confirm convention. There is a sense in which Austen, via the character of Bennet, dresses social criticism in the garb of respectability and conformity.

Again, we find this indicative as an example of an entrepreneurial tactic that precisely tries to avoid stirring up counter-acts from those with majoritarian power on their side, and instead make use of the cracks and openings in the strategic grids.[20] The entrepreneurial often works itself into the ethical, in disturbing habits delivers a form of social and civic opening up, one whose very uncertainty maintains its credentials, at least insofar as the openness is one of minor critique.[21]

As we have briefly shown above, Gilles Deleuze's work on minorization assists our analysis of how Bennet would be part of a critique that subtly transforms the dynamics between the majority and minority in the contemporary English society. Minorization makes use, in a surprising way, of the majoritarian language, the language of the dominant conception, the roles and identities and the limited range of pre-fabricated choices. Minorization describes the formation of conditions for movement; the arrangement of social forces that makes new becomings possible. Minorization would describe how Bennet would avoid being reduced into a particular role or character in her way of playfully playing the majoritarian game. In operating with the resources already provided by the majoritarian forces – the higher men – minorization brings language against and so beyond itself and so in repetition forces it into patterns of difference that then upset and corrupt the dominant strategies to which, ostensibly, it continues to subscribe.[22]

The unequal system in which Bennet "operates" allows her to resist the perfect marriage as an act within limits of the possible. This confirms the rules of the game and makes her a prominent "player." At the same time this becomes a flight line that points ahead towards what she could become. The resistance *should* properly have led up to an act of finally giving in to the perfectness of this marriage, which is also the act of submission to the patriarchal dominance and the normalcy thereof. This would only have fortified the norms of the higher men. Without struggle no glory; so she should have resisted, and then given in. Instead, Bennet's entrepreneurial moment arises in her working the other way, going into convention so deeply, so ethically, as Kierkegaard would have it, that it disturbs the surface-dwelling majority to the point they must exercise power against themselves (in the act of Darcy's transgression), thereby revealing, in a surprising way, that ultimately, "power is exercised only over free subjects, and only insofar as they are free."[23]

Chichikov

Ostensibly, the dead souls in Nikolai Gogol's novel are the serfs who have died, but institutionally remain alive because their deaths have not been reported to the authorities. Figuratively, the dead souls invoke an enslaved people, a people lacking the material, social and intellectual means to reconfigure their parlous condition as the raw material for aristocratic cruelty and administrative incompetence. Where Austen is reserved, and perhaps even negligent, in disguising the conventional abuses perpetrated by inherited power, Gogol is ruthless. He writes of a world so hollowed out by indifference, corruption, and arrogance that what passes for common sense is better configured as a survival manual than as a guide to civilized manners.

Like Bennet, Chichikov, the hero of Gogol's novel, is well acquainted with common sense, though now what passes as habitual convention is less assured, less confident, less agreeable: the "higher men" are no longer so high, indeed they are clinging on, their bureaucracy is crumbling and the intensifying stupidity and cruelty of the social system over which they preside have become a harbinger of revolutionary fervour. Chichikov, a mid-ranking bureaucrat, similar in station to Bennet, is frustrated bureaucrat, educated and with administrative skills yet constantly held back from what he felt was his rightful advancement. He has discovered, by chance, an anomaly in the census system, and has set out to exploit it. His carriage and bearing, like those of Don Giovanni, are of a well-established, culturally competent person. In each town he visits the officials in the local burghers in control of the paper processes, who he befriends and wins over with a rhetoric steeped in pathos, an awareness that is often gathered around food and drink. The mayors, the judges, the record keepers are all entranced by the novelty, the change, and the difference that the arrival of this well turned out man with his small assembly of servants bring. Chichikov's swagger is infectious. He deliberately chooses small, backward towns in which he can make an impression, and once inveigled into their lives he asks after local landowners to whom he gets introductions. His pathos extends to these aristocratic figures, attempting to ingratiate himself and win their ear. This can take minutes, or hours, and only when he feels ready does he then make his absurd request. "Have you reported your list of dead serfs to the town council?" If not, he offers to make the report himself, offering them a service. The government taxed landowners on the basis of how many serfs they owned, yet gathering these figures was always a cumbersome and lagging process, largely on account of the landowners failing to update their lists. Chichikov exploits this laziness and oversight, offering to intercede on their behalf, but in doing so also requests they sell them, these dead souls, for he has need of them:

> "You're asking for what purpose? The purpose is this: I would like to purchase the peasants ...," said Chichikov, then began to stammer and did not finish what he was saying.
> "But permit me to ask you," said Manilov, "how do you wish to purchase the peasants, with land or simply to take them away, that is, without land?"
> "No, what I'm referring to is not exactly peasants," said Chichikov. "I wish to have the dead ones ..."
> "Wha-a-t? Pardon me ... I'm a little hard of hearing, I thought I heard a very strange word ..."
> "I propose to acquire the dead ones, which, however, would still be carried on the census as living," said Chichikov.[24]

He is careful to present his proposition as a form of cleaning up and caring, reminding the owners of their troubling administrative duty to report deaths, and offering to take on the duty himself, much like a consultancy. However, his is a rather dubious, not to say outright fraudulent, move that exploits a glitch in the system. The owners are persuaded to sell because they receive money for what they relate to as exhausted assets. Chichikov does not offer them much, but it is, they suspect, better than nothing, and it relieves them of administrative burdens. What they do not realize (though some suspect him of some trickery) is that once the ownership is transferred, Chichikov can use "his" serfs as collateral for loans to then purchase land and become a landowner, "as if" he owned real serfs.[25] He has to act quickly, however, as he is legally required to register the dead serfs within a year of their death, so his paper assets have a sell by date. Hence, his scheme is a rather precise exploitation of system limits. He has identified an "entre-space" in-between the land-owner and the government system, and in entering that space the time gap between the dead serfs and registering them becomes an opportunity.

The dead souls he is buying represent a classic case of an opportunity being created; he is buying a fictitious thing, an absence, and much in the way modern financial markets work he is able to convince systems that these things carry value, at least for as long as he needs them to, then to use these possessions to gain further advantage. The dead are being animated but retain the unique quality of being frictionless, thereby over-coming the inertia of the physical markets where live serfs had problems and were problems with their needs and gripes and feckless lack of prod-uctivity had to be dealt with by their owner. In the physical economy the serfs-used physical resources were heavy; in Chichikov's economy of the dead, the serfs were unalloyed assets without demand. He could put thousands into his pocket and walk off with a non-chalant whistle. People debated how he would move them all to his newly bought piece of land in the south, a land that also did not have a river or a pond, and offered him help. He of course refused to accept such assistance, as this would reveal that there was no such problem of physical resources. Therein lies an important part of his innovation; he had made a phys-ical resource, full of friction and bodily constraints and limitation into an intangible asset that did not weigh more than a piece of paper in his pocket. There is nothing possible to realize, with all its practical challenges of adjusting to circumstances. He actualizes a virtuality by creating the hitherto unheard of in-between opportunity – to use unregis-tered dead serfs as solid collateral for a bank loan that funded his pur-chase of land.

Despite the complete absence of things, he is still able to create a flourishing market through a supremely entrepreneurial act that is predicated upon and sustained by desire. Much like Iago, Chichikov connects desires so that a proto-organizational form is emerging; an assemblage held together by this desire.[26] The transaction here is one of desire. The desire of the landowner to ease their life from bureaucratic hassle, and earning some money on the side. The desire of Chichikov to gain assets and so establish himself in higher echelons of society to which he enviously feels drawn. The desire of the town-folks looking for a local hero, one that they can talk about and one they can attribute their wishes on. Nothing is being traded here, in both senses: there is no material thing, yet a nothing (dead soul) exists to trade by way of ownership title.

Whereas Bennet follows the line drawn by common sense and explores its contours intensely in order to understand precisely how to follow it, and how to "transformatively" resist it, Chichikov is following the lines with the explicit purpose of actualizing a potential "hole." He does not need to perforate or breach the limits because his intricate knowledge of the bureaucratic system has imagined an opportunity that can be actualized. Chichikov's strength, in echo of Romanticism, is that he is as much *in* the life of common sense as he is aware *of* common sense. There is a social (and thus also economic) risk associated with this, for in poking and prodding the shakily maintained corpus of common sense knowledge, looking for places where it might still offer a yield, makes others aware that something is afoot. His scheme works because he senses the frustration and laziness in owners, he is alive to their resenting having to record and report on their activity. He also correctly reads their greed, their desire to make something for minimal effort. In correctly reading this common sense amongst the aristocrats he guesses rightly that they will always look to outsource their duty to others, whilst looking for reward. Yet caution is needed, for it is precisely the same qualities of resentment and greed that cast the serf-owning classes into an atmosphere of condescending suspicion. In some the condescension is dominant, and they look at Chichikov as a fool quickly parting from his money, and these he could exploit:

> Chichikov's purchases became a subject of conversation. Gossip went around town, opinions, discussions of whether it was profitable ... [---] All this gossip and discussion produced, however, as favorable a result as Chichikov could possibly have looked for. Namely, the rumor spread that he was no more nor less than a millionaire.[27]

Chichikov has a certain style and his swagger does work in his favour as he becomes a landowner after having conducted his business and fraternized with the important people in the city. Indeed, at the point where he is believed to be in fact a wealthy man, he is imagined to be someone of importance.

There are some though, who are more cautious in their welcome, and as much as Chichikov's scheming is catalysed in the compromising murmur of town gossip, it is also exposed. The exposure begins at a party that had ironically been arranged to honour the purchase of his "serfs," and event that is read by the guests as overstepping the mark. As a newcomer of unknown origin Chichikov should have resisted the urge for conspicuous display, he should have continued to fit in invisibly a whilst longer. With a party he was flaunting his wealth, and himself, which then made him the subject of some resentment. Just how did he come by his money? One questioning comment morphs into another as it passes through tongues and ears, each intensifying in query as how such a rapid ascent in status had been possible. Before long, the talk is of Chichikov being a philanderer scheming to seduce and elope with the Mayor's daughter, and people begin to compare notes as to just how many serfs had been bought, from whom, and why.

Chichikov has to run from the town. His mistake had been to treat it like a safe space in which to settle, rather than move through and onwards, always into open seas, he had attempted to treat the town as though it was a safe port, and in seeking refuge he had lingered long enough for the indigenous people to grow suspicious, to question his right to be there, and to turn against him. In hindsight he should have kept to the liminal spaces, to the in-between of the sea, and to look for new harbours and new business, again and again, pursuing a flight line, always leaving shore. Life in the harbour is comfortable, economized, heavy with the discursive structures upon which Chickov's fabulating can riff, but to which he can never belong.[28] Chichikov's line of flight is shut down by the party, he had stayed too long.

Having been found out, Chichikov's wandering is no longer kindled by fabulation, he is not seeking adventure, rather he is being forced by convention to hide. He has to move on, avoid the mob, and seek refuge in adding distance between him and his shattered scheme: the line between innovation and failure is a thin one. His scheme exploited common sense, but then betrayed it. The betrayal begins at the very moment of proposing the deal: his offer for dead souls so defies common sense that he stuns the interlocutor and creates an element of surprise. In this interim moment between buying the dead souls and registering them as dead he becomes a figure who, on paper, is one of considerable property on the back of which he is able to impress others, raise finance, and win standing. Yet unlike Bennett, who is able to transform common sense, Chichikov has simply exploited it, temporarily, and has done so whilst remaining thoroughly subjectified to prevailing norms (financial reward, social standing). There has been cunning, but the world has not changed in any irreversible way, new space has not been disclosed, indeed the mendacity and abuse that Gogol finds so troubling in Russian society has been confirmed and intensified in the figure of Chichikov.

Gogol's story also makes us ponder whether the "dead souls" epithet applies equally well to the small-minded authorities and insulated landowners who are so inert and dried up that, in contrast, Chichikov's arrivals are as striking as that of flaming comets. Is it because of this near-dead atmosphere that Chichikov is able to put his scheme into productive play? The most difficult landowner is the most ordinary, the one lacking casual refinement, but whose estate is in good order – the serfs well fed, the buildings repaired, the fields full. Chichikov is forced to pay a lot for these dead souls, and his rhetoric of name-dropping fails to cast light upon the business-like features of this landowner's face. He needs to make a difference by merely appearing, with swagger and all. His visit as such needs to disrupt, to break habit, and open up for the less than ordinary. This already gives him an opportunity to propose the implausible, to start to craft his opportunity. In situations where the difference cannot be made, where he cannot make an offer of himself, the opportunity falls away.

Bennet, Chichikov, and entrepreneurship

With Bennet and Chichikov we have elaborated on the element of common sense in the model of the entrepreneurship process: there is no entrepreneurship without seduction and play, but equally not so without common sense. What these characters reveal is the force of common sense and how, in its being understood diligently and intensely from within, it throws up possible lines of flight. Once discovered, Chichikov's becomes an explicit case of information asymmetry: he knows more than those he is attempting to trade with, and as the novel progresses, unique information in which he is in possession starts to leak out and the novelty loses its lustre. The timeliness of his activity becomes less and less apparent, yet he keeps going, caught within the machinations of his own scheme. He has grown used to the civic admiration that his creative scheming had organized, he wants to fit in and ascend the social hierarchy, no longer content with his established station as a minor bureaucrat.

Elisabeth Bennet is also respected and admired when she operates within common sense. Doing this skilfully is something like an investment from her side, a build-up of social capital that will protect her from when she resists the template role assigned to her as a woman. When she creatively resists in order to make space for manoeuvre as a woman, she, like Chichikov (obviously for different reasons), is met by frustration and anger. Knowing common sense is not only a source of opportunity, it is also a source of knowing how to handle the reactions you will inevitably be up against when you have breached the limits of what is presently considered as possible. Where creation requires virtuality to be actualized, the actual, in order to happen, has to settle itself into acceptable patterns.[29] Bennet's creative resistance emerges from her unrivalled capacity to listen in and attend to what prevails, but it generates ideas that can be hosted by what already exists as common sense, whereas Chichikov's couldn't. The surprise that greats Chichikov's scheme lessens once the twist is understood, it is a clever trick. Whereas the surprise that greets Bennet's betrothal to Darcy only intensifies, requiring common sense itself to shift. Hers' is a virtuality that has to create its own ways of actualization, its newness has to insinuate itself into everyday practices that are already "full" of sense, something that unfolds because of her entrepreneurial belonging to the situations she experiences so attentively.[30] Knowing when and how to leave common sense is thus also help in figuring out how to actualize the virtually real.

Bennet knows that the only resistance to play along that will help her create space for the new is one that emerges from within a perfect demonstration of knowing common sense down to its very details. Such newness has prepared its actualization by establishing tendencies, by making the new incipient, its pastness opens up towards a future.

The distinction between the possible and the virtual and the corresponding distinction between the real and the actual is one we get from Deleuze's reading of Bergson.[31] Bergson, Deleuze suggests, says that the real is in the image of the possible that it realizes. Resemblance and limitation characterize processes of realization. The virtual does not need to be realized, but rather actualized. Difference, divergence, and creation characterize the process of actualization:

> While the real is in the image and likeness of the possible that it realizes, the actual, on the other hand does *not* resemble the virtuality that it embodies. It is difference that is primary in the process of actualization – the difference between the virtual from which we begin and the actuals at which we arrive, and also the difference between the complementary lines according to which actualization takes place. In short, the characteristic of virtuality is to exist in such a way that it is actualized by being differentiated and is forced to differentiate itself, to create its lines of differentiation in order to be actualized.[32]

Realization of the possible will happen as it finds its place – via resemblance and limitation – within common sense. Actualization needs to create its lines of becoming through difference and differentiation. The challenge here is to not limit difference by thinking and acting from the already actualized. There is difference in repetition as in all processes of actualization.

Initially Chichikov's difference is stark, the novelty is almost absurd, but it lessens as what is apparently strange is revealed as instrumental scheming. In the end nothing much changes. Chichikov never leaves common sense. The opportunity arises as it does for many entrepreneurs from this combination of practical cunning and frustration in which he felt pinned down and without prospects. As with many entrepreneurs he is aware that what matters is what seems to be; appearance is everything, indeed it is really all there needs to be to create a market. The assembling is done in language, a telling of tall tales whose plausibility rests with the credulity, greed, and vanity of listeners.

Arguably, this selling of dead souls, though ingenious, is not an entrepreneurial act, save for the fact that potentially he earns some money by being cunning. In contrast Bennet forces common sense to struggle. Initially she is presented as a conformist, indeed anxious and vane, wondering what others might think of her in her situation, but gradually, as she attends (ethically) to her allotted role, the vanity wanes, and its withdrawal leaves space for a transgression that differentiates her from the standards already available in the actual life. Her action is entrepreneurial because it creates a space in which, collectively, others also experience an intensified urge to act, and in ways that create what is new.

Notes

1 Davis, P. (2017) *The Transferred Life of George Eliot*, Oxford: Oxford University Press, pp. 278–280.
2 Hjorth, D. (2015) Sketching a Philosophy of Entrepreneurship. In T. Baker & F. Welter (Eds.), *The Routledge Companion to Entrepreneurship*, London: Routledge, p. 41.
3 Schumpeter, J.A. (1947) "The Creative Response in Economic History," *The Journal of Economic History*, vii(2): 149–159.
4 Schumpeter, J.A. (1949). "Economic Theory and Entrepreneurial History," In Cole, Arthur, H. (ed.) *Harvard University Research Center in Entrepreneurial History. Change and the Entrepreneur – Postulates and Pattern for Entrepreneurial History*, Cambridge, MA: Harvard University Press, p. 68.
5 Ibid., p. 150.
6 Gartner, W.B. (2007) "Entrepreneurial Narrative and a Science of the Imagination," *Journal of Business Venturing*, 22(5): 613–627.
7 Cf. Greenblatt, S. (Summer, 1997) "The Fate of 'Culture': Geertz and Beyond," *Representations*, 59(Special Issue): 14–29. See also Van Maanen, J. (1979) "The Fact of Fiction in Organizational Ethnography," *Administrative Science Quarterly*, 24: 539–550.
8 Deleuze, G. (1998) *Essays – Critical and Clinical*, Transl. D.W. Smith & M.A. Greco, London and New York: Verso, p. iv.
9 Austen, J. [1996] (2012) *Pride and Prejudice*, V. Jones (Ed.), London: Penguin English Library, p. 265.
10 Fletcher, D. (2006) "Entrepreneurial Processes and the Social Construction of Opportunities," *Entrepreneurship & Regional Development*, 18(September): 421–440. Fletcher's theorization brings opportunity back into a processual understanding of everyday practices where, in relation to others, opportunities are socially constructed (rather than discovered).
11 See Deleuze, G. (1995) *Negotiations*, New York: Columbia University Press, pp. 113–118, where Deleuze discusses subjectification in Foucault's writing and stresses that this is a process, a process of production of subjectivity.
12 Ibid., p. 98.
13 Mary Parker Follet's (1925) definition of management resonates with Bennet's character. For Follett managers ought to try to find the law of the situation. She pioneered a more relational approach; the manager, she tried to show, would be as much responding to the workers' demands as vice-versa, both attending to the law of the situation, in order to have work managed well. Parker, F.M. (2004) *Dynamic Administration: The Collected Papers by Mary Parker Follet*, H.C. Metcalf and L. Urwick (Eds.), originally published by Harper & Brothers, 1942, New York: Routledge.
14 Deleuze, G. (2006) *Nietzsche and Philosophy*, New York: Columbia University Press, p. 170.

15 Deleuze, G. (1997) *Essays Critical and Clinical,* Minneapolis: University of Minnesota Press; Deleuze, G. and Guattari, F. (1986) *Kafka. Toward a Minor Literature,* Minneapolis: University of Minnesota Press.

16 Deleuze, G. (1998) *Essays Critical and Clinical,* London and New York: Verso, p. 4.

17 Foucault, M. (2004) *The Birth of Biopolitics,* London: Palgrave Macmillan.

18 Hirschman, A.O. (1977) *The Passions and the Interests: Political Arguments for Capitalism before Its Triumph,* Princeton: Princeton University Press, p. 59.

19 Marshall, C. (1992) "'Dull Elves' and Feminists: A Summary of Feminist Criticism of Jane Austen," *Persuasions,* 14: 39–45.

20 Hjorth, D. (2005) "Organizational Entrepreneurship – with de Certeau on Creating Heterotopias (or Space for Play)," *Journal of Management Inquiry,* 14(4): 386–398; de Certeau, M. (1997) *Heterologies – Discourse on the Other,* Transl. B. Massumi, Minneapolis: University of Minnesota Press; Colebrook, C. (2002) "Certeau and Foucault: Tactics and Strategic Essentialism," *The South Atlantic Quarterly,* 100(2): 543–574.

21 Skoglund, A., Redmalm, D., and Berglund, K. (2020) "Videography – Studying Ethical Uncertainty in Alternative Entrepreneurship," *Society and Business,* 15(4): 305–324.

22 Deleuze, G., Smith, D.W., and Greco, M.A. (1997) "Literature and Life," *Critical Inquiry,* 23(2): 225–230. Also see Colebrook, C. (1997) *New Literary Histories: New Historicism and Contemporary Criticism,* Manchester: Manchester University Press.

23 Foucault, M. (1982) *Power/Knowledge,* C. Gordon (Ed.), Hertfordshire: Simon & Schuster, p. 221.

24 Gogol, N. (2008) *Dead Souls,* Transl. D. Reyfield, New York: New York Review of Books, p. 34.

25 Gartner, W.B., Bird, B.J., and Starr, J. (1992) "Acting as if: Differentiating Entrepreneurial from Organizational Behaviour," *Entrepreneurship Theory and Practice,* 16(3): 13–32.

26 Deleuze, G. and Guattari, F. (1988) *A Thousand Plateaus – Capitalism and Schizophrenia,* London: The Athlone Press.

27 Gogol, N. (2004) *Dead Souls,* Transl. Introd. and notes by R.A. Maguire, London: Penguin Classics, p. 175.

28 See Smith, D. (1998) Introduction: A Life of Pure Immanence: Deleuze's "Critique and Clinique" Project. In G. Deleuze – essays, *Critical and Clinical,* London: Verso, xi–lvi.

29 Deleuze, G. (1988) *Bergsonism,* New York: Zone Books.

30 Applied explicitly to entrepreneurship see Dimov, D., Schaefer, R., and Pistrui, J. (2020). "Look Who Is Talking … and Who Is Listening: Finding an Integrative "We" Voice in Entrepreneurial Scholarship," *Entrepreneurship Theory and Practice.* DOI: 10.1177/1042258720914507

31 Deleuze, G. (1988) *Bergsonism,* New York: Zone Books.

32 Ibid., p. 97.

8 Organization-creation
Commerce

Transaction, calculation, commerce

For Edith Penrose the entrepreneurial venture is an enactment and organization of productive knowledge that has arisen from the constraints of history. Being entrepreneurial, and so nascent, the venture acts as a kind of refuge, albeit itself of a fledgling form: it is a space in which the standard ways of doing things have been tested and found wanting in some way, making what was historically settled as an equilibrium unsettled.

To conceptualize such a condition, Penrose uses the concept of image, based loosely on Kenneth Boulding's argument in his book *The Image*.[1] Boulding suggests knowledge arises within an organism as it senses and habitually engages with a wider environment: "[K]nowledge is not something which exists and grows in the abstract. It is a function of human organisms and of social organization."[2] This environment is never known in itself, objectively, but only in images built up through subjectively structured experience. As such images are palimpsests of perceptions that have been filtered by the senses and evaluated along scales of desirability, the desire of a collection of bodies held in play. Images grow with the subject, they gather a history, becoming sticky, to the point where they are hard to budge as they have become meaningful.[3]

Boulding is writing in a pragmatist's vein, inspired very much by John Dewey's argument that knowledge arises from embodied interactions within the organism itself, between it and other organisms, and between organisms and the wider social and natural environment.[4] Dewey uses the term "transaction" to describe this ecological intimacy between how an organism is made up "internally" and how it relates to what is outside or beyond its boundaries. Because of its transaction nature, what is novel in knowledge remains tithed to the already established, and what is an individual can only emerge from a collectivity.[5] For human organisms, it is in processes of transaction that knowledge, habit, norms, and institutions become bundled practices, and through transaction that these practices are both confirmed and modified by repeated attempts to judge, act, decide, know, and express ourselves in a particular situation.[6]

DOI: 10.4324/9781315714455-11

According to Boulding:

> The accumulation of knowledge is not merely the difference between messages taken in and messages given out. It is not like a reservoir; it is rather an organization which grows through an active internal organizing principle much as the gene is a principle or entity organizing the growth of bodily structures.[7]

Setting aside the cogency of equating internal organizing to genetic determinism (Boulding's sense of "images" working from the inside out can read a little like a "private language" argument at times), what excites Penrose about Boulding's pragmatic thinking, is first, that relational knowledge is a grounding condition of any organism, and second, this knowledge is wrapped up in the unique life patterns of how one organism attempts to apprehend itself-in-relation-to-others again and again. It is the accumulation of this experience that Penrose sees as a necessary constraining force (a history), and which is carried along in imagery. Typically the imagery sediments experience into habits, and routines, but it can also loosen patterns of action, feeling, and thought, and do so without ever invoking an external (objective) environment (an exogenous shock) or an internal (objective) subject (a mental decision).

By invoking images Penrose is adamant that the knowledge necessary to create and sustain entrepreneurial processes is, as we too have been arguing, of an affective, embodied, and relational order that can neither be grounded in either a big end or little end analysis, nor be easily packaged in distinct categories like "information" or "resources." Whilst on a superficial reading a resource can be described as a fixed and discrete entity (a qualification, e.g., or an R&D unit), phenomenologically speaking it is divisible: within each resource are myriad ways of generating productive knowledge, and these open up under imaginative pressure to think through and around them, to envisage the different ways they might be used. Recalling the distinction the philosopher Wilfred Sellars makes between "scientific images" realized through theoretical constructions and "manifest images" realized in self-conceptions of experience, the latter should not be eliminated on the grounds of immediacy, incompleteness, or delusion.[8]

Penrose argues entrepreneurship arises where personal cognitive, sensory, and affective experiences are woven with wider social, historical, and economic environments to form an image of being in business in which speculative possibility is to the fore. Typically images of business subdue speculation. It is in their nature to conform to already evaluated and agreed business patterns, resulting in accepted managerial formations and firm structure. Just as an individual organism like a human being builds up images from experience by which it orients itself towards patterns of survival and flourishing, so to do firms: their internal resources and operations constituting structures by which the world is known and from which investment decisions and production activity are forthcoming.[9]

The entrepreneurial occurs when messages apprehended as productive opportunities disturb settled images, whether it is applying existing resources in novel areas, attempting to integrate new technologies into existing patterns, or noticing how the incidental or overlooked might be taken to the centre of things.[10] The entrepreneur holds such an image in place long enough to create and pursue new organizational forms: a gathering of habituated structure, novelty, imaginative speculation, and responsibility.

The resources being used in this newly emerging entre space – whilst often meagre – protect nascent ideas, allowing them to become substantial enough not only to persuade others of their viability. It also protects them from wanton imitation. The idea has to have room to twist itself free and become self-sufficient, it cannot just be thrown onto the market without first being organized productively. It is at this point that seduction, play, and common sense begin to cohere and distill and configure into acts of transaction.

The disturbing aspects of entrepreneurial images are twofold. First comes the transactions in which the images, configured imaginatively, are bringing about new arrangements within human practice. These are the new products and methods of which Schumpeter talks in relation to creative response to change. The entrepreneurial transaction entails a knowledge production in which what is being imagined carries its own reality, "as if" it existed, even though it is only as a manifest prospect.

The second is the disturbance to the criteria of meaning by which knowledge (such as information or resources) is being judged. Here the disturbance brings into critical light the technologies of power and knowledge by which any specific image is deemed transactionally sensible. It is a disturbance at the level of what Wittgenstein would call a form of life rather than of any specific practice within it: just what counts as transaction in a commercial setting?

It is in the act of transaction that the entrepreneurial becomes actual, as a practice exposed to, and exemplary of, the prevailing forces of power and knowledge by which it is acknowledged as an organizational forming that is "of interest." The idea has been found seductive, others have played with the prospect of joining in, the venture has acknowledged the constraints of common sense to which it has to appeal, and now, finally, the transaction can (or might) unfold from this commerce. In the lessening and loosening of what is virtual and incipient, and the rise of what is actual, the forces of power and knowledge gain more momentum, they have an organizational form to compress and categorize. The forces come explicitly (symbolically) in the form of business plans, loan agreements, certification, training, regulatory compliance, legal and tax structures, and consultancy. More discursively, as technologies of power, they come in the articulation of dominant economic, environmental, and social challenges that determine where R&D funding is being directed, in logics of performativity that preclude sauntering and fixate on scaling; in the spectacle of a brand society in which it becomes almost sinful to be, or associate with, the obsolescent, and in the rise of an experiential economy in which sensation is taking precedence over material possession. Little of this can be transacted away, indeed it configures the criteria by which any transaction is made sensible. Yet it is never totalizing, indeed, as we have suggested, it is only because the subject remains a distinct possibility that power and knowledge persist as forces. The subjects of the entrepreneurial process are those who are, in some way or other, able to consciously and critically assay: those aspects of the self that are considered integral and intimate to self-development; the rules by which this self is inevitably subjugated in its belonging to and being expressed within a range of practices; and the available means and ends for of organizing and so understanding themselves.

Together these constitute what Foucault calls technologies of the self through which practices are both sustained and repaired, or meddled with and even transformed.[11] Transaction is the result of the commerce process whereby these technologies of self-organizing meld with those of power and knowledge, and in the case of entrepreneurship, doing so in ways that reach up to the edges of prevailing practice, to the point where, as Schumpeter said, creative responses to change might happen, meaning, once the transaction gets underway, the world might not be quite the same.

To elaborate on commerce and transaction we again recur to two literary characters, those of Julien Sorel from Maurice Stendhal's *The Red and Black*, and Tom Ripley, from Patricia Highsmith's *The Talented Mr. Ripley*.

Julien Sorel

Julien Sorel is born into a family of no particular means or social standing, but with ambitions nurtured by reading titles like "Memorial of St. Helena," based on conversations with Napoleon during his exile, a book "… he held dearest of all …" Sorel is hired by the major of the small, provincial town of Verrières, France, Monsieur Rênal, as a tutor to his children. The title of the novel refers to the dual-career options Sorel is presented with, coming as he does from a family of no particular means and without status or standing. It refers to the red of a military or the black of the clergy.[12] Sorel has chosen "the Black," pursuing a career in the church, which promises the faster route to being someone and acting with authority. Or is it respect and tranquillity that this book-reading young man, plagued by his father, really is after? The quick-minded, handsome young Sorel is frustrated over the fact that this gets him nowhere in the French society at the time. What he lacks is social recognition, and the prospect of this is the great desire that drives him to make politically and ethically dubious (to say the least) decisions. There is commerce to be had, social intercourse, trading of services, a quick route to respect and standing. However, Sorel seems to underestimate that common sense at the time is also a force that prioritizes status quo, that thinks Sorel should know "his place."

As a professional believer, the need to display humility does not prevent him from nurturing big ambitions for his career. He is determined to make any opportunity to get access to a life where authority will shield him from being pushed around. His extraordinary sensibility is a great power to be affected, and he thus reads his times and surroundings better than most, and knows what he can transform into a possibility, how he can seduce others to follow, and how he can play in the in-between where his life is thus located. His desire for women, however, pushes him around too and does not prevent him from seducing the mayor's wife. After having left his position in the mayor's house (and the love affair with the mayor's wife), he has a relationship with the daughter of a Marquis. The Marquis, however, runs a background check and hears rumours about the earlier affair with Madame Rênal. It transpires that it is Madam Rênal herself who has been talking. Aghast, Sorel returns to his hometown, buys guns, and shoots her. He believes he has killed her, but he lacks competence in most practical affairs, and hasn't. What follows is a constant and restless shift of opinion, including: the Marquis daughter believing Julien acted as an honourable man; Madame Rênal forgiving Julien and confessing she still loves him; and Julien oscillating between different positions not quite knowing whom he loves, who he is, or what to think about people apart from that most appear hypocrites to him, including, of course, himself, the biggest hypocrite of all. Stendhal eventually throws his hands in the air and as an author cedes to the reader – what do you think about all this?

Stendhal seems to be provoking us. Sorel's actions are anchored by an interest in self-advance, yet as a consequence, they are wayward, scurrilous, and worthy of scorn. His warrant, though, is circumstance, and his persisting question to us is: "Who is to say others would develop any differently?" After the much too early death of his mother, Julien had to cope with a harsh and violent father, often leaving him crying and with bruises. Julien was a physically weak type, his nose into books rather than others' business, a sharp mind with a fantastic memory (he can more or less recall the Bible in its entirety) but apparently not with the qualities his father sought in a son. Stendhal refers to him as a hero, yet portrays him as an anti-hero that tries to take the initiative but mostly ends up defending himself against humiliation and powerlessness. Sorel tries to move forward and upward in French society as he finds it. He is a calculating figure, and the situations he encounters demand constant calculation, shifting this way, then that. He is, though, not reducible to a gamer of the system in search of opportunities to exploit. Rather, he seeks commerce, in the original sense of social intercourse. The soft or calm settling of differences originally attributed to (*doux*) commerce suits Sorel – the avid reader, the thinker – and his *conatus* seems focused on finding that calm life.[13] The warrant for wanting settlement is his own sense of inadequacy, and how this might be compensated for, or ameliorated, with the small wins, the accumulation of currency he carries as social capital in the French society at the time. There is no wider project than securing his own outward, institutional presence.

The narrator in the book echoes the inconstancy of Sorel's life: his view and opinion is constantly shifting and changing, playing with irony, and forcing the reader to intervene and to ask, along with Sorel and Stendhal, what is it that is "me" here, or "I," and "how could we be what we are?" In this sense Sorel shares a lot with Iago, a fluid character that is not what he is, but he lacks the singular project that anchors Iago. Sorel's only project is himself, and in its social incarnation, the self is not an end, just an assembly of roles, titles, offices, duties, and access privileges.

Stendhal's conundrums are difficult, perhaps unanswerable questions, so might it not be better, in a spirit reminiscent of Kierkegaard's more gloomy moments, to fall back into a strictly calculative form of transacting, allowing oneself to be governed by prevailing technologies of power and knowledge, falling in with what counts for as long as one might? This is what Schumpeter calls adaptive response to change: Sorel's transactions are coloured by compliance with what he experiences as the necessities of a situation. Stendhal has placed Sorel in a time when – following revolutionary changes to the social orders – limited possibilities for advancement have opened up, but only to those knowing how to calculate the political and social risks involved in pursuing a career beyond the confines of their "natural station". Sorel's is one such calculating self:

> The building of the church and the sentences pronounced by the Justice of the Peace suddenly enlightened him. An idea came to him which made him almost mad for some weeks, and finally took complete possession of him with all the magic that a first idea possesses for a passionate soul which believes that it is original [...] Nowadays, one sees priests of forty with salaries of 100,000 francs, that is to say, three times as much as Napoleon's famous generals of a division [...] I must be a priest.[14]

The idea was the church, but it could as easily have been the military, either/or, it would have made little difference. Sorel did not suffer from a sense of calling or duty, he was utterly uninterested in the ethics of the practice and attempting to perform the roles skilfully, for their own sake. His relationship with them is a measured one.

Though his decisions are measured, as the novel unfolds, we witness how the technologies of self which Sorel employs are inadequate to handle the wider technologies of power and knowledge to which he is continually being made subject. There is a heaviness and bitterness to his judgement which is being twisted into strange shapes because of a sharp and frustrating distinction between what he can imagine and what he can do. His imagination – great indeed as it is based in both intelligence and a childhood where books provided the best escape or shield – attempts to feed his judgement with examples (of grandeur and ambition) to work on in his continual negotiation with circumstance, but the ideas remain stubbornly distant, even perverse, and the institutional forces to which he has submitted, those of the clergy and family, gain an imperceptible ascendancy whose slowness begins to grind his ambition down.

And here we find a reason to return to the many debates about the colour symbolism in Stendhal's title for the novel – *The Red and the Black*. Whereas there is a somewhat dominant and somewhat conventional interpretation of this as representing the military and the church – the career choice available to a man of ambition but without means, standing or status at the time – there are alternatives. Sure, the Jacobinism (red) and Clericalism (black) is a rather fortifiable option for any hermeneutician. When we look at the childhood of Sorel, however, and his drive to find a new life, we might find it more convincing – as Patrick Pollard argues well – to see in Stendhal's choice of colour, a symbolism for a carrier in the church only: black is then the humble dress of a tutor/priest, and the red represents the "high peaks of success in this same segment of society."[15] Pollar argues that there is, realistically, only one career option available to a person like Sorel, and that is through the church. This leads Pollard to summarize his analysis using a simple scheme (see below).

Sorel is living through a period where the polite forms of commerce identified by Hirschman, those whose exponents were calm, assured, and productive, was giving way to something more economic.[16] Sorel is witnessing the rise of a bourgeoisie who are well schooled in, and have respect for, the art of self-advancement.[17] So in aspiring to become someone, Sorel had to attend, continually, to an instrumental logic of getting ahead through small acts of tactical diplomacy and suggestion. That he stalls is no real surprise: it is convention that defines the limits to self-development, leaving Sorel to content himself with techniques of self-development that absolve him from relative failure, and which insulate him from the harm he causes others.

Table 8.1 Pollard's analysis of *The Red and the Black*

Red		Black	
1.	The colour of objects connected with the church	1.	The colour of a priest's frock (and similar items)
2.	Ecclesiastical preferment	2.	Ecclesiastical and social subordination
3.	(A) Energy and ambition (B) Passion (including love)	3.	(A) Melancholy (B) Intelligence

Source: Based on Pollard (1981: 331).

We can thus also read *The Red and the Black*, and thus Sorel's "adventure" as an analysis of the difficulties that entrepreneurial life entails. It is based on a heightened sensitivity for occasions that might be transformed into opportunities. It relies on a passionate receptivity for other people's capacities for being affected. Seduction would be an art firmly based on such "redness," as the life of Don Giovanni has demonstrated. A career, however, in business as in the church, Stendhal and Hirschman seem to say, also relies on the mastering of the calm passions, the doux commerce, the calculative. This describes the rise from black to red in the church, and it would differentiate the entrepreneur driven simply by passion and loosing herself in play, from the one that knows how to respect common sense, be politically wise enough to know what defeats one can "handle" on the route to commerce.

To recur to Schumpeter's distinction between creative and adaptive change, Sorel's actions are set firmly within the range of existing practices.[18] The conditions that Schumpeter sets for creative change just do not pertain. Creative change occurs in situations where it is impossible to infer effects through an analysis of existing initial conditions, *ex ante* planning is nonsensical, whereas Sorel's transactions are based on a "figuring out" of a provable landscape rather than on flashes or hunches. Creative change changes social and economic conditions for good and its force is unique, whereas Sorel's transactions confirm conditions, and could easily be undertaken by any other figure in his station in life. Finally, creative change requires the doing of new things in new ways, whereas Sorel's transactions carry the bearing of an administrative style. In short, to continue using Schumpeter's terms, Sorel's transactions are shaped by institutional forces, there is no bursting influence consequent upon "getting a new thing done."[19]

Reference could be made again to institutional entrepreneurship as we agree with Biliana Kassabova's analysis of *The Red and the Black*[20] pointing to the striking absence of revolution in the novel. The claustrophobic sense of being locked into an unliveable life, having lost his mother, being plagued by his father, autodidact and well-read, intelligent and handsome, Sorel finds his only "escape" in going into another life of being dominated by the reds of the high peaks of success in the church. He is in Schumpeter's sense "within the pale or routine," limiting his imagination to "reactive response." In the end, this makes him an excellent case for studying commerce – or so we propose – and precisely for this reason, a good example of how commerce as such is not enough for entrepreneurship. His commerce easily leads to a "boiling dry" since it plays within the game, exploits what is there, calculates risks. Entrepreneurship is a bigger process, requires constant "filling up" of the cup, cannot confine actions to gaming but needs to play, and has to act on the ambiguous, non-calculable when exploring what could become doable beyond the present limits of the possible.

Stendhal was writing in post-revolutionary France, a country that was becoming bold, indeed: "the special monomania of the early nineteenth century was overweening ambition of all sorts, stimulated by the more fluid society that was the legacy of the Revolution."[21] Yet Sorel drowns in the fluidity. Fast forward to the 1960s and we find Patricia Highsmith providing us with a brilliant analysis of "pathological ambition" in her portrait of the talented Tom Ripley. In many ways we are then in post-post-times: post the traditional society and values of France in Stendhal's times of chance, but also post the normalization of commerce in the British society and its more unashamed individual ambition. We are now in a post-war euphoria of the United States where *if you lacked* what was diagnosed as pathological ambition in early nineteenth century France, you would be considered not normal.

Tom Ripley

Tom Ripley, the central character in Patricia Highsmith's eponymous crime novel, certainly shares Sorel's ambition for a better life. Ripley is fully engaged in the business of being, calmly, clinically, rationally, utterly amoral. The novel opens with Ripley being hired by the father of Dickie Greenleaf to track down his errant son living in Italy, and to persuade the son to return to the United States and assume his natural position running the family business. Tom agrees with alacrity, wanting to escape the nastiness of an earlier fraud, and before long has ingratiated himself into Dickie's Italian life with such finesse that his constant presence is beginning to irritate Marge, Dickie's girlfriend. Ripley finds in Dickie an interesting persona, a character loved by others, easy-going, enjoying life, and he yearns to imitate and embody it, he wants it, and proceeds to take it (e.g. secretly wearing Dickie's clothes). Dickie is aware of the flattery that he has come to expect from many he meets, indeed Marge suggests Dickie might be an object of Ripley's lust. Yet Ripley does not want to partner Dickie, he wants to become him. Ripley is that sort. He soaks up his surrounds, always attentive to the potential, and Dickie is a rich source of varied experience. Finally, on a trip to San Remo, Dickie becomes exasperated by Ripley's fawning and hovering about. Ripley understands no more can be had from Dickie alive, but his death still holds possibilities: he strikes and kills him. With Marge away, Ripley assumes Dickie's identity, taking over the apartment and finances. This is, of course, also the start of the huge task of avoiding all of Dickie's friends' questions and inquiries (Ripley also ends up killing Freddie, one of Dickie's friends, who gets too suspicious), as well as tricking the Italian police investigating the death of Dickie and Freddie by sliding between being Dickie and being Ripley, depending on who is looking where. The novel ends without denouement or resolve: Ripley convinces Mr Greenleaf that Dickie's inheritance should come to him, he convinces the police that Dickie (who has "disappeared") was the more likely suspect for killing Freddie, and he needs to convince himself of nothing, for he is forever mobile, constantly adjusting: un-freighted by morals, which we left on the dock as he un-birthed, Ripley just travels, he is watching others and others are watching him, and amid the twists and turns there is a disorientation and loosening of cause and effect: who is responsible here, can anyone even be responsible in such fluidity? Ripley living alongside others in their surface appearance, hiding in the rippling declivities of civilized manners, is an agent of pure pragmatism: Dewey should be proud. Ripley reads situations as a kite follows currents of air, utterly unaware of St Augustine's question: "Who am I?" Ripley's experience has no relief: he is conscious without conscience.

Inadequate explanations for his behaviour can come from his childhood (as can explanations for Highsmith's). Like Sorel, Ripley is a life that, early on, is shaped by an inability to overcome or get past people and the forces that dominate them. His solution was to master the art of multiplication: operating with a palette of characters, moving smoothly across surfaces, working towards positions in life he admires and desires, always feeding his talent. In this he is much like Iago, a versatile social chameleon whose scheming is predicated on an inner sense of injustice. Unlike Sorel, Ripley is not limiting himself to an either-or logic of red or black, military or clergy, and unlike Iago, he carries no bitterness. He is not interested in already available roles or offices into which a self can willingly jump (or not, in Iago's case), and conform as best they can. Ripley is not interested in already existing allocations, he is a transactional figure, someone who has the measure of things, along with the charm and imitative skills to become anyone.

> "Oh, I can do a number of things – valeting, babysitting, accounting – I've got an unfortunate talent for figures. No matter how drunk I get, I can always tell when a waiter's cheating me on a bill. I can forge a signature, fly a helicopter, handle dice, impersonate practically anybody, cook – and do a one-man show in a nightclub in case the regular entertainer's sick. Shall I go on?" Tom was leaning forward, counting them on his fingers. He could have gone on.[22]

Ripley can never pause. There is no consideration or indebtedness.[23] His stories are all ad hoc, extensions to previous extensions: "[I] always thought it would be better to be a fake somebody ... than a real nobody."

Ripley's shapeshifting mobility, or agility, carries hints of the modern corporate form: not the conglomerate behemoths of yesteryear, but the agile, digitally enhanced, untaxable corporations whose global presence is grounded in their unchallenged absence. His desires are akin to those "that propel the fantasy of corporate personhood."[24] There is something in this view, but Wagers observes how, in Ripley's urge to continually destroy his past and begin anew, working from a clean slate, there is also something profoundly American and something entrepreneurial in him.[25] The American Dream has historically served the collective imagination with a set of ways to conduct oneself as a successful man – being a Rugged Individual, a Golden Boy, or the Horatio Alger that takes himself from rags to riches.[26] Highsmith plays with this, for he is an adventurer, a chancer, travelling as lightly as gossamer, yet his skills are riddled with amoral brutality, and he has no soil, he can never belong to a nation, or to others; he is his own turning world.

In the character of Ripley, the talent for seducing others into his scheming, the skills required for playfully rewarding these others as they come along, and an intimate and detailed knowledge about the common sense that holds human practices in place, all come together in one body, but through multiple characters. In Ricoeur's terminology, we can describe Ripley's elaborate and gradually more complex emplotment as an effort to synthesize the heterogeneous characters such that a narrating self is in control (and can keep up).[27] At the same time, to his multiple audiences, Ripley sustains himself through techniques of multiplication reminiscent of the conversational interplay in Schlegel's *speil*: ironic play and buffoonery.

At the core of Ripley's talents is this agility in becoming different selves without compunction, and with an intensity of will, that allows him to see and pursue potential that is hidden or non-existent to most others. This is a key characteristic of audience-sensitivity, of being able to vary your performance depending on the nature of the crowd/listener(s), attentive to the various ways one might persuade them and have them come along. This, in turn, seems to be a requirement for commerce to happen. Social intercourse – the original meaning of commerce, and central to the *doux* commerce idea that this is a soft and gentle way of handling disputes amongst people – would more likely emerge from a person creating relationships on the basis of audience-sensitivity.[28] The "with-ness" that is the meaning of *com-* in commerce is of course still important for merchandise (*-merce*) to be traded and thus money-making to happen. Again, audience-sensitivity would be key to establishing this withness, and Ripley masters this art. Expansion of interests when taking place via commerce was, to most people, understood as *doux*, gentle, polishing, though Karl Marx was far less encouraging, believing the polishing more an abrasion of dignity and hope.[29] We see the history of gentleness, the social intercourse part, as key to understanding commerce as an entrepreneurial achievement. It has to be passionately interested in the other's interest and in winning them over.

Again, Ripley is a case in point, whilst also demonstrating how reflection has to accompany such interest in the "other" to achieve successful commerce. Ripley's skill for living through a fluid personality and a normalized chameleon style makes him open up possibilities for commerce almost everywhere.[30] However, at the same time, both Marx' critique and Ripley's ethical and relational failures show that for commerce to work well – that is, as an investment in relationships and further commerce and not as exploitation or abuse of relationships – it needs to be based on a respect for the other and the otherness of the other. Entrepreneurship and ethics is a complicated relationship and we can learn a lot from Iago and Ripley, Don Giovanni and Sorel about this dilemma that will always present itself when you have understood what roles, templates, and logics that have institutionalized and normalized thinking and behaviour such that you can go passed that line and venture into the hitherto unexplored.[31]

Despite (and because of) his acumen, Ripley remains a renegade figure whose obsessive interest in self-oriented scheming strikes us as abnormal, and certainly amoral. Indeed, as many commenters of Highsmith's novel point out, one of the brilliant if disarming experiences of reading the novel is reflecting on how closely aligned, and mutually accommodating, the normal and psychopathic can become. Ripley knows all there is to know of good and evil, without ever feeling their resonance; it is as if the common sense he exploits so mercilessly is sedimented in practices to which he will never be properly privy. He runs asymptotic to the limits of practices, studying them but never experiencing them, and so can we really claim this to be in any way entrepreneurial if by such the world is being disclosed differently in some way? Not entirely. Entrepreneurship is the full process of seduction-play-common sense-commerce. Ripley touches on it, indeed his exceptional talent for adjusting to the situation, reading the potential, for tendering possibilities into opportunities, and acting on carries all the vestiges of what we are arguing is entrepreneurial.

Sorel, Ripley, and entrepreneurship

What we witness in Ripley, and what is lacking in Sorel, is the capacity to create the conditions for agreeable transactions to take place. He knows how to make others agreeable to the proposition; he knows how to loosen the seemingly rigid; he knows how to make questionable what had thus far passed as solid truths. Sorel is content to choose from those already made available, whereas Ripley creates the setting from which organizing might begin anew and to take hold, in even the most unlikely of situations. Where one becomes suspicious he seems able to find others who will come along with him, following one line of flight after another, opening up avenues for action that most people would never imagine. We are, apparently, a long way from the rose-tinted view of commerce Hirschman reports and discusses as popular in the early dawn of capitalism.[32] Yet Ripley understands the forces of commerce to be close to those Hirschman elaborates on, at least in the form of face–face dealings that he is exploiting. It is because people have acquired manners and have learned to deliberate that there are patterns in values and activities, patterns that Ripley can exploit. Ripley could not operate in a rapacious world, he needs the trust and credulity of others. He needs protocols with ready-made characters that offer people templates for how to behave, logics to follow, and roles to hide behind. In this sense, Ripley, as we have hinted a number of times above, is more of a failed institutional entrepreneur. He can negotiate events as they tumble over themselves, motivate others to join his scheme, and provide visions that fascinate.[33] Yet ultimately Ripley's project is to take over, to possess, to become what he is currently not, and his efforts at shapeshifting are alive to, but unconstrained by, law or common-sense standards. This lends his commerce both an utterly self-centred and destructive quality: his affective power is dedicated to his own advance, a little like Don Juan, though strangely sexless.

Somewhat in the same vein as Don Juan, though, there is a violence in the way Ripley literally forces the space of opportunity open, without a care for how the scheming might go awry, or hurt others. This is also why Ripley is only partly demonstrating commerce. He cannot go all the way because he cannot care enough for the interests of the other. Commerce is, in this sense, immanent to social intercourse, and the sociality of "social intercourse" relies on a balance, a care, a reciprocity. There has to be value in the relationship, in the dealings with the other, lest the other simply become a stone to be stepped on. Again, entrepreneurial commerce is an investment in the next trade. Ripley is, in this sense, very different: his venture is an escape from a history of being dominated to a future of being dominating. He has no need for the stepping stones after he has stepped on them. He is alive to how, almost inevitably, his surface dwelling will only distract people so long: they will grow suspicious and begin to question the authenticity or accuracy of what he says, who he portrays. He is alive to prevailing forms of common sense, but to keep tapping this awareness across the multiple situations that he has deliberately brought together becomes a precarious experience. Within events, he always seems to be postponing his own fall, almost on the point of tripping, then scheming to be elsewhere, leaving some of those he has seduced, played with and persuaded out of joint and uncertain, whereas others he is able to keep in play just a little longer, always moving.

What we take from Ripley, whilst cautious of his amoral and destructive wake, is a sense of how commerce is actualized in a deal, in a trade, but without its being managed. The managerial revolution of the nineteenth and twentieth centuries built more competitive companies, as well as a new social class.[34] At the culmination of this era in the mid-1900s, managerialism dominated not only the corporate landscape of large businesses, but nearly all organizations, and most notably the management of social relations undertaken by (and increasingly on behalf of) governments.[35] Invoking Ripley and Sorel, in the company of our other characters, disturbs this settlement quite profoundly, not least because in each of them the conceit of control is being left to one side, none of them take up a bridle in their hand. Rather they flow with currents, drift, hurry, pause, all the whilst attempting to write themselves into events rather than trying to canalize them. In this the fabrication of organization is set against management, though it remains essential to it.

Notes

1 Boulding, K. (1956) *The Image,* Ann Arbor: University of Michigan Press. Penrose, E. (1959) *The Theory and Growth of the Firm,* Oxford: Oxford University Press, pp. 89–90.

2 Boulding, K. (1956) "General Systems Theory – The Skeleton of Science," *Management Science,* 2(3): 197–208, 197.

3 Meaning is a gathering of those particular external environmental occurrences that act as a message, either as an occurrence that could be acknowledged but is ignored, or as one that conforms to and confirms the established logical and aesthetic (sensory and affective) evaluative structures from which the image is formed, or which disturbs these structures in some way, requiring adjustment or transformation.

4 Vanderstraeten, R. (2002) "Dewey's Transactional Constructivism," *Journal of Philosophy of Education,* 36(2): 233–246.

5 Sullivan, S. (2001) *Living Across and through Skins: Transactional Bodies, Pragmatism, and Feminism,* Bloomington: Indiana University Press.

6 Dewey's ideas are resonant with more contemporary ideas of practices as found, for example, in Schatzki's theoretical developments: Schatzki, T.R. (1996) *Social Practices: A Wittgensteinian Approach to Human Activity and the Social,* Cambridge: Cambridge University Press; Schatzki, T.R. (2002) *The Site of the Social: A Philosophical Account of the Constitution of Social Life and Change.* University Park: The Pennsylvania State University Press; Schatzki, T.R. (2005) "The Sites of Organizations," *Organization Studies,* 26(3): 465–484.

7 Boulding, K. (1956) *The Image,* Ann Arbor: University of Michigan Press.

8 Indeed, even to claim to know something is to be part of, and open to, a world that is not inherently thinkable: meaning has to be worked at continually, and thereby remain alive to discrepancies between concepts of objects and our experience of them. See Shaviro, S. (2014) *The Universe of Things,* Minneapolis: University of Minnesota Press, p. 120, 157.

9 See Foss, N. (2002) Edith Penrose: Economic and Strategic Management. In C. Pitelis (Ed.), *The Growth of the Firm: The Legacy of Edith Penrose,* Oxford: Oxford University Press, pp. 147–164, 156; Ravix, J. (2002) Edith Penrose and Ronald Coase on the Nature of the Firm and the Nature of Industry. In C. Pitelis (Ed.), *The Growth of the Firm: The Legacy of Edith Penrose,* Oxford: Oxford University Press, pp. 165–178, 169.

10 Spinosa, C., Flores, F., and Dreyfus, H.L. (1997). *Disclosing New Worlds: Entrepreneurship, Democratic Action, and the Cultivation of Solidarity,* Boston: MIT Press.

11 Foucault, M. (1984) "The Courage of Truth" in his *Lectures at the Collège de France 1983–1984,* Transl. G. Burchell, London: Picador, pp. 1–22.

12 The red is also said to be about dreams, revolution, and Marie-Henri Beyle (Stendhal's birth name was Marie-Henri Beyle and Stendhal one of the many, but the most famous, pen name he used) did serve in Napoleon's army. The black is perhaps also, in his personal life, representing the realistic necessity of life. In addition, this being an ironic novel, some readers reason – due to "The Red and the Black" also being considered as a study of the impossibilities of finding truth and what the true self is – that the red and the black are the colours of roulette and thus that it brings chance and the necessity of chance to the fore. See Translator's note, Burton, R., in Stendhal (2004) *The Red and*

the Black, Transl. by B. Raffel, Introd. by D. Johnson, New York: Random House Modern Library Classics.

13 Hirschman, A.O. (1977) *The Passions and the Interests – Political Arguments for Capitalism before Its Triumph*, Princeton: Princeton University Press, p. 1989.

14 Sorel, the main character, speaking, from Stendhal (2004) *The Red and the Black – A Chronicle of 1830*, Transl. B. Raffel, Introd. by D. Johnson, Notes by J. Madden, New York: The Modern Library, p. 23.

15 Pollard, P. (1981) "Colour Symbolism in 'Le Rouge et le Noir,'" *The Modern Language Review*, 76(2): 323–331, 328.

16 As Hirschman points out, at the turn of the nineteenth century "interest-motivated behavior and money-making were considered to be superior to ordinary passion-oriented behavior." Hirschman, A.O. (1977) *The Passions and the Interests: Political Arguments for Capitalism before Its Triumph*, Princeton: Princeton University Press, p. 58.

17 Julien played his cards so well, that in less than a month of his arrival at the house, M. de Rênal himself respected him. (Chapter 7, *The Red and the Black*).

18 Schumpeter, J. (1947) "The Creative Response in Economic History," *Journal of Economic History*, 7(2): 149–159.

19 Schumpeter is deliberately (and perhaps irresponsibly) agnostic on the question of the beneficial or injurious effects of the creative response to change, consigning the consideration to a case-by-case basis. His interest in, and support for, the entrepreneurial class is as a force of disruption that prevents tradition from ossifying. Desire matters more than its direction or object.

20 Kassabova, B. (2020) "What Was to Be Done? Missing Revolutions in Stendhal's The Red and the Black and Charterhouse," *Clio*, 47(3): 313–330.

21 Goldstein, J. (1987) *Console and Classify: The French Psychiatric Profession in the Nineteenth Century*, Cambridge: Cambridge University Press, p. 159, quoted in Kete, K. (2005) "Stendhal and the Trials of Ambition in Postrevolutionary France," *French Historical Studies*, 28(3): 467–495, p. 469.

22 Highsmith, P. (1955). *The Talented Mr. Ripley*, New York: Vintage Crime, p. 58.

23 Borch, C. (2005) "Urban Imitations: Tarde's Sociology Revisited," *Theory, Culture & Society*, 22(3): 81–100.

24 Wagers, K. (2913) "Tom Ripley, In: Patricia Highsmith's Corporate Fiction," *Contemporary Literature*, 54(2): 239–270, p. 250.

25 Ibid., p. 250: Wagers refers to: Fisher, P. (1999) *Still the New World: American Literature in a Culture of Creative Destruction*, Cambridge: Harvard University Press.

26 Sarachek, B. (1978) "American Entrepreneurs and the Horario Alger Myth," *The Journal of Economic History*, 38(2): 438–456.

27 Ricoeur, P. (1992) *Oneself as Another*, Transl. K. Blarney, Chicago: University of Chicago Press; Rasmussen, D. (1995) "Rethinking Subjectivity: Narrative Identity and the Self," *Philosophy & Social Criticism*, 21(5/6): 159–172.

28 See critique of the overly positive interpretation of doux commerce, which is also voiced by Hirschman, in e.g. Oman, N.B. (2016) *The Dignity of Commerce – Marlets and the Moral Foundation of Contract Law*, Chicago: The University of Chicago Press.

29 Marx ridiculed doux commerce, believing it utterly violent. Das Kapital, Vol. I, Chapter 24, Section 6, referred to by Hirschman in *The Passions and the Interests*, p. 62.

30 Stolarek, J. (2018) "Fluid Identities and Social Dislocation in the Face of Crime, Guilt and Ethics in Patricia Highsmith's The Talented Mr Ripley and The Tremor of Forgery," *Brno Studies in English*, 44(2): 145–156.

31 See Harris, J.D., Sapienza, H.J., and Bowie, N.E. (2009) "Ethics and Entrepreneurship," *Journal of Business Venturing*, 24(5): 407–418; Hannafey, F.T. (2003) "Entrepreneurship and Ethics: A Literature Review," *Journal of Business Ethics*, 46(2): 99–110. And also McCormick, M., Buttrick, H., and McGowan, R. (2018) "Ethics and Entrepreneurship: Should We Be Teaching Students the Inevitable Moral Dilemmas That Challenge All Entrepreneurs?," *Journal of Learning in Higher Education*, 14(1): 29–36.

32

> Commerce attaches [men] one to another through mutual utility. Through commerce the moral and physical passions are superseded by interest ... Commerce has a special character which distinguishes it from all other professions. It affects the feelings of men so strongly that it makes him who was proud and haughty suddenly turn supple, bending, and serviceable. Through commerce, man learns to deliberate, to be honest, to acquire manners, to be prudent and reserved in both talk and action.

Hirschman, A.O. (1982) "Rival Interpretations of Market Society: Civilizing, Destructive, or Feeble?," *Journal of Economic Literature*, 20: 1463–1484, 1465.

33 Battilana, L., Leca, B., and Boxenbaum, E. (2009) "How Actors Change Institutions: Towards a Theory of Institutional Entrepreneurship," *The Academy of Management Annals*, 3(1): 65–107; Svejenova, S., Mazza, C., and Planellas, M. (2007) "Cooking up Change in Haute Cuisine: Ferran Adrià as an Institutional Entrepreneur," *Journal of Organizational Behaviour*, 28(5): 539–561.

34 Chandler, A.D. (1977) *The Visible Hand – The Managerial Revolution in American Business*, Cambridge and London: The Belknap Press of Harvard University Press. Also, Burnham, J. (1941) *The Managerial Revolution – What Is Happening in the World*, Westpoint: Greenwood Press.

35 Deetz, S. (1992) *Democracy in an Age of Corporate Colonization – Developments in Communication and the Politics of Everyday Life*, New York: State University of New York Press.

Part III

9 Entrepreneurship as fabrication

Introduction: via literary imagination towards fabrication

In theorizing entrepreneurship, our book has never strayed far from Schumpeter, from Penrose, or from Spinosa, Flores, and Dreyfus. It has been written in their company, not least because for all of them there is an intimacy between entrepreneurship and history, whether this is a concern with how economies thought innovation develop over time, with the use innovation and creativity make of history as a source of imagination, legitimation, and inspiration, or with an apparent intimacy between organizational form and the ongoing accumulation and development of the entrepreneurial venture. Our theorization of the entrepreneurship process – Seduction →Play →Common Sense →Commerce – relies on imagination and organization-creation at each move in the process. Elsewhere we have theorized entrepreneurship as: Invention × Entrepreneurship = Innovation.[1] By this we mean that imagination, the virtual, new ideas, an anomaly is what makes organization-creation (entrepreneurship) necessary and, when making an organizational form through which the new can be offered, the result is innovation (actualized virtuality that generates value for the organization offering it by adding value to the users/customers). The idea of the new, the invention, the anomaly that requires the creation of an organization is thus the force that impinges as a seduction on the body that thereby becomes individuated as potential entrepreneur. The first step in actually becoming an entrepreneur – which would require accomplishing the whole process (seduction, play, common sense, commerce) – is to seduce others to assemble around the idea of the virtually new.[2] Again, this makes the idea of the new important.[3] However, at each stage in our process, imagination becomes central in order for the assemblage to be kept together and to solve challenges that seek to prioritize status quo. How to play requires imagination, how to handle common sense requires imagination, and how to accomplish commerce also requires imagination. What we are saying here is that at each move in the entrepreneurship process, there is a swarm of multiple differential relationships of ideas that could become,

DOI: 10.4324/9781315714455-13

where selection and creation are required for one to be actualized into the lived everyday world of practices.

Imagination, in Deleuze's reading of Kant's discussion of aesthetics in the *Critique of Judgement* (a book that changes the general discourse on art and aesthetics), is important in this regard as it teaches us how a free agreement of the faculties (understanding, reason, imagination) is possible. The key here, and the problem for Kant as he tries to build a philosophical system, is that there are no objects that are necessarily subject to aesthetic judgement, it is all optional, and hence contingent. There is this free movement since the critique of judgement has no domain proper to it. Deleuze explains:

> In aesthetic judgement, the imagination cannot attain a role comparable to that played by the understanding in speculative judgement, or that played by reason in practical judgement. The imagination is liberated from the supervision of the understanding and reason.[4]

This is indeed an important reflection by the process philosopher Deleuze, since it adds an additional explanation to why we have sought new knowledge of the entrepreneurship process in the aesthetics of literary character and writing. Deleuze's thinking provides yet another analogy to our model of the entrepreneurship process, for which common sense plays an important role, as he further explains how imagination works:

> Kant also says that imagination, in esthetic judgement, "schematizes without concepts." This is a brilliant formulation, though not quite exact. Schematizing is indeed an original act of the imagination, but always in respect to a determinate concept of the imagination. Without a concept from the understanding, the imagination does something else than schematizes: it *reflects*.[5]

Understanding delivers concepts to imagination, without which it does not freely speculate but rather reflects. Deleuze, moreover, is not satisfied with Kant's ideas on imagination, for it still limits thinking to the thinker. Deleuze places more emphasis on ideas and on thinking as something that happens to the thinker. In this sense he is more in agreement with what we argued earlier was Foucault's emphasis on the uneasy intimacy between subjectification and the subject (the knowing subject as the known subject, the thinking subject as the subject of thought). Here desire plays an important role in making subjects receptive – passionate – for ideas that induce thinking. When this happens imaginatively, in aesthetic judgement, understanding plays a role (as a discursive force on thinking) in imagination's schematizing. Thus, for entrepreneurship, when imagination seeks ways to create the organization missing for the virtual idea to become actual, the desire to see this actualized drives thinking and assembling, and understanding provides concepts. It does so both as a subjectifying, enterprising force of self-management and self-realization, and an entrepreneurial force of questioning actual limits.

Fiction, and specifically literature, can foster such understanding. In Vaihinger's "as if" philosophy, for example, the power of fiction lies with its metaphorical capacity to approach the unknown from within the known. The understanding wrought by fiction connects "what is" with "what could be," the "as" with the "if," showing "[T]he necessity (possibility or actuality) of an inclusion under an *impossible* and *unreal* assumption."[6] Recal romanticism: "literature is the power of fiction itself: not making a claim about what the world *is*, but about the imagination of a possible world."[7] It is the power to think with what is unreal and impossible and to consider how affect initiates and drives this thinking. For Vaihinger literary work provides a space for imagination and consciousness to vie with one another: imagining things otherwise, "as if" this were the case, forcing what is real to account for itself, delineating the boundaries of the "given" using correlations of possibility.[8]

Again, this is central to how we understand entrepreneurship: entrepreneurship is not primarily about what the world is, but about imagining possible worlds. Entrepreneurship is not equal to imagination, nor is it reducible to bricolage (creatively making do with what is at hand) or craft or making. When we re-imagine, re-think, and re-write entrepreneurship in this book, we have come to the conclusion that the concept that describes it most precisely is one that signifies a process that includes imagining, seductively describing, playfully organizing, political agility in navigating common sense, and business sensibility before possible commerce. We suggest, somewhat provocatively perhaps, that the concept of fabrication holds these parts together in a whole.

When Giorgio Agamben investigates imaginative power, he describes this as a "knowledge that does not know, but enjoys, and as a pleasure that knows."[9] Thus, taste or aesthetic judgement is from the beginning (Agamben's genealogical enquiry starts long before Kant) an in-between problem (or opportunity). When Agamben analyses Kant's treatment of this problem, discussing aesthetic judgement, he further notes that:

> It is in Kant's *Critique of the Power of Judgement* (1790) that the conception of the beautiful as an excessive signifier as well as of taste as the knowledge and enjoyment of this signifier find their most rigorous expression. From the first page, Kant in fact defines aesthetic pleasure as an excess of representation over knowledge.

This excessiveness, going back to Deleuze, can be likened to imagination that cannot be put in place or fully guided by a concept. Kant says that "... since to bring a representation of the imagination to concepts is the same as to expound it, the aesthetic Idea can be called an inexpoundable representation of the imagination (in its free play)."[10] On this Agamben comments: "The excess of imagination over understanding grounds beauty (the aesthetic idea), just as the excess of the concept over the image grounds the domain of the supersensible (the Ide of reason)."[11] Recalling Ricoeur's view of imagination allowing understanding built on the ruins of literal interpretation, we may elaborate on Agamben's excess and say that it is not only imagination that is at home in "free play" but that thinking that is provoked by imagination enjoys free movement as long as concepts cannot direct it fully into place – there is still conceptual building going on. This excess of the aesthetic over knowledge, the literary image of a possible world, can be thought of as creating an opening. This opening has a strong seductive force, which entrepreneurship makes use of to attract desire and assemble resources. All that has been actualized becomes history, and it is only "... by leaving history to reenter the immanence of the field of potential that change can occur. [...] there is an opening for this. It is called style."[12] Becoming, Massumi continues, "is inextricably aesthetic (stylistic) and ontological (emergent)."[13] Entrepreneurship is not a new idea, entrepreneurship is today a practice, but entrepreneurial becoming is evolving all the time. It is possible due to style, the aesthetic, an individuation, a node of expression, of the collective becoming in a new firm, the result of entrepreneuring. Again, we suggest calling this entrepreneurship process *Fabrication*. Charles Spinosa, in the context of a volume that discusses and develops the meanings and implications of a practice turn in contemporary theory, analyses how such leaving history and re-entering the immanence of the field of potential happens:

> A practice engages a new circumstance that cannot be easily accommodated with the considerations of the telos (appropriateness, familiarity, vulnerability, and mood). Hence, an imposition is required, and that imposition is itself retrospectively normalized.[14]

Entrepreneurship is a practice that is by its fixation with anomalies/ novelty set on a course where it will hit the limit of practice and therefore demand from the process that an imposition is created, that new organization is created, such that the entrepreneurial process is moved beyond the limit of the actual as set by practice and guided by a telos (characterizing how competitors do, or typically describing the advices given by consultants or business school professors or accelerator managers).

Background and context to the concept of fabrication

Conceptualizing entrepreneurship as *fabrication* enables us to think, study, and analyse entrepreneurial becoming as a breaking free from history – its practices, institutions, and telos – through the aesthetic difference a style-variation accomplishes in articulating an idea of the new, seductive enough to affect and assemble others.

Entrepreneurship continues to evolve as practice by leaving history and "re-enter the immanence of the field of potential" (as Massumi put it above). What breaks it free is its aesthetic force, its style-driven variation, how it affirms the multiplicity of differential relations leading from the virtual to the actual. Fabrication's seductive, joyful speculation, making a claim about the possible world, hits the world with an imaginative excess over knowledge. There are no concepts that precisely can capture this force, and instead an opening, a clearing is made. Moving into that clearing means joy and pleasure – this too is an aesthetic experience – and play can then happen. These are the two affective parts of the process, where the force of "literary fiction" and the desire to create assembles people and resources. This is needed for the process to tackle common sense – all the existing solutions' resistance to the new; all the reasonable objections; all the politically motivated negations – and find ways to move ahead towards commerce. Commerce would be the final confirmation that fabrication successfully enabled entrepreneurship to leave history and reenter the process of actualizing the new by differentiating it, offering a value to a potential customer that through commerce became an actual customer.

When Spinosa, Flores, and Dreyfus[15] enquired into entrepreneurship they related it to history or world-making. Entrepreneurship, in their conceptualization, is the practice of skilfully dealing with the world (things, people, practices) of starting and growing an organization by virtue of their having become acutely sensitive to prevailing dispositional styles and how these might alter. The experiential grounding of this skill, they point out, and backed up by phenomenological study, is neither abstract reflection nor cognitive processing, but affective-bodily engagement that discovers and latches onto anomalous experience, and finds here the location of difference to which others might be enjoined. Some bodies (including bodies of ideas, styles of thinking, but also teams, relationships, and people) have at times what Spinosa et al. call a heightened sensitivity for the potential of anomalies.[16] Rather than dissolve or avoid them, they investigate their potential.

Spinoza (the seventeenth century philosopher) talks about passion and Deleuze develops this away from passivity and to affectivity. Deleuze places emphasis on a power to be affected, which would explain why ideas "come to" some bodies and not other. In this processual conceptualization of passion, Massumi defines it as "… an incipience of action in readiness potential."[17] Fabrication, in portraying a future wanted state, relies on sympathy for where there is incipience of action in readiness potential (as Massumi describes passion), such that bodies can be affected, assembled, and become part of the becoming of the new.

Entrepreneurship becomes the process of disclosing new styles grounded in a diligent, intelligent, and immersed familiarity with the existing ones. In other words, entrepreneurship unfolds from within a history of existing practices, it is a gathering, emulating, toying with, and then twisting of what is already there. In its intimacy with history, entrepreneurship is also conservative: there is a necessary respect for what "is," because this is the agreeable soil in which what is different, surprising, or disturbing can take root.[18]

In its ambivalent respect for history, entrepreneurship is not unique, indeed it shares its enthusiasm with all manner of ritualistic and institutional practice, ranging from religions to the legal profession. Where it diverts from other practices, and enjoys distinction, is when it takes hold of history, and roughs it up, affeered, even, that what "is" there, by way of established practice, is becoming so weighty, so restrictive, that its very solidity is reason enough for critique, attempts to loosen the seemingly fixed. History is something to be respected and be wary of: it runs along rails of truth that have been fabricated. Management has become a practice of straightening out these rails through organizational settings such that the future becomes a diagrammatic plot running straight between past-present and future; it is a repeated attempt to figure out how to place history onto an abstract grid. Entrepreneurship does not oppose the grid or offer alternative grids: it is a disposition, not a rival dogma. Rather, it is a practice in which grids are experienced as spaces of twisting mystery: they delineate spaces in which the actual is giving way to the virtual. It is a grid of hesitations, of hand-drawn nuances, of alignments and placings whose surface order barely contains the new openings emerging from beneath.[19] In this sense, entrepreneurship is sensitive to the cracks in the strategic grid that holds the official history in place and affirms such cracks as potential openings by varying the style of engagement.

This is at least how Penrose envisaged entrepreneurs relating to and embodying history. Its effect was one of constrained flexibility; any process of economic creativity and growth began from an already existing condition, a restraining equilibrium of habituated forces. The necessity of these gridded conventions (routines, values, aspirations) is of an institutional order, not a natural one (and patterns of the grid remind us of this), and in being so they can be authored anew, and give rise to new sources of authority whose legitimacy cannot rely on existing criteria of what is right or good. These too have to be made anew:

> The entrepreneurial performance involves, on the one hand, the ability to perceive new opportunities that cannot be proved at the moment at which action has to be taken, and, on the other hand, will power adequate to break down the resistance that the social environment offers to change. But the range of the provable expands, and action upon flashes or hunches is increasingly replaced by action that is based upon "figuring out."[20]

Figuring out is not entrepreneurial. As Penrose suggests, it is more imaginative than that, more an awareness of how the gridded plotted lines of instituted repetition can be twisted anew.

If management is figuring out (as in solving), then entrepreneurship is fabrication. Fabrication comes from the Latin *fabrica* means "something skillfully made or constructed," but in addition carries dubious connotations of unreal things being made up. Both meanings, however, seem indispensable for creation – that it starts a process of making something up, imagining, fabricating. The crucial skill of the entrepreneur – which is a process that is mainly collectively composed – as we have tried to analyse and discuss above is this sensitivity before anomalies that interrupt the smooth ongoing plotted nature of an already instantiated world in which we are immersed and bodily engaged. The entrepreneurship process keeps to and coordinates the established order in ways that transform it by differentiating; by varying the style of engaging with people, things, and practices.

We can easily see how this relates to our emphasis on the role of assemblage as a proto-organizational form enabling us to grasp what is there before there is a new organization, a new firm, or business. There is a tendency, Spinosa, Flores, and Dreyfus say, that certain skills draw other skills together into more productive wholes. Tendencies are resources that the entrepreneurial process draws upon throughout. Tendencies, Massumi has defined for us already, as "pastnesses opening directly onto a future, but with no present to speak of." A tendency is thus futurity that is a fantasy for those that do not want to create an organization through which it can become actual. For those that do, it is a virtuality to be actualized. This requires creation as all new ideas, fantasies, fabulations, or visions do. Plans typically prolong, extend, and squeeze more out of less and are operationalized, implemented, or decided to the extent that they draw on existing resources. Such processes require management. However, resources that do not exist need to be created. This is entrepreneurship, an organization-creation process that seduces/assembles people that agree with this desire to actualize the virtual into an assemblage, a proto-organizational form that progresses towards an organization (a new firm, a new business) via play, common sense, and commerce. This is a fabricating process – fiction and making joined.

Spinoza would back this up with reference to his concept of joy: if skills can be made to agree with each other, the productive capacity of the domain constituted by related skills increases and a joyful life, life with greater capacity to create, to make, would follow. The concept of assemblage gives us the possibility to describe this collective belonging before there is an organization, which means we extend organization theory into the field where the challenge is to understand entrepreneurship.

When we deal with configurations of things, people, and practices, skilfully held together in a more productive whole such as an assemblage, this can be describing what Katz and Gartner referred to as the *emerging organization*.[21] What emerges out of the assemblage would then be a new organization, a start-up (beginning again). Whether this is a successful start-up or not is a question of whether the value it has been able to offer through its new organization is indeed acknowledged as such by others (potential users, customers). Start-ups occur always in an already organized world, full of alternative value-offerings. Imagination, the sensing of a virtual reality that has not become actualized yet, has to see through such an established gridded order and convincingly articulate the idea of how something is concealed, is missing, or could be taken further. Imagination would thus "disturb" such a world-in-order and open up a space for difference. Sensing an anomaly, central to how Spinosa, Flores, and Dreyfus describe the start of an entrepreneurship process, is often related to an idea of the new. When you realize that cars could run on battery, and you have an idea of how this could be actualized, this is initially the anomaly that gradually makes the fact that almost all cars run on fuel that is bad for the planet into the new anomaly (or a no longer neutral normality). When you get the idea that a plastic card can mediate monetary transactions, that anomaly is what gradually makes the use of physical money into the new anomaly (or at least no longer a neutral normality). However, apart from idea-driven anomalies, based on virtualities that make the world missing what could become actual, anomalies can also be practice-based, accidental style changes. Someone had to use x instead of the conventional y in a situation, and the potential change of practice incipient in that difference can be sensed as an anomaly by someone that hangs on to it and affirms it.

Present styles of skilfully coordinating people, resources, and practices, in a world in which existing organizations are operating, could also be the source of frustration or friction that drives the opening of an organization-creation process. What is crucial for this to happen, either from imagining, from accident, or from a style-threatening anomaly, is a body's power to be affected, to pick up the tendencies, to know where there is passion, to know how to seduce/be seduced, to be leading astray onto the unexplored land. With a power to be affected there is a possible entrance of a virtuality of transformative kind, often via a story that describes the virtually real such that joy – increased productive capacity – becomes incipient and attractive enough to assemble people and resources into an assemblage, a proto-organizational form, an emerging organization.

In this concluding chapter, we would like to performatively apply our ideas – demonstrating skilful dealing if you like – so as to enquire into the possibilities of this book's ideas having the function of disturbing the style of entrepreneurship research (and, by implication, practice) in such a way that it represents a virtuality, an idea of transformative kind, enabling this practice of entrepreneurship research to become something new. We believe the previous chapters provide discussions, opportunities to make use of as we try to achieve this end: transforming entrepreneurship research by adding a new process model, made from literary inspiration, of the entrepreneurship process. As with all entrepreneurship processes, following the introduction above, this would require a skilful, imaginative making – a fabrication – in order for this new theorization to disclose "entrepreneurship research" in a new way.

Review

We have located entrepreneurship in an array of fictional characters from literature and used literature in this way to arrive at entrepreneurship in a new way, for a particular reason: it is where we find entrepreneurship vividly present in life. Our interest in imagination, the artificial, and literature as a source for understanding life is one we share with Sarasvathy, Gartner, Spinosa, Flores, and Dreyfus, as well as Geertz and Greenblatt. In our literary sources, we find entrepreneurship engaged, embodied, and passionate. We wanted to affirm literature's power to tear "perception from its human home"[22] and allow us to sense what entrepreneurship – as part of actualized, lived life – could possibly become. Literature, in concentrated form, brings us life with affect and intensity (resonance). In this sense literature is only partly about what it means to us and more about what it does to us. It moves (wonder) us and our thinking by generating affect: it makes us reboot our thinking by having us see possible worlds. It is, therefore, entrepreneurial in the sense that we are moved into the playful, the aesthetic experience where concepts are not capturing thought but where we have to imagine how to move on. We relate to literature not only as representative but also as productive. "Literature has the power to mobilize desire, to create new pre-personal investments, and enables thought and affects that extend beyond the human."[23] Literature helps us make entrepreneurship leave history and reenter the immanence of the field of potential: it can now become something new by being differentiated. Our way (see below) is characterized by bringing the affects and intensities from literature with us into the organization of them into ideas that challenge the concept of entrepreneurship and moves it beyond the sense it has in history. Process thinking's empiricism is thus an acknowledgement of that fiction is at the heart of any analysis that stays with experience: "because it exposes the productions and extensions of ideas from their affective components."[24] Our new model of the entrepreneurship process provides a new interval that can bring new actuality out of the virtual.

Our way, through literature, to engage with and study entrepreneurship beyond history is also an approach that embraces the romanticist endorsement of imaginative thinking, whilst remaining suspicious of its tendency to elevate the personal above the circumstantial (a tendency we also witness in entrepreneurship itself). Romanticism thrives by living through a cracking or breaking down of the institutional continuity of an everyday, embodied, immersed lived experience, and entrepreneurs too have been sensing, describing, and exploring such fragmentary life. Through its imaginary effort the novel became possible, a form of writing in which the interiority of a subject and the exteriority of subjection were shown yielding to one another in patterns of resisting, enhancing, complying, and abjuring, thereby creating form. We have learned from such forms, and notably the characters in whom becoming a subject is revealed as a continual elaboration of negotiation of subjection.

These characters – Dalloway, Pippi, Sorel, Ripley, Chichikov, Don Giovanni, Iago, Bennet – are not entrepreneurs. Rather, in their thought, feeling, and action we find expressions of what, when placed in company, we have been striving to call the entrepreneurial process. Taken separately, these characters do not evoke images that help us to better describe and analyse the whole entrepreneurial process. Taken as a whole, they do because of the interaction between them and its (the interaction's) effect. There is desire for actualizing the virtually new, to move beyond what is presently actual. This desire affects seduction such that it is given a direction and is as such prevented from becoming an end in itself. It is thus only partly Don Giovanni's seduction, and only partly Iago's seduction. It is seduction to join a road not taken, a direction even without a road, and find joy in making "moving ahead" possible together. It shares with Don Giovanni and Iago the affective intensity that belongs to listening to a story where you have to know how it ends and where you have a real sense of being part of making a particular end happen. Studies of this have appeared in entrepreneurship- and organization studies research: narrative approaches[25] have studied how stories affect the entrepreneurship process' success in dealing with scepticism or reluctance. Cultural entrepreneurship and institutional entrepreneurship studies have focused on how stories are part of attracting resources and breaking normative regulations, templates, and role constraints reproducing institutionalized behaviours.[26] To this we have added the theoretical context of a process model for entrepreneurship, and the affective dimension that is central for being alert to seducation as a concept, as well as for understanding the role of desire in the organization-creation process.

That particular kind of seduction is then related to play, making play interact with seduction and both being affected by that interaction (interaction-in-the-making being a relation). This play is also not Pippi's or Mrs Dalloway's play. Only partly so, since Pippi's rebellion and Mrs Dalloway's party mood and loosening of rigid social roles (which of course Pippi does too) have some but not perfectly overlapping contexts with entrepreneurship processes. The latter needs more to reward the seduced with play as a sense of freedom and possibility. Play is also a necessity when you need to find out, beyond the regulations, institutions, roles, and templates of the actual, what becoming-actual of the virtual needs in order to create its way through. Play too has been part of entrepreneurship research,[27] but again the processual and affective is what we better see and understand when using literature as empirical sources.

Although we might, for pedagogical reasons, exaggerate a sense of linearity here, our process model of entrepreneurship informs us that play emerges from seduction and is on its way to a relationship (an interaction-in-the-making) with common sense. However, seduction may also be understood as initiated by an urge to play, to relativize the practices and perceptions that hold dominant normality in place. Play, no doubt on its way towards commerce in most entrepreneurship processes, will also soon encounter common sense as that which defines the anomaly – the virtuality – you hang on to and want to see actualized as the source of new value. Will and energy to battle common sense in our model are surely fuelled by having seduced others to join and follow. Versions of battling common sense appear all over the entrepreneurship research literature. Indeed, Schumpeter's vibrant concept of "creative destruction" targets the challenge. However, resonant with what seems to have been the personal style of Schumpeter,[28] and indeed Schumpeter as a conceptual persona[29] in modern entrepreneurship research, the concepts are, from a process philosophical perspective, somewhat over-dramatic in exaggerating the impacts on the actual, on what is, on, for example, the institutionalized. What we show with our model is that something more tactical, transformatively insinuating (as de Certeau would conceptualize tactics) does the work better. Common sense needs to be understood and dealt with rather than destroyed, in order to create receptivity for the new. Yet, it is in battling common sense that the intensity of the image of the new is sensed. Intensity is here incipience, as we have earlier described, and this means that tendencies to actualize the new press upon the actual to find a way to completion. Common sense has to understand the point and acknowledge the difference as attractive enough to have value, or, common sense is the source of awe, dazzlement, wonder, the equivalent of an aesthetic experience where imagination is called on to freely identify a concept to make sense, to acknowledge the new.[30]

Commerce, in our process philosophical model of entrepreneurship, is more to be understood as what takes us back into the role of a traditional rational decision maker. The potential customer is made into a potential customer by the affective impact a novelty has on her/him after encountering the experience that called on imagination to make sense (of the new). "There is no calculus of risk independent of an individual's affective self-relation to uncertainty." Massumi points out,[31] wherefore rationality and affectivity are joined in self-interest. The individual, processually, affectively, is seen as the result of having collected oneself from the dividual multiplicity that we sense affectively. We are many and that room of multiple is where affect is sensed as we move around by intensities. Economy calls upon us as individuals with self-interest. The decision to buy is made by a dividual having decided to make commerce as an individual with an interest. Massumi calls this the infra-individual – the endpoint and starting point of the economy. Sorel and Ripley are certainly more moved and moving around on the infra-individual level, as dividuals with an urge to collect themselves as individuals but struggling to find a way to do so that gives them joy. Yet, from all their attempts to achieve commerce, we learn the role of affect also for this to happen.

"This makes the economy more affectively activating than it is effect-ively rationalizing," Massumi points out.[32] Again, entrepreneurship and organization studies research is full of commerce, but only lately have affect come into the picture[33] and this book is added to this.

The images that these characters give us are images of what it is to experience and imagine seduction, play, common sense, and commerce. Potentially we might have chosen other characters but have been limited by our own histories and their familiarity, at which we attempt to push.[34] These characters are emblematic and exemplaric in the sense that the actuality of seduction, play, common sense, and commerce have inspired authors to imagine how they are loved out in new stories. The fact that all these stories have reached immense popularity and are indeed considered classics by most readers and critics only contest to the resonance they have with readers' lives in an endless variation of contexts.

Entrepreneurship and fabrication

To describe this process we cannot come up with a better example of world-making and things forming than entrepreneurial fabrication. Literature has helped us find a language for expressing this sensing of a world disintegrating, falling apart, cracking, and opening up to the new, this event-potential, in ways that upset the easy and casual ways of the already institutionalized. In this sense, as pointed out in Chapter 3, fiction can reinvest language with the wealth of experience, with affect, passion, intensity, which is often lost in a theoretical language that still carries the burden of Galilean distance and Cartesian detachment. Entrepreneurship, such as our point of departure, is a desire for disclosing new opportun-ities and their potentiality and this process starts with a power to be affected by anomalies or sensing of tendency in view of imaginative futures. To explore such desire, to understand this affect, to enquire into how it assembles resources and makes new worlds happen, literature had to become our faithful companion. And the romantic urge for "else-where" holds the forces of a de-territorializing or uprooting move, the sensing of a pull from an image of where we could be, what we could do, that generates movements. The movement that fascinates us in this book is the one we refer to as the entrepreneurship process, and have modelled according to seduction, play, common sense, and commerce.

Entrepreneurship, when made known via literature and philosophy, is that process that tenders incipient newness (opportunity) into fru-ition by allowing the world/what is/the actual to be cracked/breached/de-territorialized in a move towards "foreign territory." This process will always be surveilled by the guardians of the dominant view, the institutionalized habits, the strategy that have bestowed upon bodies their functions in a prescribed place – the world of normal. Getting away from there, an urge we connected to the Romantic view in the opening of this book, is based on a desire for and opening to the affect of what is other, and requires a seductive move that affirms the playful (venturous), respects common sense, and targets commerce as a kind of receipt that a re-territorialization was indeed possible and has been accomplished: desire became productive in new ways.

This might give birth, from within the fertile grounds of an assemblage, to a new organization, often called a start-up or a venture.[35] We have not been able, this book argues, to describe this creation process, entrepreneurship, in such a realistic language until we acquainted it with literature. Literature gave us a language of immersed life, lived life fully engaged, fully attached. The point with experiencing affect, the intensity of the life of the characters we have studied, is that affect typically pauses the normal action-reaction circuit and makes us passionate. Learning this from literature enables us to understand how new ideas come to us and how they affect others (to join the entrepreneurial process). Imagination, at the same time involuntary and elicited, as Massumi suggests, shows us the no-difference between perception, cognition, and hallucination.[36] This is the delirious of imagination, and literature as delirium. Deleuze describes this as a force of imagination that keeps us evolving, on the move, nomadic in ways we see are intimately related to entrepreneurial restlessness and passion for loosening the seemingly fixed for the purpose of creating hitherto missing values and life made possible by such. Entrepreneurship would then be what "forces itself out of its usual furrows," "disorganising its own forms," and "encourage ruptures and new sproutings."[37] This is close to being another way of saying what Schumpeter said with "creative destruction."

From there, literary imagination, delirious thought affecting us by showing possible life rather than what life is, from the many adventures of such lives that we have enquired into throughout this book, emerges a new language in which entrepreneurship is made intelligible in a different way that we hope makes a difference. This chapter will develop what difference this difference makes for entrepreneurship research in particular. We will summarize and conclude and make use of the learnings already before we have reached the back cover of the book. In this sense we demand from ourselves to be performative, to demonstrate what being affected by this book does to us as entrepreneurship scholars.

Shortly summarizing the basis for our model

We can claim that we have been seduced by this book's ideas, seduced by entrepreneurship itself, and perhaps even, if we are self-critical, by the preponderant and apparently irresistible self-making discourse of enterprise. Obviously, we were seduced by the ideas that we brought into the composition that resulted in this book. Yet we hope to have been led somewhat astray by entrepreneurship, rather than simply accede to the despotic demands of enterprise. In that sense we feel to have been led astray into a playful process, struggling with entrepreneurship research's common sense for what entrepreneurship is and how to study it, and aiming for delivering an interesting result to the publisher that, ultimately through commerce, reaches out to you, the reader. This is organization of writing and publishing of the book. We therefore know the ideas from having lived them, and believe we can witness from experience that this book could move entrepreneurship research thinking. We have also tested the core model and its implications for analysis in many conferences, seminars, and PhD courses. Amid such occasions we have met with generative feedback and stories from researchers' and teachers' lives where listeners have already started to imagine what it could mean for them in their everyday practice. It is thus with some (critical) confidence that we conclude on and demonstrate what this book can do.

Romanticism and human nature was a theme that allowed us to describe entrepreneurship as that process that imagines and seeks to clear new land, because of a desire to see what life beyond the limit of the present could mean for opportunities that pressed themselves upon the actual everyday practices. This desire, we argued, is producing the curious body whose power to be affected nurtures and is nurtured by this desire. Openness to the other, a power to be affected that Spinoza says is based on having incomplete ideas, ideas that are in-between what prepares me proper for action, and the situation where I need to collaborate to increase my productive capacity. This drives the entrepreneur into encounters with others, and to the extent that their ideas agree with the others', their capacity to produce increases and they experience joy. "The process of desire," said Deleuze, "is called joy."[38] When you are interested in entrepreneurship as a process that forms firms to actualize new value, the proto-organizational start of this process is the time of the assemblage. The assemblage is the collective necessity for productive capacity to increase, and the joy of this happening is what provides motivational force to the assemblage, which is held together by desire. It follows that the emphasis on risk as a differentiating factor identifying the entrepreneur as different from managers, small-business owners, and folks in general, which is a debated and yet persistent idea in entrepreneurship research, is to a large extent a result of missing desire and joy of creating possible worlds.[39] Risk is tied in with an ontology of being, seeing the individual as a subject that spots opportunities "out there" and calculates whether it is worth acting on them. When we turn to an ontology of becoming, we understand that to the extent that risk is involved, it is not about disturbing what is there so much as about not reaching agreement with others, not reaching increased productive capacity, not actualizing enough of the imagined new world for it to pay off in terms of joy.

We thus turned to imagination and the language of **fiction** and the primary form of expression where most of us read it – **the novel**. Fiction, otherwise, is of course part of our everyday, the way we speak and the way we plan. Every plan, every strategy, every imagination of what could become but is not yet are examples of fiction. In the case of the entrepreneurship process, we can talk about a narrative groping for ways (handles) to bring the virtual into the actual. Soon enough this turns into an organizational groping that we call assembling. Anticipations of how the virtually real can become actual are always formulated as fictions. Plans and numbers do not change that. Our choice to make fiction our "empirical basis" for a renewal of our processual understanding of entrepreneurship is based on the need to stay with life and learn entrepreneurship from the language that is spoken from the edge of the actual. Most of us know how fiction plays a part in our scholarly quest for knowledge as we often abductively grope for how to make the swerving matter we seek to understand describable. When Karl Weick reasons his way towards the conclusion that theorizing in the social sciences (including economics) cannot rely on validation, because the process depends on images, maps, metaphors to grasp what they study, and that theory construction centres on imagination and artificial selection, what is missing is a reflection on how this is performed in his own text, how the text writes him, and in his case the concealed nature of this framing, somewhat ironically, is stark.

Similar concerns can be brought to bear in entrepreneurship research: just how much of what is being studied is itself structured by the framing being brought to the field? Relatedly, studies might better consider just how productive might fictional structures be when it comes to understanding the entrepreneurial, not just through theory but also as a practice.[40] Conjectures are sprung out of thick-description born imaginations that acquire prototypical qualities in helping people make sense of their predicament. However, when that predicament is about how to make people believe in and help actualize the virtually new, the primary effect of a conjecture is how it makes the fiction of what will come retrospectively into a prototype for what has achieved the status of "being there." The intensity of the conjecture's image is a question of how strong, with what force, it tends towards its future. Intensity is here both incipience and a selection – some but not all will be actualized. What will be actualized is a question of the intensity of the tendencies given in the conjectural vision of a wanted future: tendencies are "pastness opening directly onto a future, but with no present to speak of" (as Massumi has put this).[41] Timing, context, and the joy provided by the assemblage would be part of how swift filling this present with what is missing for it to become that future happens. Retrospectively, this would be described as the potential of the conjectural vision to become actualized. Potential is futurity and pastness combined into a spring that provides force to actualization.

The language that escapes the real, the institutionalized, the habituated, the language of making entrepreneurship leave history and enter potential becoming is equally the language of a **desire** to escape and subvert, the language of entrepreneurial fiction. The novel's power to affect its readers, the way it intrudes on the real world, we suggest, is paralleled by the entrepreneurial fabrication's power to affect other bodies, to intrude into lived life and seduce them into the process (seduction – play – common sense – commerce). The truth that fiction has us experience – how we recognize the pain a poet describes or the love that makes a character in a novel sing – is **affectively** carried. The intensity of the affect comes not primarily from how well the story corresponds to some reality (the location of which is a matter of contextually based validation), not from its representational quality, but from what the author/narrator wants to achieve – its productionist quality. How much we are affected by a fiction, or an entrepreneurship story of a future to come, is a question of what that story wants, as expressed by an author/narrator, and how that resonates with our lives. This is the question of agreement or lack thereof, in Spinoza's terms, between forces. When they agree, we experience joy (increased productive capacity), and when not, sadness (decreased productive capacity).

Assemblage, finally, is the concept we propose as capturing this proto-organizational form that is formed before an organization is created, and that is more than a network. Assemblages are all about increasing the productive capacity of related bodies, also bodies of thought. Assemblages are held together by desire. Assemblages are both concrete – as in a start-up process – and abstract, as in the specific relationships between forces that affect what bodies can do together. Passion is a key part of how assemblages work, since passion answers how I am affected by others and other forces, and how I in turn affect them. Assemblages are distinctly entrepreneurial to the extent that they cannot be subject to management, which would make desire reduced to interest and assemblage reduced to organization. "Reduced" is not a lower form or less valuable form. We use it simply to describe that assemblages and desire are more than that – they are multiplicities with potential trajectories of becoming. This also means they are limited (and thus reduced) to one specific form when they are made into a specific interest and the specific organization that is designed to achieve that interest. Actualization necessarily involves selection apart from differentiation when one of the virtualities is created. This is probably why the concept of assemblage has not appeared frequently in management research. Management, as already Mary Parker Follet noted, is the practice of getting people to get things done with reference to one general interest that gives priority to efficient execution, the control of which is the domain and expertise of management. This move from desire to desire being coded into a particular interest inevitably happens in the creation of new firms. It does not mean it is wrong, but it means we have then entered a *managerial* world. Management is needed, for what we have created also needs to be used efficiently and in a controlled manner. Entrepreneurship, however, has to be created and re-created as its nature is to be processually ephemeral, creating organization by fuelling desire to venture, playfully, into the assemblage.

There is thus, as previously pointed out, a time for entrepreneurship and a time for management. We note that it is in the time of mature equilibria, when the desire to move beyond the common sense fringe of what is considered valuable, that entrepreneurship's seductive forces are intensified. On both sides of the unhinged equilibria, in the border land of seduction and play, this is the peak time of entrepreneurship. When we move away from the region of an equilibrium, this is when the proto-organizational process of forming an organization is intensified.

In this sense we are Schumpeterians. Schumpeter suggested that entrepreneurship's innovative impact on the economy was characterized by unhinging it from equilibrium. On a more macro-economic level, you can thus say that equilibria drive the entrepreneurial desire to explore a common sense stability, the balance achieved by existing knowledge being at work in a market. That is the time of entrepreneurship. This, on a more micro-social level, is when the world – always temporally and spatially defined by a specific social context – is opened to being seduced into processes of becoming. This is, our theory proposes, the time of Don Giovanni and Iago, the time of being led astray, into the venturous. The seduction-play-common sense-commerce process allows us to say something new and more about entrepreneurship. Let us elaborate further on this new capacity and what it can mean for entrepreneurship research.

Researching entrepreneurship anew

When we in 2008 engaged with the neo-Kantian-pragmatist philosopher Hans Vaihinger's work in order to analyse and better understand William Gartner's contribution to entrepreneurship research, we emphasized the importance of imagination.[42] Vaihinger engaged with Kant's philosophy, where, as we have discussed above, in The *Critique of Judgement,* imagination plays a key role in "performing" the free play that helps us extend thought to make sense of aesthetic experiences. What we discussed above in terms of the importance of imagination for describing, analysing, and understanding entrepreneurship as the process of actualizing the virtually new, seems to have been a problem or challenge for thought that Vaihinger too focused on, and for which he developed his "as if" philosophy.

Gartner draws on this in the early development of a constructionist theorization (with inspiration from Weick's work) of entrepreneurship. This characterizes the 1990s in European–Scandinavian entrepreneurship research, inspired by and inspiring Gartner. In a curious piece from 1993 – "Words lead to deeds" – Gartner turns to literature, T.S. Eliot's Four Quartets, to suggest the generative analogy between falling in love and the emerging organization. To us, an indirect reference to affect as central to the time of organization-creation. Organizational emergence, what we in this book would describe as the time of assembling, of entrepreneurial organization-creation, is to the existing organization what falling in love is to being in a relationship, Gartner suggested. Later, he turns towards the narrative and subsequently the practice-based approaches to entrepreneurship processes.[43] A thread that runs through this work is attention

to imagination, to acting "as if." The emerging organization is ontologically different from the existing organization. This theme, running through
processual entrepreneurship studies, not only places emphasis on the relationship between the virtual and the actual, on actualization as creation,
but also on the importance of understanding the process as such. The
arrow in mid-air is ontologically different from the arrow resting at the
nock point by the string, and it is ontologically different from the arrow
that has reached the target: these are potentiality-arrow, flying-arrow,
and having-hit-or-missed-arrow.[44]

"As if" thinking is thinking beyond and ahead of fixing language, it
moves thought freely, before it is caught by concepts, so as to pragmatic-
ally speculate, to foretell how the virtual can be made actual. This is resonant with a process thinking that upgrades thinking's creative capacity
and its role and function in steering action into worldmaking:

> While it is thought which must explore the virtual down to the ground
> of its repetitions, it is imagination which must grasp the process of
> actualization from the point of view of these echoes or reprises. It is
> imagination which crosses domains, orders and levels, grasping the
> unity of mind and nature, moving endlessly from science to dream
> and back again.[45]

Where Kant steps back a bit after having discovered the power of
imagination, Deleuze and Guatarri step forth, affirming imagination as a
directedness-towards the world, an opening of a world as such, a springing-
forth that then allows the formation of subjects and understanding given
the work of concepts "invading" the free space opened by imagination.[46]
The process of fabrication is the work of making use of this opening
for the purpose of making an organization of people, resources, practices,
and things where this is missing for new value to be offered to others. Once
organized, there remains a continual awareness that further openings are
possible, indeed desirable, that is insofar as the entrepreneurial, insofar as
it is more than just commercial enterprise, releases the collective capacity
for and expression of critique.[47]

When we started on the project of re-thinking, re-conceptualizing,
and re-writing entrepreneurship, upgrading the role of imagination,
fabulation, and (now) fabrication has been central to it. Schumpeter's
emphasis on creativity and Spinosa, Flores, and Dreyfus' emphasis on
worldmaking and philosophy have all partaken in this. What we have
added, in this book, is the result of approaching entrepreneurship via process philosophy and literature, and it has brought us to the more intimate
conversation with organization theory, and the framing concepts of
affect, desire, and assemblage. With process thinking comes an empiricism that seeks to stay with bodies, action, the visceral, timing, location,
but the deed and movements before doers and positions. Then, we argue,
there is a natural direction where seduction initiates and opens up the

venture for people. This is how you get attracted to joining the assemblage. This is how you get constructed as a co-creator by the desire to explore what value can be achieved when moving beyond the fringe of the established order. What distinguishes the entrepreneurial process is a desire to create organization amongst people, resources, things, ideas, affects, such that the pursued value is actualized in the sense offered to those that would have to confirm it by becoming customers. Joining the assemblage is initially an event as much as a decision. Bodies are attracted, like in a magnetic field, by the sharing of desire to see an idea or image become actualized. This desire achieves an individuation through intensifying forces such that an affective event of potentiality is set up. This field constructs the subject missing for this field to become productive of a process that will ultimately actualize the idea of the new (the virtual becoming actual). Attention to desire adds to the way affect has been entered into entrepreneurship research lately, where the relation between affect and cognition tends to dominate.[48] It brings us to the level of the process and to the relation, to the interaction-in-the-making, rather than to who is related. It, thus, brings us to the organization-creation process and how assembling characterizes its becoming.

The reward for the passionate body, having a power to be affected that draws you into this field of intensity, is play-free movement. This movement is in turn intensified to the extent it is shared with others agreeing with your desire to actualize. Agreement means increased capacity, which means joy. This sense of belonging to a productive whole is often fuelled by an image, a story that provides a narrative "line of flight" that suggests how the already more, the virtual, can be furthered into its incipient next-ness, how the world can be rolled into its newness. Most entrepreneurship processes would go through the seduction-play-common sense-commerce process several times before a stable enough trade has become established for there to be reasons to formalize an organization.[49] This happens as a result of dealing with common sense and understanding how much it needs to be integrated into the stories of the new in order for "the world" to understand and appreciate the proposed value. Gradually, desire has to find a language through which it can express itself and "do the job" of creating an organization out of the assemblage. It means that there needs to be a socially accepted coding of desire into interests. Such interests are easily translated into business language – marketing plans, strategies, recruitment needs, funding proposals, product- and service portfolios – for which there are multiple templates in place.

This language and those templates have since the Second World War been productive of a dominant subjectivity – the manager.[50] Gradually, management leans into the new organizational equilibrium the desire to move beyond the fringe of things, to increase freedom of movement, is quelled and left waiting in the wings. When this happens, subject-positions have been stabilized, the assemblage has solidified into relations of forces that are in place: management is dominant and entrepreneurship is the dominated. We get a hierarchy, and we get social roles, responsibilities attached to those, and a sense of inside and outside, a collective identity. In short, we have arrived at an organization, with its institutions, where management conceives of problems of control and efficiency: meantime the entrepreneurial waits, witnessing the hierarchy and stirring anew.

To recap: what does this model mean for describing, researching, and analysing entrepreneurship?

Seduction

Seductions come in many forms, but indications of their existence often appear in the embodiment of desire – expressed by a person with a story to tell, a new plot, which opens up something within the grid: "look, see, it might be done like this instead." It is not, though, a story offering a rival grid. Nowadays, in the wake of political and educational systems that have "installed" support for entrepreneurship in the shape of entrepreneurship-ecosystems and business school programs and student-incubators, there are plenty of competitions that ask the "storytellers" to squeeze their fabulations into the format of a business plan, business model canvas, and customer value propositions often in design thinking infused value proposition design processes.[51] Business schools and universities alike have launched student incubators, and national policy systems are falling over one another to champion entrepreneurship- and innovation ecosystems using business incubators and accelerators.[52] The risk here is that all of this has become part of a grid, which too is productive of its world. Seeing entrepreneurship, opportunity, value is easily reproductive of this particular framing. It is perhaps primarily a managerial style of figuring out how to do more with less, and it easily comes to dominate too early in the start-up process and so confine what, ostensibly, is unconfined.[53] The opening up of the world through imagines of the new can thus quickly be closed by the normalization of a particular way of seeing the world and thus what needs to be done to place another successful start-up in it.

Given our model of the entrepreneurial process, this problem of too much management too early in the process can be described as desire being coded as interest, when it should have been allowed to continue to overspill a bit longer, as desire. An interest aligns with, and falls into, the furrows that a strategy has pointed out in relation to goals: it is an investment in a particular achievement. This breaks desire's capacity to configure and hold an assemblage together, and it seeks the organization in the proto-organizational condition in which seduction and play thrive.[54] The desire-directed assemblage proliferates like a poetic bubbling and swarming, just like how Michel de Certeau describes creation: "In reality, creation is a disseminated proliferation. It swarms and throbs. A polymorphous carnival infiltrates everywhere, a celebration …"[55] It operates as a multitude, in the plural, and is effectively reduced into "one" when the prose of interest is introduced as an interstice that seeks to achieve a particular output. The creation process is then, in Bergson's analysis, reduced to an execution of the possible, the implementation of a plan. The actualization of the virtual, creation by differentiation, is then lost and newness reduced to moreness.

Like in the business of Iago's (Chapter 5), his stories mobilize desire, they swarm and throb, operating as a multitude, "in the plural": his desired actuality – getting rid of Othello – has multiple virtualities through which this could become achieved. His infiltrations are at work everywhere, providing fodder to the great fire that eventually will destroy almost everyone. The force holding this carnevalesque identification and gathering of fodder together is desire that maintains a potential for organization in the assemblage. Desire directs material flows, as a social force, and brings bodies together so as to increase their productive capacity and thereby – Spinoza would say – the joy of living.[56] Iago continuously feeds this fire through the dark poetry of what could become, seductive and playful adventures are described as promises that will be fulfilled if those that listen agree to get led astray and join.

Iago's desire is itself stirred by his having been rejected from what he felt was his rightful position, and being refused the role deputy, he refuses all fixed identities and like Don Giovanni, he gives himself up to movement.[57] But unlike Don Giovanni, who is almost a caricature of desire-as-movement, Iago consciously enlists others in the loosening of gridded order. This loosening can be described as a lack of character in the sense that nothing is fixed long enough to be found.[58] The rhizomatic nature of Don Giovanni's and Iago's stories, and their corresponding self-narratives, is a way to operate with the multitude as a style of movement, rather than using a specific form, answering to a socially coded version of desire as a particular interest. If there is any form for the rhizomatic multiplicity, it is the assemblage, held together by desire. Desire does not settle in a gridded structure (like the business plan, the business model canvas) but makes the assemblage into the nomadic home for desire. If a structure is pressed upon it, the wings get clipped, movement and flight becomes secondary, interest takes over, and desire becomes muted in ever more dexterous patterns of figuring out.

There is a long history in entrepreneurship research of focusing on the individual entrepreneur being held in relations with other individuals but with little attention being paid to the more elusive contextual atmosphere of language or affect.[59] Some of this also sought to find the traits or psychological "profile" that would explain the success of some rather than others. Although most of these ghosts are laid to rest, subsequent approaches still maintain a fixation on individual units, albeit ones held in wider systems such as clusters or ecosystems.[60] Those studies focusing on the relational qualities of context, resonate in non-individualistic cultures, yet have had a hard time influencing mainstream thinking because, it seems, of their tolerating what is contingent, opaque, and unpredictable. More recent efforts to research entrepreneurship without recourse to the firm grounding of identifiable variables, and which focus instead immersive, experiential study, seem promising in this regard, as do proposals to turn attention to affect (although here we also caution against what can appear as a return to the individual [body]).[61] Our proposal to research entrepreneurship as a "seduction-play-common sense-commerce" process of organization-creation requires attention to context, relations, language (as discourse and narrative). In this sense we build on yet challenge previous research to move entrepreneurship research ahead by bringing this into an integrative model that opens up new ways to research and know entrepreneurship.

Play

Play also comes in many forms and shapes. Limiting ourselves here to the study and practice of entrepreneurship, play still has many functions in that process. In our process it follows upon seduction, but the model is also said to be open in the sense that entrance into it can happen at any of the phases that we, for analytical-theoretical purpose, have separated. Indeed, as the *poetry of business* the entrepreneurship process is as such making use of play in the sense of an in-between, a gap, a potential for movement. Opening from seduction the entrepreneurship process mobilizes people, persuading them that going astray has a reward. If we understand this from the perspective of Spinoza's philosophy of force, body, and *conatus*. Once swept away by a convincing promise, the process becomes a playful search for productive capacity in spaces that are, by their nature, somewhat disorienting. The freedom is one of moving without a script, acting in order to know and organize what otherwise remains ephemeral and difficult to maintain (Vaihinger's philosophy of "as if").[62]

Play, when understood as being integral to an "as if" practice, comes in the continuous loosening of the seemingly fixed in order to free up space for movement to which others also become affectively implicated. A power to be affected, related via passion to a power to affect, is perhaps also what we understand as openness. As Deleuze puts it, reading Spinoza:

> when we encounter a body that agrees with our nature, one whose relation compounds with ours, we may say that its power is added to ours; the passions that affect us are those of *joy*, and our power of acting is increased or enhanced.[63]

What we want to emphasize is that openness and play are intimately related to the use of space, to the attractiveness of space as a playground. Deleuze suggests this joy of increased capacity to act can be described as "the correlate of speculative affirmation."[64] "Speculative affirmation" could also be a description of a playful move towards what is not but could become, and as such it exposes players to the difference that marks out the processes of innovation by which play begins to sediment into patterns of established order, or what we have called common sense.[65]

Play is a surprisingly rare theme in entrepreneurship research. If the exclude role-playing (in the context of learning entrepreneurship) and game-playing as a way to train scenarios (also most often in educational contexts), play as a free movement, as experimentation and imaginative, semantic innovation – play/ing is a rare concept in entrepreneurship research. Steyaert encourages us to experiment more, to consider the ontological politics of methods, as we re-conceptualize how we perform ourselves as entrepreneurship scholars.[66] In organizational research, recent work has suggested that the concepts of organizational creativity, play, and entrepreneurship provide a framing for researching organizational renewal and change.[67] Play is notoriously slippery as a concept, but if we see it as the absence of a regulating centre, as a space for fabulation in the absence of concepts guiding thought we find it helps us focus on the process – on playing – and see that the individual is but a node of expression of the play.[68] The subject (the agent, the actant) is new value and playing is the organization-creation process that makes new value achieve being through seduction, play, common sense, and commerce. As we have tried to indicate in this book, imagination, aesthetic judgement, and taste, the realm of problems we typically refer to aesthetics, seems like a fruitful place to start when trying to relate entrepreneurship and play.[69] Robert Chia's early plea for a more entrepreneurial scholarship is an ambition that has inspired and hopefully animated this book. It also brings together skills that need to be cultivated in entrepreneurial practice whether in organization-creation of in entrepreneurial scholarship; sensitivity, style, beauty of ideas:

> Intellectual entrepreneurship implies a conscious and deliberate attempt on the part of academics themselves to explore the world of ideas boldly and without the undue inhibitions of disciplinary restraints, so as to cultivate the necessary sensitivity and style of thinking that is capable of inducing in aspiring entrepreneurial managers an intimate sense for the power and beauty of ideas, and an eye for the bearing of one set of ideas on another.[70]

It also reminds us that in the world of academia, common sense is often effective as "inhibitions of disciplinary restrains" and as such these are important to understand – as we have argued and shown in our model – in order for a more entrepreneurial practice to emerge. We could of course not agree more with Chia's reflection that: "I believe that recourse to literature and the arts provides the best means of stimulating the 'powers of association' in young, fertile minds."[71] And we share with him the emphasis on the Whiteheadian truth that Business School education, like all university education, must cultivate imaginative acquisition of knowledge, and that this must too be exemplified in how research in entrepreneurship creates knowledge:

> Thus the proper function of a university is the imaginative acquisition of knowledge. Apart from this importance of the imagination, there is no reason why business men, and other professional men, should not pick up their facts bit by bit as they want them for particular occasions. A university is imaginative or it is nothing – at least nothing useful.[72]

Common sense

One of the most common ways to force the entrepreneurial process to accept what is already in place – what habits, routines, logics, customs, templates, roles, norms, and standards that already provide backdrop to customers' understanding of what is valuable and not – is the business plan. Historically, in entrepreneurship practice, the business plan holds a most prominent place as common sense. The business plan – or business model canvas, or customer value proposition, or strategy – is part of the entrepreneurial curriculum and ecosystem, it belongs to the very basic ground from which new ventures are, institutionally speaking, born as facts, registered in start-up statistics.[73] For quite some time (1980s and 1990s), whether the business plan was really needed to begin a venture, whether it made any difference to the success of a venture, seemed secondary to its being an institutional expression of intent.[74] One would always have to watch out for the tendency that the business plan becomes less of a tool to ensure economic viability than a way to discipline the entrepreneurial subjects, legitimizing the limits that define the norms of enterprising. That would indeed be more interesting to incubator managers and venture capitalist firms than to the entrepreneurial process. Jane Austen's Elisabeth Bennett is constantly identifying where the limit of the normal is presently drawn. Her respect for that boundary is being constantly acknowledged as she moves in society, confirmed in her small actions, thoughts and feelings of sense and sensibility. Yet in being so attentive and attuned as she is, she becomes alive to the slight absurdity of these conventions, and hence of their possible transgression: the persistent asking of "what" and "how" soon spills over into asking "why?"

The entrepreneur is of course also there, at the limit, in order to figure out how limits can be breached without the breach being rejected as an intolerable move. How can a difference be created without disconnecting from common sense's capacity to perceive value in the proposal? In this sense, and from a process perspective, entrepreneurship processes also benefit from being forced to acquaint themselves with what the dominant normality is, what is expected of them according to the institutionalized templates, norms for behaviour, and roles through which to exercise agency.[75] This draws the line and makes it easier not only to follow suit but also to transgress, differentiate, create.[76] Bennett asks: "… what is the difference in matrimonial affairs, between the mercenary and the prudent motive? Where does discretion end, and avarice begin?" searching for this line, in order *not* to cross it. But in making the line explicit, ipso facto, what is beyond the line comes into view as a horizon of possibility. The entrepreneurial process is there, at the edge, precisely to learn how to cross it cleverly, thereby using the receptive capacity of those coming along with the proposal. Play as a respectful way of handling the limit is thus intimately related to an ethics of finding life-affirming ways for actualizing the virtual, creating a differentiating line of introducing the new into contexts of everyday practices in a way that makes it graspable as valuable.

At its heart, an ethics of entrepreneurship is about this capacity to stay in the "open" and absorb differences, without slavishly acceding to them. This also makes clear the difference between ethics and morality. Morals refer to prescribed standards and principles demanding compliance – behaviour and thought either conform or fall short – whereas an ethics of entrepreneurship concerns the struggle to cope with practical questions of right and wrong in ordinary settings where any threshold of compliance often disappears in a grey fog of equivocation and contingent event. Here ethics requires we remain with life, figuring how to live well within what is an increasingly fragile ecology of life forms, rather than invoke a law or principle that rejects complexity for the sake of simplicity.[77] Ethics is precisely this relation, with the other, that is cancelled as soon as you give in to the monophonic totality of a rule. Entrepreneurship encourages experiment with everyday norms and habits, that which directs common sense, in ways that acknowledge what is "other" without confining it within a specific set of (economic) established value requirements.[78]

We might reserve the concept of entrepreneurship to describe the condition (i.e. the entrepreneurial) whereby this imaginative power – well-demonstrated by both Elisabeth Bennett and Chichikov – finds expression when it brings what is already known into questionability: always asking what the current situation requires one not to know. Here, we find entrepreneurial agency as relationally constituted movement from belonging to disclosing, a creative response to being affected by both the virtually new and the historically and communally constituted. A keen sensibility before common sense is a key condition for knowing how space for play can be opened and used. To the extent that one can convince others of one's belonging, as one acknowledging the limits that are part of holding the present order in place, you can be trusted to negotiate those limits. Bennett and Chichikov are masters of convincing others that they are one of them, that they belong. Chichikov takes time to study the locals, informing himself of how to talk and act, who to know, in order to pass as someone that is acting within the limits of common sense. This is how breaching common sense in Chichikov's case passes as plausible and doable. The result is often the "why did not someone think of this before?," to which the entrepreneurial answer is: they all did; they all precisely *just thought*.

Researching the relationship between common sense and entrepreneurship processes is exemplified in institutional entrepreneurship, where studies have come to focus on the social embeddedness of actors and acknowledge how institutions – much in line with what we have reflected upon above – both enable and constrain action and creativity.[79] Institutional entrepreneurship research also has pointed to creativity as a "heretic" combination of logics following the awareness of where boundaries are drawn (as stressed by Chia, see above, when discussing entrepreneurial imagination).[80] What in institutional entrepreneurship is described as field-level events (regulatory changes, technological disruption, and so on) that make space for entrepreneurial initiative is something we have related to in the play phase of our model.[81] Playing moves in play-space and adds to loosening the seemingly rigid, that is, the institutionalized constraint. Possibilities to play would also increase with the level of heterogeneity amongst multiple institutional logics in place in a field.[82] This enables multiple in-betweens, entre-spaces, where playing becomes potential. It seems to us that institutional entrepreneurship is a field of research where our entrepreneurship process model can bring analyses further.

Commerce

In Montesquieu's words: "... whenever there is commerce, there the ways of men are gentle," but in the entrepreneurial process, it is an amiability that can hide a certain single-minded selfishness, indeed viciousness.[83] So it is, at least, with Patricia Highsmith's Tom Ripley, who is making his way via gentle manners that disguise a severe intent. Highsmith's book is full of descriptions of Ripley trying to learn the gentle ways necessary to those – like Dickie – able to move smoothly in the social landscape. As he acts and acts anew, he spills into an irreversible project of becoming someone else, accumulating his persona, possessions, and aspiration, and what began as a mere opening becomes an all-consuming lifestyle. There is a passion in Ripley, one that characterizes much in the way of enterprise, as Montesquieu was to remark:

> One commerce leads to another: the small to the medium; the medium to the large; and the person who was so anxious to make a little money places himself in a situation in which he is no less anxious to make a lot.[84]

Ripley reveals what it is to insinuate oneself into the commercial setting, to make oneself agreeable, to become part of what Hirschman calls a cohesive community based on commercial ties. Those in the community benefit financially, but also socially and emotionally, and Ripley learns and exploits this, carefully but without any regard for the lives he touches.

The same might be said of entrepreneurship: the value being created is not just economic.[85] Conventional economic knowledge would have it that revenue growth and return on capital generate a cash flow that together represents value accumulation (or value growth). Launching a new product or expanding an existing market are considered to be means of creating value: entrepreneurship is a process of creating and launching new products or services, and the firm providing such. Value, however, is also a function of actual performance – of a service, product, or firm – and expected performance. What something is worth for an investor, a consumer, or a user is a combination of what it does for you today plus what you expect it to do for you in the future, the immanent "next-ness" of the entrepreneurial process which assures people that virtual value will become actual. This is where the stories, the strategies, the brands, the "aura" of a business are important carriers of potential value.[86] Yet the ever-present risk (ethically speaking) is, as with Ripley's enterprise, these values are only ever serving self-centred accretions of personal gain, and so actually serve to sever the organization from its wider environs into which it might properly develop relations of care, but which all too often become territorialized as relations of commerce. Ripley's commerce fails because it is an attempt to write others into his own history, rather than write himself into theirs: the lives of others become resources, plain, and simple. His is a desire that lacks joy, his smile is slow to come, held fast by calculation.

As a quartet, seduction, play, common sense, and commerce, constitute a form of entrepreneurship in which the venture – the fabrication of an organization – is not a struggle to institute formal structures, but a continual enquiry into limits and how to live with them. It is a preparedness to ask just why it is people act and think in the ways they do. As the enquiry takes shape, an organization gathers, but it does so in relation to vulnerability, to exclusion, and to the immediate necessity of a performance. The playful, imaginative, affective exchange of tendencies and suggestions is inherently unruly and its beauty is insubstantial. There are no sovereigns or subjects, no grand challenges or visions, no fast formulae or inviolate standards. Everything is being encountered as a fluency, taking place in the yellow light (the in-between light), in the greyness of multiplicity, the ambiguity that calls for decision, and the entrepreneur is the fragment that desires it to be so.

Notes

1 Hjorth, D. (2012) "Introduction: Entrepreneurship in Organizational Contexts." In D. Hjorth (Ed.), *Handbook on Organizational Entrepreneurship*, Cheltenham: Edward Elgar, pp. 1–18.

2 Studied also in Fletcher, D. (2006) "Entrepreneurial Processes and the Social Construction of Opportunity," *Entrepreneurship & Regional Development*, 18(September): 421–440, with a focus on the construction of opportunity; and in Dimov, D. and Pistrui, J. (2020) "Recursive and Discursive Model of and for Entrepreneurial Action," *European Management Review*, 17: 267–277, with a focus on discursive action and perception, time, and context.

3 Dey, P. (2016) "Destituent Entrepreneurship: Disobeying Sovereign Rule, Prefiguring Post-Capitalist Reality," *Entrepreneurship & Regional Development*, 28(7–8): 563–579.

4 Deleuze, G. (2004) *Desert Islands – and Other Texts, 1953–1974*, D. Lapoujade (Ed.), Transl. M. Taormina, Los Angeles and New York: Semiotext(s), pp. 58–59.

5 Ibid., p. 59 (emphasis in original).

6 Vaihinger, H. (1952). *The Philosophy of 'as if': A System of the Theoretical, Practical and Religious Fictions of Mankind*, London: Routledge & Kegan Paul. (Original work published 1911) p. 93. (emphasis in original).

7 Colebrook, C. (2002) *Gilles Deleuze*, London: Routledge, p. 12 (emphasis in original).

8 As a neo-Kantian Vaihinger remained committed to fictions being mental productions (and so what he called false) whose utility comes in allowing subjects to think through conditions, they are the equivalent of counterfactuals in a chain of reasoning, they are useful falsehoods allowing the thinker to test the robustness of ideas. Deleuze and others would be far more equivocal about absorbing fictional concepts into such a mechanical, purposive view of reasoning. For a good overview of Hans Vaihinger's method see Kobow B (2014) "How to Do Things with Fictions: Reconsidering Vaihinger for a Philosophy of Social Sciences," *Philosophy of the Social Sciences*, 44(2): 201–222.

9 Agamben, G. (2017) *Taste*, York: Seagull Books, p. 22.

10 Kant, I. (1892) *The Critique of Judgement*, Indianapolis: The Online Library of Liberty, p. 179.

11 Agamben, G. (2017) *Taste*, York: Seagull Books, p. 48.

12 Massumi, B. (2002) *Parables for the Virtual – Movement, Affect, Sensation*, Durham and London: Duke University Press, p. 77.

13 Ibid., p. 78.

14 Spinosa, C. (2001) "Derridian Dispersion and Heideggerian Articulation: General Tendencies in the Practices That Govern Intelligibility." In T.R. Schatzki, K. Knorr Cetina, and E. Von Savigny (Eds.), *The Practice Turn in Contemporary Theory*, London: Routledge, pp. 199–212.

15 Spinosa, C., Flores, F., and Dreyfus, H. (1997) *Disclosing New Worlds – Entrepreneurship, Democratic Action, and the Cultivation of Solidarity*, Cambridge: MIT Press.

16 *Disclosing New Worlds* is written in a similar spirit to that of Nelson Goodman's *Ways of Worldmaking* (1978, Indianapolis: Hackett). Goodman argues that practices are never fixed by correlations to an actual world, but organizational forms whose viability is less a function of truth that it is utility, coherence, probability, attractiveness. Hierarchies within and between worlds are, then, possible, but never fixed: worlds are there to be made.

17 Massumi, B. (2015) *The Power at the End of the Economy*, Durham and London: Duke University Press, p. 62.

18 Spinoza emphasized agreement as the ground of ethics, the experience of productive affect emerging from mutually resonating bodies.

19 In Agnes Martin's hands, for example, the painted grid becomes a repetitive imagining of community – the hand-drawn dots and cells become the thought of trees, trees in company, neither abstract nor sacred, they trees that tend to acknowledge one another, to acknowledge the need for mutual space which is similar. She gives expression to a regularity that comes from listening, not from ordering and planning and designing.

20 Schumpeter, J. (1947) "The Creative Response in Economic History," *Journal of Economic History*, 7(2): 149–159, 157.

21 Katz, J. and Gartner, W.B. (1988) "Properties of Emerging Organizations," *Academy of Management Review*, 13(3): 429–441.

22 Colebrook, C. (2002) *Gilles Deleuze*, London: Routledge, p. 136.

23 Ibid., p. 145.

24 Ibid., p. 86.

25 For example, Aldrich, H. and Fiol, M.C. (1994) "Fools Rush in? The Institutional Context of Industry Creation," *Academy of Management Review*, 19(4): 645–670; Hjorth, D. and Steyaert, C. (Eds.) (2004) *Narrative and Discursive Approaches in Entrepreneurship*, Cheltenham: Edward Elgar; Downing, S. (2005) "The Social Construction of Entrepreneurship: Narrative and Dramatic Processes in the Coproduction of Organizations and Identities," *Entrepreneurship: Theory & Practice*, 29(2): 185–204; *Journal of Business Venturing*, 22(5); Ericson, M. (2010) *A Narrative Approach to Business Growth*, Cheltenham: Edward Elgar; Fletcher, D. and Watson, T.J. (2007) "Entrepreneurship, Management Learning, and Negotiated Narratives: 'Making It Otherwise for Us – Otherwise for Them,' " *Management Learning*, 38(1): 9–26.

26 Lounsbury, M. and Glynn, M.A. (2001) "Cultural Entrepreneurship: Stories, Legitimacy, and the Acquisition of Resources," *Strategic Management Journal*, 22(6/7): 545–564; Lounsbury, M., Gehman, J., and Glynn, M.A. (2019) "Beyond *Homo Entrepreneurs*: Judgement and the Theory of Cultural Entrepreneurship," *Journal of Management Studies*, 56(6): 1214–1236; Garud, R., Jain, S., and Kumaraswamy, A. (2002) "Institutional Entrepreneurship in the Sponsorship of Common Technological Standards: The Case of Sun Microsystems and JAVA," *Academy of Management Journal*, 45(1): 196–214; Garud, R., Hardy, C., and Maguire, S. (2007) "Institutional Entrepreneurship as Embedded Agency: An Introduction to the Special Issue," *Organization Studies*, 28(7): 957–969; Battilana, J., Leca, B., and Boxenbaum, E. (2009) "How Actors Change Institutions: Towards a Theory of Institutional Entrepreneurship," *Academy of Management Annals*, 3(1): 65–107.

27 Schumpeter, J.A. (1947) "The Creative Response in Economic History," *Journal of Economic History*, November: 149–159; Gartner, W.B., Bird, B., and Starr, J.A. (1992) "Acting as If: Differentiating Entrepreneurial from Organizational Behavior," *Entrepreneurship: Theory & Practice*, 16(3): 13–31; Papers in the Special Issue: Hjorth, D., Strati, A., Drakopoulou, D.S., and Weik, E. (2018) "Organizational Creativity, Play and Entrepreneurship: Introduction and Framing," *Organization Studies*, 39(2–3): 155–168.

28 McCraw, T.K. (2007) *Prophet of Innovation – Joseph Schumpeter and Creative Destruction*, Cambridge and London: The Belknap Press of Harvard University Press.

29 The conceptual persona is Schumpeter as how the thinker is represented by the concepts made known through his work and the work's reception. It is difficult to think "creative destruction" without Schumpeter as a conceptual persona "interfearing" with that concept. Dionysus or Antichrist would be the conceptual persona of Nietzsche, Socrates the conceptual persona of Plato, and the "creative destructor" or the "going-against-the-grain" figure would be the conceptual persona of Schumpeter. See on conceptual persona: Deleuze, G. and Guattari, F. (1994) *What Is Philosophy*, London and New York: Verso.

30 This being related to imagination's role in Kant's philosophy of aesthetics, where it is not constrained by the understanding and ruled by cognition, but moves more freely to make sense, for example, by making new syntheses of concepts. Deleuze also has a theory of the aesthetic experience as affectively bringing us into a jolt where we have to re-calibrate, to think anew, in order to find our bearings.

31 Massumi, B. (2015) *Power at the End of Economy*, Durham and London: Duke University Press, pp. 4–5.

32 Ibid., p. 13.

33 Delgado García, J.B., De Quevedo Puente, E., and Blanco, M.V. (2015) "How Affect Relates to Entrepreneurship: A Systematic Review of the Literature and Research Agenda," *International Journal of Management Reviews*, 17(2): 191–211.

34 With Gaston Bachelard we may say that imagination is best studied in the literary as its inspired actuality, and that imagination is not primarily about forming images of reality, but about forming images that go beyond reality (Bachelar, 2014: 71). See Bachelard, G. (2014) *On Poetic Imagination and Reverie*, Putnam: Spring Publications.

35 Vesper, K.H. (1980) *New Venture Strategies*, Upper Saddle River: Prentice-Hall; Drucker, P.F. (1985) *Innovation and Entrepreneurship – Practice and Principles*, London: Heinemann; Fisher, G., Kotha, S., and Lahiri, A. (2016) "Changing with the Times: An Integrated View of Identity, Legitimacy, and New Venture Life Cycles," *Academy of Management Review*, 41: 383–409; Überbacher, F. (2014) "Legitimation of New Ventures: A Review and Research Programme," *Journal of Management Studies*, 51: 667–698.

36 Massumi, B. (2002) *Parables for the Virtual – Movement, Affect, Sensation*, Durham and London: Duke University Press, pp. 206–207.

37 Deleuze, G. and Guattari, F. (1986) *Kafka: Toward a Minor Literature*, Minneapolis: University of Minnesota Press, p. 28.

38 Deleuze, G. and Parnet, C. (2002) Dialogues II. Transl. by H. Tomlinson and B. Habberjam, 'The Actual and the Virtual' Transl. by E. Ross Albert. London/New York: Continuum, p. 74.

39 See Stewart, W.H. Jr. and Roth, P.L. (2007) "A Meta-Analysis of Achievement Motivation Differences between Entrepreneurs and Managers," *Journal of Small Business Management*, 45(4): 401–421; Haffziger, D.W., Hornsby, J.S., and Kuratko, D.F. (1994) "A Proposed Research Model of Entrepreneurial Motivation," *Entrepreneurship: Theory & Practice*, 18(3): 29–42; McClelland, D.C. (1961) *The Achieving Society*, Princeton: D. Van Nostrand; Carland, J.W., Hoy, F., Boulton, W.R., and Carland, J.A.C. (1984) Differentiating Entrepreneurs from Small Business Owners: A Conceptualization. *The Academy of Management Review*, 9(2): 354–359.

40 For some indicative examples of entrepreneurial studies that take aesthetic forms of fiction making explicitly, and seriously, see Skoglund, A., Redmalm, D., and Berglund, K. (2020) "Videography – Studying Ethical Uncertainty in Alternative Entrepreneurship," *Society and Business*, 15(4): 305–324. Popp, A. and Holt, R. (2013) "The Presence of Entrepreneurial Opportunity," *Business History*, 55(1): 9–18; Anderson, A., Drakopoulou, D.S., and Jack, S. (2009) "Aggressors; Winners; Victims and Outsiders: European Schools' Social Construction of the Entrepreneur," *International Small Business Journal*, 27(1): 126–133; Steyaert, C. and Bouen, R. (1997) "Telling Stories of Entrepreneurship: Towards and Narrative Contextual Epistemology for Entrepreneurial Studies." In R. Donckels and A. Miettinen (Eds.), *Entrepreneurship and SME Research*, London: Routledge, pp. 47–64; Nordqvist, M. and Gartner, W.B. (2020) "Literature, Fiction, and the Family Business," *Family Business Review*, 33(2): 122–129; Anderson, A.R. (2005) "Enacted Metaphor: The Theatricality of the Entrepreneurial Process," *International Small Business Journal*, 23(6): 587–603; Smith, R. (2015) "Entrepreneurship and Poetry: Analyzing an Aesthetic Dimension," *Journal of Small Business and Enterprise Development*, 22(3): 450–472; Holm, D.V. and Beyes T. (April 2021) "How Art Becomes Organization: Reimagining Aesthetics, Sites and Politics of Entrepreneurship," *Organization Studies*, April 2021, doi: 10.1177/0170840621998571. O'Connor, E.S. (2007) "Reader Beware: Doing Business with a Store(y) of Knowledge," *Journal of Business Venturing*, 22(5): 637–648.

41 Massumi, B. (2002) *Parables for the Virtual – Movement, Affect, Sensation*, Durham and London: Duke University Press, p. 30.

42 Hjorth, D. and Johannisson, B. (2008) "Building New Roads for Entrepreneurship Research to Travel by: On the Work of William B. Gartner," *Small Business Economics*, 31: 341–350.

43 Saras Sarasvathy (Sarasvathy, S. (2021) "Even-If: Sufficient, Yet Unnecessary Conditions for Worldmaking," *Organization Theory*, 2: 1–9) invokes Vaihinger, referring to Milton Friedman's project of developing a positive economic science though use of "as if" theories and hypotheses. Friedman's spirit lacks the sense of anarchic magic that Woolf found lighting the hearth of Keynes' view of the market. Specifically, Friedman cannot consider the "What is?" question as anything other than a correlation problem connecting language (concepts) and reality. For Woolf, Keynes' was more a magus figure, alive to how reality is being performatively created, not related to.

44 As we know by now, this image is Henri Bergson's, explaining the need for new ways to conceptualize creative becoming.

45 Deleuze, G. (1994) *Difference & Repetition*, London and New York: Continuum, p. 220.

46 Colebook, C. (1999) *Ethics and Representation – from Kant to Post-Structuralism*, Edinburgh: Edinburgh University Press, pp. 68–71.

47 See Verduijn, K., Dey, P., Tedmanson, D., and Essers, C. (2014) "Emancipation and/or Oppression? Conceptualizing Dimensions of Criticality in Entrepreneurship Studies." *International Journal of Entrepreneurial Behavior and Research*, 20(2): 98–107.

48 Garcìa, J.B.D., Puente, E.D.Q., and Mazagatos, V.B. (2015) "How Affect Relates to Entrepreneurship: A Systematic Review of the Literature and Research Agenda," *International Journal of Management Reviews*, 17:

191–211; Grégoire, D.A., Cornelissen, J., Dimov, D., and van Burg, E. (2015) "The Mind in the Middle: Taking Stock of Affect and Cognition Research in Entrepreneurship," *International Journal of Management Reviews*, 17: 125–142.

49 Klofsten, M. (2002) *The Business Platform: Entrepreneurship and Management in the Early Stages of a Firm's Development*, Luxemburg: European Commission.

50 Burnham, J. (1941) *The Managerial Revolution – What Is Happening in the World*, Westpoint: Greenwood Press; Chandler, A.D. (1977) *The Visible Hand – The Managerial Revolution in American Business*, Cambridge and London: The Belknap Press of Harvard University Press.

51 And these can be very useful tools, as the work from Alexander Osterwalder and team have shown.

52 Isenberg, D. (2014) "What an Entrepreneurship Ecosystem Actually Is," *Harvard Business Review*, May: 2–5. Dee, N.J., Gill, D., Lacher, R., Livesey, F., and Minshall, T. (2012) "A Review of Research on the Role and Effectiveness of Business Incubation for High-Growth Start-Ups," Centre for Technology Management, Institute for Manufacturing, University of Cambridge, No. 2012/01.

53 Alexandersson, A. (2015) Incubating Businesses. Doctoral Thesis. Växjö: Linnaeus University Press; Henriques, C.T. (2016) In Search of Entrepreneurial Learning: Towards a Relational Perspective on Incubating Practices. Doctoral Thesis. Copenhagen: CBS Press.

54 Hjorth, D. (2014) "Entrepreneuring as Organization-Creation." In R. Sternberg and G. Kraus (Eds.), *Handbook of Research on Entrepreneurship and Creativity*, Cheltenham: Edward Elgar, pp. 97–121.

55 De Certeau, M. (1997) *Heterologies*, Minneapolis: University of Minnesota Press, pp. 139–140.

56 Deleuze, G. (1988) *Spinoza: Practical Philosophy*, Transl. R. Hurley, San Francisco: City Lights Books. See also Hjorth, D. and Holt, D. (2014) Spinoza. In J. Helin, T. Hernes, D. Hjorth, & R. Holt (Eds.), *The Oxford University Press Handbook of Process Philosophy and Organization Studies*, Oxford: Oxford University Press, pp. 78–93.

57 Iago: "Heaven is my judge, not I for love and duty,/ But seeming so, for my peculiar end: For when my outward action doth demonstrate /The native act and figure of my heart /In compliment extern, 'tis not long after/But I will wear my heart upon my sleeve/For daws to peck at: I am not what I am." Don Giovanni "Idiot! You scream in vain. Who I am you'll never know!"

58 Robert Musil's *Der Mann Ohne Eigenschaften*, mocking the 1930s' fascist fascination with militant force and paranoid worshiping of authority, is an example of how a suggested movement that escapes a socially coded and authorized investment of desire as interest in a specific production, is received as an anomaly. Hjorth, D. and Steyaert, C. (2006) American Psycho – European Schizo: Stories of Managerial Elites in 'Hundred' Images. In P. Gagliardi and B. Czarniawska (Eds.), *Management Education and Humanities*, Cheltenham: Edward Elgar, pp. 67–97.

59 Gartner, W.B. (1989) " 'Who Is an Entrepreneur?' Is the Wrong Question," *Entrepreneurship Theory and Practice*, 13(4): 47–68. See also Ramoglou, S., Tsang, E.W.K., and Gartner, W.B. (2020) " 'Who Is an Entrepreneur?'

Is (Still) the Wrong Question." *Journal of Business Venturing Insights*, 13: e00168.

60 Chell, E. (1985) "The Entrepreneurial Personality: A Few Ghosts Laid to Rest," *International Small Business Journal*, 3: 43–54.

61 As good examples of studies showing contextual sensitivity see Johannisson, B. and Nilsson, A. (1989) "Community Entrepreneur: Networking for Local Development," *Entrepreneurship and Regional Development*, 1: 3–19; Dimov, D. and Pistrui, J. (2020) "Recursive and Discursive Model of and for Entrepreneurial Action," *European Management Review*, 17: 267–277; for study of context see Baker, T. and Welter, F. (2018) "Contextual Entrepreneurship: An Interdisciplinary Perspective," *Foundations and Trends in Entrepreneurship*, 14(4): 357–426; Welter, F., Baker, T., and Wirsching, K. (2019) "Three Waves and Counting: The Rising Tide of Contextualization in Entrepreneurship Research," *Small Business Economics*, 52: 319–33; for study of process see Steyaert, C. (2007) " 'Entrepreneuring' as Conceptual Attractor? A Review of 20 Studies," *Entrepreneurship and Regional Development*, 19: 453–477 and also Brattström, A., Delmar, F., Johnson, A.R., and Wennberg, K. (2020) "A Longitudinal Project of New Venture Teamwork and Outcomes." In Gartner, W.B. & Teague, B.T. (Eds.), *Research Handbook on Entrepreneurial Behavior, Practice and Process*, Cheltenham: Edward Elgar Publishing, pp. 309–334; for study of affect see Baron, R.A. (2008) "The Role of Affect in the Entrepreneurial Process," *The Academy of Management Review*, 33(2): 328–340; and for study of contingency see Ramoglou, S., Gartner, W.B., and Tsang, E.W. (2020) " 'Who Is an Entrepreneur?' Is (Still) the Wrong Question," *Journal of Business Venturing Insights*, 13: e00168. doi.org/10.1016/j.jbvi.2020.e00168.

62 Vaihinger, H. (1952 [Original work published 1911]) *The Philosophy of "as if": A System of the Theoretical, Practical and Religious Fictions of Mankind*, London: Routledge & Kegan Paul; Smythe, W.E. (2005) "On the Psychology of 'As If,' " *Theory Psychology*, 15: 283–303.

63 Deleuze, G. (1988) *Spinoza – Practical Philosophy*, San Francisco: City Lights Books, pp. 27–28.

64 Ibid., p. 29.

65 See Dubini, P. and Aldrich, H. (1991) "Personal and Extended Networks Are Central to the Entrepreneurial Process," *Journal of Business Venturing*, 6(5): 305–313 and Chaston, I. and Scott, G.J. (2012) "Entrepreneurship and Open Innovation in an Emerging Economy," *Management Decision*, 50(7): 1161–1177.

66 Steyaert, C. (2011) "Entrepreneurship as In(ter)vention: Reconsidering the Conceptual Politics of Method in Entrepreneurship Studies," *Entrepreneurship and Regional Development*, 23(1–2): 77–88.

67 Hjorth, D., Strati, A., Dodd, S.D., and Weik, E. (2018) "Organizational Creativity, Play and Entrepreneurship: Introduction and Framing," *Organization Studies*, 39(2–3): 155–168.

68 As in Immanuel Kant's (1892/1951) analysis of the aesthetic experience in *Critique of Judgment*, Transl. J.H. Bernard, New York: Hafner Publishing. See also Derrida, J. (1967/1978) "Structure, Sign, and Play in the Discourse of the Human Sciences." In *Writing and Difference*, Chicago: The University of Chicago Press, pp. 278–294.

69 See, for example, Cornelissen, J. (2013) "Portrait of an Entrepreneur: Vincent van Gogh, Steve Jobs, and the Entrepreneurial Imagination," *The Academy of Management Review,* 38(4): 700–709; Kier, A.S. and McMullen, J.S. (2018) "Entrepreneurial Imaginativeness in New Venture Ideation," *Academy of Management Journal,* 61(6): 225–295; Thompson, N.A. (2018) "Imagination and Creativity in Organizations," *Organization Studies,* 39(2–3): 229–250. Dey, P. and Mason, C. (2018) "Overcoming Constraints of Collective Imagination: An Inquiry into Activist Entrepreneuring, Disruptive Truth-Telling, and the Creation of 'Possible Worlds,'" *Journal of Business Venturing,* 33(1): 84–99. Find a good start here: Bjerke, B. and Rämö, H. (2011) *Entrepreneurial Imagination. Time, Timing, Space and Place in Business Action,* Cheltenham: Edward Elgar; Gartner, W.B. (2007) "Entrepreneurial Narrative and a Science of the Imagination," *Journal of Business Venturing,* 22(5): 613–627.

70 Chia, R. (1996) "Teaching Paradigm Shifting in Management Education: University Business Schools and the Entrepreneurial Imagination," *Journal of Management Studies,* 33(4): 409–428.

71 Ibid., p. 411.

72 Whitehead, A.N. (1927) "Universities and Their Function," *Address to the American Association of the Collegiate Schools of Business,* available at: la.utexas.edu/users/hcleaver/330T/350kPEEwhiteheadunivfxtable.pdf, accessed May 25, 2021.

73 Katz, J. (2003) "The Chronology and Intellectual Trajectory of American Entrepreneurship Education 1876–1999," *Journal of Business Venturing,* 18(2): 283–300. Isenberg, D. (2014) "What an Entrepreneurship Ecosystem Actually Is," *Harvard Business Review,* May: 2–5.

74 Lange, J.E., Mollov, A., Pearlmutter, M., Singh, S., and Bygrave, W.D. (2007) "Pre-Start-Up Formal Business Plans and Post-Start-Up Performance: A Study of 116 New Ventures," *Venture Capital,* 9(4): 237–256.

75 This includes the broader cultural setting, within which the designation of entrepreneurial is itself a contested condition, drawing ire as often as eulogy. See Dodd, S.D., Jack, S., and Anderson, A. (2013) "From Admiration to Abhorrence: The Contentious Appeal of Entrepreneurship across Europe," *Entrepreneurship & Regional Development,* 25(1–2): 69–89.

76 Garcia-Lorenzo, L., Donnelly, P., Sell-Trujillo, L., and Imas, J.M. (2018) "Liminal Entrepreneuring: The Creative Practices of Nascent Necessity Entrepreneurs," *Organization Studies,* 39(2–3): 373–395.

77 For a provocative prognosis for entrepreneurship studies see Dodd, S., Anderson, A., and Jack, S. (2021) "'Let Them Not Make Me a Stone' – Repositioning Entrepreneurship," *Journal of Small Business Management,* DOI: 10.1080/00472778.2020.1867734.

78 Alasdair MacIntyre conceptualizes this willingness to acknowledge what is "other" from everyday norms and habits as effective practical reasoning. This reasoning is the ability to consider why doing x is a good way to achieve y, and why y is a good (how it contributes to one's own vitality and that of others). "Effective" is being understood as making action possible, affirming life. This requires: the ability to distinguish having reasons from having *good* reasons; to critically evaluate how "effectiveness" is understood; and to have shared understanding of the norms and habits into which one is thrown that is sufficiently developed and nuanced to imagine alternate and equally legitimate

sets of actions, roles, and goods. MacIntyre, A. (1999) "Social Structures and the Threats to Moral Agency," *Philosophy*, 74: 311–329.

79 Leca, B., Battilana, J., and Boxenbaum, E. (2008) *Agency and Institutions: A Review of Institutional Entrepreneurship,* Cambridge: Harvard Business School.

80 Leca B. and Naccache, P.A. (2006) "Critical Realist Approach to Institutional Entrepreneurship," *Organization,* 13(5): 627–651. Garud, R., Hardy, C., and Maguire, S. (2007) "Institutional Entrepreneurship as Embedded Agency: An Introduction to the Special Issue," *Organization Studies,* 28(7): 957–969.

81 Battilana, L., Leca, B., and Boxenbaum, E. (2009) "How Actors Change Institutions: Towards a Theory of Institutional Entrepreneurship," *The Academy of Management Annals,* 3(1): 65–107.

82 Clemens, E.S. and Cook, J.M. (1999) "Politics and Institutionalism: Explaining Durability and Change," *Annual Review of Sociology,* 25(1): 441–466.

83 Montesquieu, Charles de Secondat de, 1758, Book XX, Chapter 1, On Commerce, Quote is Transl. by Hirschman. Quote is from p. 60 in Hirschman, A.O. (1977) *The Passions and the Interests – Political Arguments for Capitalism before Its Triumph.* Princeton, NJ: Princeton University Press.

84 Ibid., Vol. XX, p. 4.

85 Fayolle, A. (2007) *Entrepreneurship and New Value Creation,* Cambridge: Cambridge University Press; Korsgaard, S. and Anderson, A.R. (2011) "Enacting Entrepreneurship as Social Value Creation," *International Small Business Journal,* 29(2): 135–151; Vozikis, G.S., Bruton, G.D., Prasad, D., and Merikas, A.A. (1999) "Linking Corporate Entrepreneurship to Financial Theory though Additional Value Creation," *Entrepreneurship: Theory & Practice,* 24(2): 35–45.

86 Björkman, I. (1998) *Sven Duchamp – Expert på aura Production,* Stockholm: Stockholms Universitet. See special issue in the *Journal of Business Venturing,* 22, 2007.

Index

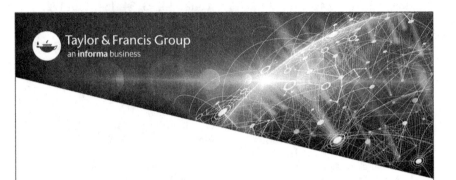

Printed in the United States
by Baker & Taylor Publisher Services